A Nation Dedicated to Religious Liberty

A Nation Dedicated to Religious Liberty

The Constitutional Heritage of the Religion Clauses

Arlin M. Adams and Charles J. Emmerich

FOREWORD BY WARREN E. BURGER

University of Pennsylvania Press
Philadelphia

Library of Congress Cataloging-in-Publication Data

Adams, Arlin M.
    A nation dedicated to religious liberty: the constitutional
heritage of the religion clauses / Arlin M. Adams and Charles J.
Emmerich; foreword by Warren E. Burger.
        p.   cm.
    Includes bibliographical references and index.
    ISBN 0-8122-8250-7. — ISBN 0-8122-1318-1 (pbk.)
        1. Freedom of religion—United States—History.   2. Church and
state—United States—History.   3. Religion and state—United
States—History.   4. Freedom of religion—United States—History—
Sources.   5. Church and state—United States—History—Sources.
6. Religion and state—United States—History—Sources.   7. United
States—Constitutional law—Amendments—1st.   8. United States—
Church history.   9. United States—Religion.   I. Emmerich, Charles
J.   II. Title.
BR516.A32   1990
323.44'2'0973—dc20

90-36248
CIP

To
my wife, Neysa Cristol Adams,
for her endless patience and warm support over the years,
To
my sister, Donna Emmerich Carlson (1943–1986),
with great admiration for her missionary work in Africa

The history of law must be a history of ideas. It must represent, not merely what men have done and said, but what men have thought in bygone ages. The task of reconstructing ancient ideas is hazardous, and can only be accomplished little by little. If we are in a hurry to get to the beginning we shall miss the path.

Sir Frederic Maitland

Contents

Foreword

Some extremists see the risk of an "established" or "state" church looming up when any state action benefits one or all religions. This view rests on Jefferson's "wall of separation," which is sometimes a useful methaphor to create the image of a separate church and state but which is hardly part of orderly legal analysis. A literal "wall of separation" is surely not what the draftsmen of the religion clauses had in mind in 1789; to the contrary, they recognized, as have many decisions of the Supreme Court over the past 200 years, that no perfect or absolute separation is possible. Although some would read Jefferson's "wall" as a clause in the Constitution, rather than a comment in a letter, the Court has allowed such obvious "aids" to religion as school bus transportation for parochial school students and tax exemptions for churches and church-sponsored schools. Beyond that, the Supreme Court has held that opening legislative sessions with a prayer, as Congress has done with government-paid chaplains for more than 200 years, does not conflict with the establishment clause. These "aids" to religion have not brought us closer to a "state church" as those words have meaning in history. The risk of a legislative act creating a state church is about as likely as a dictatorship in our country.

Surely Justice William O. Douglas was sensitive to the objectives and nuances of the establishment clause and yet we find him writing in *Zorach v. Clausen*:

> We are a religious people whose institutions presuppose a Supreme Being. We guarantee the freedom to worship as one chooses. We make room for as wide a variety of beliefs and creeds as the spiritual needs of man deem necessary. We sponsor an attitude on the part of government that shows no partiality to any one group and that lets each flourish according to the zeal of its adherents and the appeal of its dogma. When the state encourages religious instruction or cooperates with religious authorities by adjusting the schedule of public events to sectarian needs, it follows the best of our traditions. For it then respects the religious nature of our people and accommodates the public service to their spiritual needs. To hold that it may not would be to find in the Constitution a requirement that the government show a callous indifference to religious groups. That would be preferring

those who believe in no religion over those who do believe. Government may not finance religious groups nor undertake religious instruction nor blend secular and sectarian education nor use secular institutions to force one or some religion on any person. But we find no constitutional requirement which makes it necessary for government to be hostile to religion and to throw its weight against efforts to widen the effective scope of religious influence.

It is perhaps annoying to establishment clause absolutists that the same First Congress that adopted the religion clauses also provided for paid chaplains in the House and Senate. Most courts open much in the same manner as the Supreme Court with the recital, "God save the United States and this Honorable Court." Surely that is a prayer—albeit brief and to the point—but is in keeping with traditions and practices going well beyond two centuries of nationhood. Hundreds—if not thousands—of classical religious paintings and great religious sculpture from the past are found in galleries supported by taxes—and the acquisition of many religious art objects is financed with tax dollars. That this may *aid* religion has not troubled most people any more than tax exemption of church buildings and contributions to maintain churches and church teachers.

Yet, as in other areas of constitutional law, the dissenters citing Jefferson's "wall" serve a significant purpose. Their challenges are not unlike road signs, warning drivers to slow down for construction ahead or a slippery road ahead. But the risk of benefits granted to church-supported schools and universal provision of school transportation and textbooks to students in public, private, and religious schools has been a deliberate legislative policy and has not brought us any closer to a state church.

Our system encourages pluralism, both political and religious. Debate is the American way, and a continuing examination of the religion clauses is useful to ensure that even if others exhibit covert or overt hostility to religions, courts will preserve the neutrality that the Founders intended.

In the continuing debate over the clauses, the authors provide a careful yet brief examination of America's rich tradition of religious freedom. They have taken a broad and complex area of study and presented it in a readable and thought-provoking manner. By so doing, they have made an important contribution in assisting citizens to gain a greater appreciation of our nation's commitment to religious liberty.

WARREN E. BURGER

Acknowledgments

A Nation Dedicated to Religious Liberty is based on an article entitled *A Heritage of Religious Liberty*, which appeared in the University of Pennsylvania Law Review, May 1989. The article was an expansion of the Owen J. Roberts Memorial Lecture, "The Religion Clauses—The Past and the Future," delivered by Judge Adams on November 19, 1987, under the auspices of the University of Pennsylvania Law School, the Order of the Coif, and the Law Alumni Society. We express appreciation to the William Penn Foundation and to the Law School, particularly the Owen J. Roberts Memorial Lecture Fund, for financial assistance in the preparation of this book. We also gratefully acknowledge the encouragement of Robert Mundheim, former Dean of the Law School, and of Colin Diver, the present Dean.

In preparing this book, the authors appreciate the research assistance of Fred Beuttler, doctoral student in history at the University of Chicago, and of Andrew Walko, Jay Spiegel, Robin Rovell, and Timothy Longacre. Thanks also are extended to Frances Boettger, Eve Gibson, and Helen Kina for their administrative help. Finally, we appreciate the thoughtful assistance of the University of Pennsylvania Press, especially Arthur Evans, former Associate Director, and Ernie Gonsalves, Business Manager of the University of Pennsylvania Law School.

Introduction

Recognizing that an examination of history can be hazardous as well as fruitful, we will address the historical meaning of a constitutional provision that represents one of America's great contributions to Western civilization.[1] The First Amendment of the United States Constitution declares, "Congress shall make no law respecting an establishment of religion, or prohibiting the free exercise thereof. . . ."[2] This provision, known as the religion clauses, contains two prohibitions against Congress: the first is referred to as the establishment clause, the second as the free exercise clause. The sixteen words of the clauses, so simple yet capable of so many different interpretations, have sparked intense contemporary debate.

In considering the meaning of the religion clauses, chapter 1 of this book will survey the history of American religious liberty, chapter 2 will examine the Founding Fathers' views, chapter 3 will discuss the core value of religious liberty, and chapter 4 will identify the constitutional principles that implement this value. Understanding these principles is more than an abstract intellectual exercise, for they provide an essential context for guiding the resolution of modern religious liberty issues.[3] To this end, chapter 5 will apply these principles, by way of example, to three current issues: the voluntary meeting of student religious groups in public high schools, known as the equal-access controversy; religious symbolism in public life, particularly the inclusion of invocations and benedictions in high school graduations; and the task of defining religion for constitutional purposes.

1. The Historical Roots of American Religious Liberty

[T]he fundamental principles of civil and religious liberty . . .
form the basis whereon these republics, their laws and
constitutions, are erected.

Northwest Ordinance, 1787

The American Founders were influenced greatly by theologians and philosophers who reflected on the religious conflicts that occurred in the wake of the Reformation. From Martin Luther and John Calvin they inherited the view that God had instituted "two kingdoms"—a heavenly one where the church exercised spiritual authority and an earthly one where the civil magistrates exercised temporal authority.[1] A liberal Roman Catholic tradition represented by Erasmus and Thomas More also exerted influence in the colonies, inspiring the Lords Baltimore and the Carrolls of Maryland to rethink the proper relationship between church and state. In *Utopia*, first published in 1516, More presented an ideal republic committed to religious freedom; the work created a literary genre and "provided arguments for the French *Politiques*, the latitudinarians, the Deists, and those who adhere to a liberal optimism."[2] The Puritan poet John Milton, confidant of Oliver Cromwell and friend of Roger Williams, helped shape colonial thought by seeking to prove in 1659 that "for belief or practice in religion according to this conscientious persuasion no man ought be punished or molested by any outward force on earth whatsoever."[3]

From Williams, John Clarke, and William Penn, the Founders learned that state control of religion corrupted faith and that coercion of conscience destroyed true piety. From the theorists Algernon Sidney and John Locke, they appropriated concepts such as inalienable rights, government by popular consent, and toleration for the religious beliefs of others. The

Founders used these concepts in justifying the American Revolution and in drafting the Declaration of Independence and the Constitution. In *A Letter on Toleration*, published anonymously in 1689, Locke advanced social and political reasons for toleration based on his exposure to England's religious strife and his association in Holland with religious refugees. He concluded that civil magistrates should tolerate every religious group except those that pose a threat either to the security of the state or to the moral well-being of society.[4] These diverse ideas, derived largely from the intellectual currents flowing from the Reformation, influenced the colonists in developing not only their religious but also their political institutions.

Colonial Background

The Virginia Company's settlements in America were motivated largely by economic considerations, but its early charters and laws also disclose a deep concern for planting true religion in the New World.[5] The famous Lawes Divine, Moral and Martial (1610–11), the first English legal code in the New World, required daily church attendance and imposed harsh penalties for blasphemy, breaking the Sabbath, and speaking maliciously against the Trinity, God's holy word, or Christian doctrine.[6] When Virginia became a royal colony in 1624, its Anglican Church settled into a pattern of preferred governmental status that endured until the Revolutionary War. This establishment was characterized by public support, glebe lands, compulsory church attendance, punishment of blasphemy, religious test oaths, and the suppression of dissenting views.

New England was settled by Puritans, dissenters who came to America after unsuccessful attempts to purge England's Anglican establishment of its allegedly "popish" tendencies.[7] The Pilgrims of Plymouth Bay were separatist Puritans who had repudiated the establishment. They demonstrated their commitment to higher law, a social compact based on covenantal theology, and government by consent in the Mayflower Compact of 1620.[8] The nonseparatist Puritans who founded the Massachusetts Bay Colony still recognized the Anglican Church and thus were less tolerant than their Pilgrim brethren, setting up a theocentric commonwealth premised on Old Testament law. Their magistrates and ministers cooperated in expelling dissenters, enforcing church attendance, limiting the electoral franchise to church members, and supporting the Congregational churches through taxation.[9] Contrary to common misconception, however, the Puritans made enduring contributions to America's heritage of religious liberty by repudiating ecclesiastical courts and by distinguishing civil and religious authority. The impact of Puritanism on colonial thought can hardly be overstated, for as a prominent historian states, it "provided the moral and religious background of fully 75 percent of the people who declared their independence in 1776."[10]

The civil and religious turmoil in seventeenth-century England not only caused the Puritan migration but also inspired dissenters to look to America as a place for carrying out colonial experiments predicated on religious freedom. The Lords Baltimore, from an aristocratic Roman Catholic family, attempted heroically, but unsuccessfully, to foster religious toleration in Maryland.[11] Maryland's Act Concerning Religion (1649), the first law in America to afford a measure of religious freedom, stipulated that no professing Christian should "henceforth be any ways troubled, molested or discountenanced for or in respect of his or her religion nor in the free exercise thereof . . . nor any way compelled to the belief or exercise of any other religion against his or her consent."[12]

Rhode Island was founded as a haven for dissenters by two ministers, Roger Williams[13] and John Clarke. Williams devoted his life to expounding a theological basis for separation of church and state, authoring the classic theological condemnation of religious persecution, *The Bloudy Tenent, of Persecution, for Cause of Conscience*, in 1644.[14] In the work's preface, Williams enumerated twelve fundamental propositions; the tenth and eleventh read:

> Tenthly, an enforced uniformity of religion throughout a nation or civil state, confounds the civil and religious, denies the principles of Christianity and civility, and that Jesus Christ is come in the flesh.
> Eleventhly, the permission of other consciences and worships than a state professes, only can (according to God) procure a firm and lasting peace (good assurance being taken according to the wisdom of the civil state for uniformity of civil obedience from all sorts).[15]

The deeply pious Williams ranks as one of the foremost advocates of the pietistic view that a wall of separation must be maintained to protect the church from worldly corruption. He announced the wall of separation metaphor over 150 years before Thomas Jefferson's famous letter to the Danbury Baptists, writing in 1644 that when Christians "have opened a gap in the hedge or wall of separation between the garden of the Church and the wilderness of the world, God hath ever broke down the wall itself, removed the candlestick, etc., and made his garden a wilderness, as at this day."[16]

The contributions of the Baptist minister John Clarke, Williams's co-worker and close friend, are often overlooked. Clarke condemned religious intolerance in *Ill Newes from New-England: Or a Narative of New-Englands Persecution* (1652), which recounted the persecution of two Baptist friends and himself at the hands of the Puritan magistrates in Lynn, Massachusetts. Appealing to the golden rule and emphasizing that Jesus ruled his kingdom with a spiritual not a temporal sword, the tract argued that the use of force to coerce conscience in religious matters disrupted the peace and prosperity of a nation and made "men dissemblers and hypocrites."[17] Clarke's most important contribution to Rhode Island was the procurement in 1663 of the Charter of Rhode Island and Providence Plantations, which confirmed the colony's democratic form of government and liberal tradition of religious freedom.[18] According to the charter, Rhode Island's settlers desired "to hold forth a lively experiment, that a most flourishing civil state may stand and best be maintained . . . with a full liberty in religious concernments."[19]

The Quaker leader William Penn devoted his life to securing liberty of conscience as a God-given right beyond the dominion of government.[20] Combining the roles of religious leader and political statesman, Penn expounded his views on religious liberty in numerous tracts. In *The Great Case of Liberty of Conscience* (1671), he stressed that coercion of conscience destroyed authentic religious experience and "directly invade[d] the divine prerogative."[21] As a proprietor of West New Jersey, Penn was a principal drafter of the settlement's fundamental law, the Concessions and Agreements of West New Jersey of 1677.[22] The document reflected the Quaker belief that only God ruled the conscience, declaring that because no man "hath power or authority to rule over men's consciences in religious matters," no settler shall be "in the least punished or hurt, either in person, estate, or privilege, for the sake of his opinion, judgment, faith or worship towards God in matters of religion."[23]

As sole proprietor of Pennsylvania, Penn served as the colony's first governor and drafted its first constitution, the Frame of Government of 1682. In this document, a landmark in constitutional history, Penn sought to establish a theocentric society without resorting, as had the Puritan commonwealths, to coercion of conscience. The Frame of Government guaranteed that those who acknowledged God "shall, in no ways, be molested or prejudiced for their religious persuasion, or practice, in matters of faith and worship, nor shall they be compelled, at any time, to frequent or maintain any religious worship, place or ministry whatever."[24] While affording broad religious freedom to theists, it restricted public offices and the franchise to Christians, prohibited labor on the Sabbath, and attempted to foster public morality by outlawing "wildness and looseness," such as sexual offenses, profanity, drunkenness and revelry, stage plays and various games, and serious felonies.[25] The guarantees of religious liberty in the famous Pennsylvania Charter of Privileges of 1701 were similar, with the notable difference that liberty of conscience was made inviolable.[26] The Frame of Government and Charter of Privileges illustrate a tension that persisted in Penn's thought—that of reconciling expansive religious freedom with the civil order's interests and the belief that society's welfare depended on a shared moral consensus. Penn's "holy experiment" flourished, tending to prove that social stability could be enhanced by liberty of conscience. Delaware, part of Pennsylvania until 1701, shared the Quaker leader's legacy of religious freedom.

In the half century preceding the Revolution, Rhode Island, Pennsylvania, Delaware, New Jersey, and New York afforded broad religious liberty. New Jersey and New York had nominal establishments, but their multiplicity of religious groups resulted in de facto religious freedom. The Southern colonies continued to maintain Anglicanism, but the establishments in the Carolinas and Georgia were not formidable. While the Puritans' conception of church and state, known as the New England Way, endured with remarkable vitality, the Congregational establishments were eroded by the increased diversity resulting from the Great Awakening, a series of religious revivals in the mid-eighteenth century.[27]

Religious leaders, such as the Baptist Isaac Backus and the Presbyterian John Witherspoon, joined with political activists, such as James Otis and Samuel Adams, in opposing British tyranny. The colonists' growing outrage found classic expression in Otis's popular pamphlet, *The Rights of the British Colonies Asserted and Proved* (1764), which emphasized the supremacy of natural law.[28] "Kingcraft and priestcraft," Otis stated, "have fallen out so often that 'tis a wonder this grand and ancient alliance is not broken off forever. Happy for mankind will it be when such a separation shall take place."[29] In *A State of the Rights of the Colonists* (1772), drafted by Samuel Adams and his Sons of Liberty, Boston colonists enumerated their fundamental rights on the eve of the Revolution; among these was a "natural right to worship God according to the dictates of [one's] own conscience."[30] Asserting that "our Ancestors came over to this Country that they might not only enjoy their civil but their religious rights," the document denounced the various attempts "to establish an American Episcopate."[31]

Religious Liberty in the New Nation

The ideas that shaped colonial attitudes on the eve of the Revolution included the supremacy of natural law, the concept of inalienable rights, the importance of a written constitution, and government by popular consent.[32] The Declaration of Independence largely embodied these views, drawing heavily on English legal theory, the Whig political tradition, and Puritan covenant theology.[33] Although it did not explicitly address the issue of religious freedom,[34] the Declaration rested on broadly theistic presuppositions and contained four references to the Deity: "Nature's God" and "Creator" in the first two paragraphs and "Supreme Judge of the world" and "Divine Providence" in the concluding paragraph.[35] The document's most famous words disclose its theistic premise: "We hold these truths to be self-evident, that all men are created equal, that they are endowed by their Creator with certain unalienable Rights, that among these are Life, Liberty and the pursuit of happiness."[36]

While reflecting Enlightenment concepts such as "Nature's God" and the social compact theory, the Declaration was of necessity a consensus document subject to both deistic and pietistic interpretations. A broadly theistic position was necessary, for according to one assessment its fifty-six signers represented six different denominations, including thirty-four Anglicans, thirteen Congregationalists, six Presbyterians, one Baptist, one Quaker, and one Roman Catholic.[37] Yet the signers generally agreed that a transcendent Creator had conferred certain inalienable rights that were beyond the dominion of human government. The Declaration of Independence, as well as the Constitution and the Articles of Confederation, comprise the organic or fundamental law of the United States. As rector of the University of Virginia, Jefferson authored a resolution on reading materials for the law school that listed the Declaration and Washington's Farewell Address as two of the "best guides" for understanding "the distinctive principles of [American] government."[38]

At the direction of the Continental Congress, all the states except Rhode

Island and Connecticut adopted constitutions between 1776 and 1780.[39] The Virginia Declaration of Rights, drafted principally by George Mason, guaranteed the free exercise of religion and served as a model for other state charters. James Madison served on the committee that wrote the Declaration, playing a critical role in deliberations concerning article 16, the document's provision on religious liberty. Troubled by the committee's adoption of Mason's wording, which afforded only "the fullest Toleration in the Exercise of Religion," Madison proposed an amendment guaranteeing that "all men are equally entitled to enjoy the free exercise of religion." The convention agreed with Madison's proposed revision.[40] As adopted, article 16 read:

> That religion, or the duty which we owe to our Creator, and the manner of discharging it, can be directed only by reason and conviction, not by force or violence; and therefore all men are equally entitled to the free exercise of religion, according to the dictates of conscience; and that it is the mutual duty of all to practise Christian forbearance, love, and charity towards each other.[41]

In line with a rich heritage of religious freedom, the Pennsylvania Declaration of Rights of 1776 prohibited compulsory attendance at or support of worship and provided that "all men have a natural and unalienable right to worship Almighty God according to the dictates of their own consciences."[42] The New Jersey Constitution of 1776 also granted broad liberty of conscience, specifically prohibiting the government from compelling attendance at worship or from forcing persons to support churches or ministers.[43] Delaware's Declaration of Rights of 1776 contained a liberty of conscience provision mirroring Pennsylvania's. Its first constitution prohibited the "establishment of any one religious sect in this State in preference to another," and its second guaranteed the free exercise of religion and proscribed compulsory attendance at or support of worship.[44] The New York Constitution of 1777 guaranteed "the free exercise and enjoyment of religious profession and worship, without discrimination or preference, . . . *Provided*, That the liberty of conscience, hereby granted, shall not be so construed as to excuse acts of licentiousness, or justify practices inconsistent with the peace or safety of this State."[45]

Along with Virginia, the other Southern states that recognized broad religious rights were North Carolina and Georgia.[46] Maryland's new constitution granted complete religious liberty only to Christians, and authorized a general tax "for the support of the Christian religion."[47] South Carolina's second constitution, adopted in 1778, established the "Christian Protestant religion" in great detail, but its constitution of 1790 broadly guaranteed religious freedom.[48] In keeping with its Congregational establishment, the Massachusetts Constitution of 1780 protected an individual's right to worship God according to "the dictates of his own conscience," but granted equal treatment only to Christian denominations, allowed public support for "Protestant teachers," and authorized the legislature to require attendance at religious instruction.[49] New Hampshire's first constitution did not mention religion, but its constitution of 1784 contained provisions similar to those of the Massachusetts Constitution of 1780.[50] Although Vermont did not join the Union until 1791, it adopted a constitution in 1777 with a religious freedom provision similar to that of the Pennsylvania Constitution of 1776.[51]

In the decade following independence, the Continental Congress authorized legislative and military chaplains, provided for the importation of Bibles, and proclaimed days of thanksgiving, prayer, and fasting.[52] The Articles of Confederation, adopted by Congress in 1777 and ratified in 1781, served as the nation's fundamental law before the Constitution. The Articles referred to the "Great Governor of the world" in article XIII and provided the model for federal noninterference in state religious affairs.[53] Under article II, the states retained sovereignty over all matters except those "expressly delegated to the United States." In article III, the states pledged to assist one another when attacked "on account of religion, sovereignty, trade, or any other pretence whatever," but the document nowhere delegated any authority in religious matters to the federal government.[54]

The Northwest Ordinance of 1787, the most important legislative act preceding the Constitution, established a republican form of government and a bill of rights for the Northwest Territory, a region that now includes Ohio, Indiana, Illinois, Michigan, Wisconsin, and part of Minnesota.[55] According to the preamble, the bill of rights was promulgated to extend "the fundamental principles of civil and religious liberty, which form the basis whereon these republics, their laws and constitutions, are erected." Article I declared, "No person, demeaning himself in a peaceable and orderly manner, shall ever be molested on account of his mode of worship, or religious sentiments, in the said territory." The Founders recognized the importance of religion to the republic in article III: "Religion, morality, and knowledge being necessary to good government and the happiness of mankind, schools and the means of education shall forever be encouraged."[56]

The period between 1776 and the Constitutional Convention in 1787 witnessed heightened efforts in the struggle against the remaining establishments.[57] The campaign in Virginia, called the "Virginia struggle," was especially important because of the involvement of George Mason, Patrick Henry, James Madison, and Thomas Jefferson.[58] Indeed, no other historical episode has influenced the Supreme Court's interpretation of the religion clauses more than the Virginia experience.[59] In the mid-eighteenth century, Virginia's Presbyterians and Baptists joined deists in aggressively agitating for religious equality. Samuel Davies, perhaps the most respected dissenting minister in the South, led the Presbyterians in establishing the Hanover Presbytery as a formidable institution in the struggle.[60] In a famous memorial submitted in October 1776, the Presbytery petitioned the legislature to repeal all laws "which countenance religious dominations" so that those of "every religious sect may be protected in the full exercise of their several modes of worship, and exempted from the payment of all taxes for the support of any church whatever, farther than what may be agreeable to their own private choice, or voluntary obligation."[61] The Baptists proved even more zealous, denouncing all governmental support for Anglicanism and providing essential political underpinning for Madison's battle against a general assessment for religion.

Prior to passage of the Declaration of Rights in 1776, Virginia had required citizens, through a compulsory tax, to support the state's established Anglican Church. The legislature abolished this compulsory tax for nonmembers of the Church in 1776 and for members in 1779. Five years later, however, the issue arose in a somewhat different context. In 1784, the General Assembly considered Patrick Henry's Bill Establishing a Provision for Teachers of the Christian Religion, commonly called the Assessment Bill, which would require all citizens to pay a modest annual tax for the support of the Christian religion.[62] The bill accommodated both the religious and nonreligious taxpayer; the former could designate the church that would receive his tax, while the latter could give the assessment to "seminaries of learning within [his] Count[y]."[63]

With the Assessment Bill all but enacted, Madison and others persuaded the General Assembly to postpone voting on the bill and to submit it for public comment. The public, particularly the state's religious dissenters, responded with a flood of critical petitions. During the legislature's adjournment, Madison wrote the *Memorial and Remonstrance Against Religious Assessments*,[64] a forceful condemnation of the tax measure as "a dangerous abuse of power" that violated every man's inalienable right "to render to the Creator such homage and such only as he believes to be acceptable to him." Liberty of conscience, Madison asserted, was "precedent, both in order of time and in degree of obligation, to the claims of Civil Society." He insisted that "the same authority which can force a citizen to contribute three pence . . . for the support of any one establishment, may force him to conform to any other establishment in all cases whatsoever."[65] Widely distributed before the General Assembly reconvened, the *Memorial and Remonstrance* generated such popular and political opposition to the Assessment Bill that the measure died in committee in December 1785. Although Madison's document figured prominently in the assessment controversy, the tax measure's defeat could not have been achieved without the support of Virginia's religious dissenters.

The defeat of the Assessment Bill cleared the way for Madison and others to achieve the enactment of Jefferson's Bill for Establishing Religious Freedom in 1786.[66] Madison spearheaded this effort because Jefferson was serving at the time as Minister to France. The Act, which marked the virtual end of the Anglican establishment in Virginia, denounced as "sinful and tyrannical" attempts by civil and ecclesiastical rulers to assume "dominion over the faith of others."[67] It placed Virginia's various religious groups on an equal legal footing, declaring:

> That no man shall be compelled to frequent or support any religious worship, place, or ministry whatsoever, nor shall be enforced, restrained, molested, or burthened in his body or goods, nor shall otherwise suffer on account of his religious opinions or belief; but that all men shall be free to profess, and by argument to maintain, their opinion in matters of religion, and that the same shall in no wise diminish, enlarge, or affect their civil capacities.[68]

The Baptist minister John Leland led his denomination in support of Jefferson's bill and worked for complete disestablishment in Virginia. Leland's most famous defense of religious liberty was *The Rights of Conscience Inalienable* (1791), which maintained that because religious freedom is an inalienable right "every man ought to be at liberty to serve God in that way that he can best reconcile it to his conscience."[69] In rejecting the traditional notion that a state could not survive without a religious establishment, Leland maintained that legal enforcement of religious orthodoxy caused hypocrisy, alienated religious groups from one another, inhibited economic prosperity, transformed the church into a political creature, and kept "from civil office, the best of men."[70]

Disestablishment of Anglicanism in the other Southern states was achieved more easily than in Virginia.[71] North Carolina and Georgia lacked the clergy and ecclesiastical resources to build anything but nominal establishments. In South Carolina, the efforts of the Presbyterians, led by the Reverend William Tennent, hastened the abolition of the establishment. The South Carolina Constitution of 1790 failed to provide for an establishment and guaranteed free exercise without "discrimination or preference."[72] Maryland abandoned its Anglican establishment during the Revolution, but adopted a modified Erastian policy and continued to prefer Anglicanism. For Jews and other non-Christians, complete religious liberty in Maryland came only after a long and bitter battle.

The Constitutional Period

By 1787, it was evident that national unity could not be achieved under the Articles of Confederation. During that summer, fifty-five delegates representing twelve states gathered in Philadelphia to amend the Articles, but decided instead to draft a new form of government. Deeply divided between advocates of state sovereignty and a strong federal government, the delegates overcame significant differences and on September 17 submitted the new Constitution to the state ratifying conventions. The only reference to religion was in article VI, which provided that federal and state officials "shall be bound by Oath or Affirmation, to support this Constitution; but no religious Test shall ever be required as a Qualification to any Office or public Trust under the United States."[73]

Given the long history of religious test oaths, this provision was a significant achievement. As the first Lord Baltimore and William Penn could readily confirm, civil authorities in the Anglo-American tradition had effectively used such oaths to identify dissenters, particularly Catholics and Quakers, and to exclude them from public life. In seventeenth-century England, Parliament enacted a maze of legislation to support the Anglican establishment, including oaths of supremacy and allegiance requiring civil and religious leaders to recognize the monarch as head of both church and state and to renounce all foreign rulers, temporal and spiritual. Refusing to take such oaths because of a belief in papal authority, Catholics were regarded as unpatriotic and deprived of civil liberties such as the right to vote, hold public office, and present grievances in court. Quakers refused on Biblical grounds to subscribe to oaths or "swear" allegiance to the Crown and therefore received similar treatment.

The American colonists adapted English test oaths to support Anglican and Congregational establishments. State constitutions enacted during the war commonly required test oaths for holding public office. Only Protestants could hold public office in New Jersey or sit in the legislatures of Georgia, South Carolina, and New Hampshire, and only those professing "the Christian religion" could hold public office in Maryland or serve in high government positions in Massachusetts.[74] North Carolina limited public offices to those who believed in God, the truth of the Protestant religion, and the divine authority of both the Old and New Testaments.[75] Even the states influenced by Quakerism enforced religious tests. Before taking their seats, Pennsylvania legislators had to declare: "I do believe in one God, the creator and governor of the universe, the rewarder of the good and the punisher of the wicked. And I do acknowledge the Scriptures of the Old and New Testament to be given by Divine inspiration."[76] Delaware went further by requiring all officeholders to profess belief in the Trinity and the divine inspiration of the Bible.[77]

The federal test oath clause was primarily the work of Charles Pinckney, an Episcopalian lawyer from South Carolina. Early in the Convention he introduced the so-called Pinckney Plan, which included a proposal that "[t]he legislature of the United States shall pass no law on the subject of religion. . . ."[78] The Convention never acted on this proposal, probably because most delegates believed such a clause unnecessary. The federal government was limited strictly to enumerated powers and therefore possessed no authority over religion. The Convention, however, approved Pinckney's proposed ban on religious tests with little debate. According to Luther Martin of Maryland:

> [The test oath clause] was adopted by a great majority of the convention, and without much debate; however, there were some members so unfashionable as to think, that a belief of the existence of a Deity, and of a state of future rewards and punishments would be some security for the good conduct of our rulers, and that, in a Christian country, it would be at least decent to hold out some distinction between the professors of Christianity and downright infidelity or paganism.[79]

Although the Convention adopted the test oath ban with virtually no discussion, the provision provoked vigorous debate in several of the state ratifying conventions. In Connecticut, Federalist Oliver Ellsworth defended the federal ban on religious tests in a series of newspaper letters signed, "A Landholder." In *Landholder, No. 7* (1787), he answered those who attacked the clause, concluding that its "sole purpose" was to secure "the important right of religious liberty" and that "[a] test-law is the parent of hypocrisy, and the offspring of error and the spirit of persecution."[80]

Isaac Backus, an Antifederalist delegate in the Massachusetts convention, supported the Constitution because of its provision prohibiting religious test oaths. Imposing such oaths, Backus reasoned, violated a principle evident by reason and Scripture "that religion is ever a matter between God and individuals." He added:

> And let the history of all nations be searched from [Constantine's] day to this, and it will appear that the imposing of religious tests hath been the greatest engine of tyranny in the world. . . . Some serious minds discover a concern lest, if all religious tests should be excluded, the Congress would hereafter establish Popery, or some other tyrannical way of worship. But it is most certain that no such way of worship can be established without any religious test.[81]

In Virginia, Madison and Edmund Randolph defended the Constitution against the assertions of Antifederalists, particularly Henry, that the absence of a bill of rights placed religious freedom and other fundamental liberties in jeopardy. Madison stressed that there was "not a shadow of right in the general government to intermeddle with religion," and that the best security for religious freedom was America's multiplicity of sects, "for where there is such a variety of sects, there cannot be a majority of any one sect to oppress and persecute the rest." Agreeing that the nation's variety of religious groups would "prevent the establishment of any one sect," Randolph applauded the ban on test oaths in article VI on the ground that it "puts all sects on the same footing," thereby allowing "[a] man of abilities and character, of any sect whatever," to serve the republic.[82]

In the North Carolina ratifying convention, James Iredell, soon to become a Supreme Court Justice, emerged as a leading spokesman for the federal test oath clause. Like other Federalists, he argued that Congress possessed no authority in religious matters and defended the clause on historical and pragmatic grounds. Stressing the historical evils caused by test oaths, Iredell remarked that America had shown "that a man may be of different religious sentiments from our own, without being a bad member of society." He considered the ban "one of the strongest proofs that could be adduced, that it was the intention of those who formed this system to establish a general religious liberty in America." On pragmatic grounds, Iredell denounced test oaths as ineffective — a person of integrity would refuse to subscribe to an oath inconsistent with his or her convictions, while an individual of "base principles" would not hesitate to take an oath in the interests of political expediency.[83]

The federal test oath clause apparently had a liberalizing effect on the states. The Pennsylvania Constitution of 1790 contained a much weaker religious test than its constitution of 1776, and by 1793, Delaware, South Carolina, Georgia, and Vermont had removed religious tests from their constitutions. The revision of Pennsylvania's test oath of 1776 resulted in part from the efforts of Philadelphia's Jewish community. In December 1783, the city's one synagogue submitted a memorial to the civil authorities objecting to the requirement that state legislators acknowledge the divine inspiration of the Old and New Testaments. Four years later, Jonas Phillips, a Philadelphia Jew, petitioned the Federal Constitutional Convention concerning the same provision.[84] The Pennsylvania Constitution of 1790 accommodated the Jewish requests, requiring only that state officials acknowledge "the being of a God and a future state of rewards and punishments."[85] Despite the decline of religious test oaths, they endured until 1961, when the Supreme Court invalidated a Maryland law requiring notary publics to declare a belief in God.[86]

Although Federalist leaders made assurances that the national government exercised only enumerated powers, the absence of a bill of rights in the Constitution evoked strong protests among the populace and in the state ratifying conventions.[87] Even though Pennsylvania and Maryland ratified the Constitution without recommending any amendments, some delegates criticized the document for failing to guarantee basic rights. New Hampshire, New York, and Virginia approved the Constitution by close votes, but all three states suggested amendments that included religious liberty guarantees.[88] New Hampshire's proposed eleventh amendment read, "Congress shall make no laws touching religion, or to infringe the rights of conscience."[89] Almost certainly drafted by Samuel Livermore, this provision played an important role in the legislative history of the religion clauses.[90] When the First Congress met in New York in 1789, it faced the dual tasks of launching the new government and addressing the demand for a bill of rights.

On June 8, 1789, Madison introduced a series of amendments in the House of Representatives. To fulfill a campaign promise made to Baptist constituents, he included a provision guaranteeing religious freedom: "The civil rights of none shall be abridged on account of religious belief or worship, nor shall any national religion be established, nor shall the full and equal rights of conscience be in any manner, or on any pretext, infringed."[91] He also proposed a clause exempting persons "religiously scrupulous of bearing arms" from military service and a clause stating that "[n]o State shall violate the equal rights of conscience."[92]

Pressed by the need for organizing the new government, the House took little action on these recommendations until August 15, 1789, when it debated a proposal that "no religion shall be established by law, nor shall the equal rights of conscience be infringed."[93] Representative Sylvester questioned the wording of the proposed amendment, expressing the fear — with no recorded explanation — "it might be thought to have a tendency to abolish religion altogether." Representative Gerry recommended that the amendment be changed to read "that no religious doctrine shall be established by law." Stressing that the people strongly desired a religious freedom guarantee, Daniel Carroll thought the "phraseology" less important than insuring the inclusion of such a guarantee. He emphasized that "the rights of conscience are, in their nature, of peculiar delicacy, and will little bear the gentlest touch of governmental hand."

Madison apprehended the meaning of the religious freedom proposal "to be, that Congress should not establish a religion, and enforce the legal observation of it by law, nor compel men to worship God in any manner contrary to their conscience." He noted that some of the state conventions had concluded that a specific amendment was needed to prevent Congress from using its power under the "necessary and proper" clause to "make laws of such a nature as might infringe the rights of conscience, and establish a national religion." When Representative Huntington objected that the proposal might prove "extremely hurtful to the cause of religion," Madison responded by recommending the insertion of "national" before religion:

[Madison] believed that the people feared one sect might obtain a pre-eminence, or two combine together, and establish a religion to which they would compel others to conform. He thought if the word "national" was introduced, it would point the amendment directly to the object it was intended to prevent.

Representative Gerry took exception to the term "national" because it would confirm the fear of Antifederalists that "this form of Government consolidated the Union" and would invade the authority of the states. Madison withdrew his motion, but disagreed that the words "no national religion shall be established by law" implied a national government. The House then passed Livermore's motion to adopt the New Hampshire ratifying convention's proposed eleventh amendment, "Congress shall make no laws touching religion, or infringing the rights of conscience."

On August 17, the House debated Madison's conscientious objector clause and adopted the provision prohibiting the states from "infring[ing] the equal rights of conscience."[94] Three days later, it adopted a conscientious objector provision, as well as an amendment based on wording recommended by Fisher Ames of Massachusetts: "Congress shall make no law establishing religion, or to prevent the free exercise thereof, or to infringe the rights of conscience."[95] This amendment and others, including the prohibition against state infringement of conscience, were forwarded to the Senate on August 24.[96]

The record of the Senate debates is fragmentary because the body met in secret. Evidence suggests, however, that the Senate took a guarded approach concerning the House's religious freedom amendment. On September 3, the Senate rejected several proposed revisions of the amendment, including one that read: "Congress shall make no law establishing any particular denomination of religion in preference to another, or prohibiting the free exercise thereof, nor shall the rights of conscience be infringed."[97] On September 7, the Senate rejected the clause prohibiting the states from violating the equal rights of conscience and, two days later, adopted a religious freedom provision that was significantly narrower than the House version: "Congress shall make no law establishing articles of faith or a mode of worship, or prohibiting the free exercise of religion. . . ."[98]

Unable to agree on several proposed amendments, including the religious freedom provision, the two houses referred the matters to a joint committee consisting of Senators Oliver Ellsworth of Connecticut, Charles Carroll of Maryland, and William Paterson of New Jersey, and Representatives Roger Sherman of Connecticut, John Vining of Delaware, and

James Madison of Virginia. This group produced the present wording of the First Amendment. Unfortunately, no record of their deliberations has been preserved; consequently the authorship of the amendment and precise intent of the committee remain uncertain.

In addition to framing the religion clauses, the First Congress revised the Northwest Ordinance of 1787, appointed paid chaplains for the House and Senate, and passed a resolution requesting the President to proclaim "a day of public thanksgiving and prayer, to be observed by acknowledging, with grateful hearts, the many signal favors of Almighty God."[99] On September 25, 1789, President Washington submitted twelve proposed amendments to the states. What is now the First Amendment was the third of these articles.

The ratification proceedings in the state assemblies offer only limited evidence concerning the meaning of the religion clauses.[100] The most illuminating debates occurred in Virginia, where the House of Delegates and Senate argued for two years over whether the amendments adequately secured individual rights. The Senate objected that the establishment clause restrained Congress only from "passing laws establishing any national religion" and that, unlike the Virginia Declaration of Rights, it did not prevent the general government from levying taxes to prefer "any particular denomination of Christians . . . over others."[101] Despite these objections, the Senate finally acquiesced and, on December 15, 1791, Virginia became the necessary eleventh state to ratify the Bill of Rights.

Commentary on the legislative history of the religion clauses is voluminous.[102] Unfortunately, scholars have generally approached this history with the aim of either proving or disproving the nonpreferentialist thesis. According to this thesis, the Framers intended the clauses to prohibit preferential treatment for a particular religion, but not support for religion in general.[103] It is questionable whether the rich and diverse history of the religion clauses can be reduced to such a simplistic formula. Rather than imposing a thesis on history, scholars should examine history independently of presentist concerns. As will become clear in subsequent chapters, the Framers held a range of views on the interaction of religion and government and approached the subject with political and philosophical concerns broader in scope than the focus of the nonpreferentialist debate.[104]

The First Amendment by its language restricted only the national government, leaving authority over religious matters to the states. In 1845, the Supreme Court affirmed this limitation in *Permoli v. Municipality No. 1 of*

New Orleans.[105] In *Permoli*, a Roman Catholic priest who performed a funeral in accordance with his faith was fined under an ordinance that prohibited anyone from exposing a corpse or performing funeral rites in any Catholic church. Instead, the ordinance required the use of a specially designated municipal chapel. In rejecting the priest's contention that the free exercise clause shielded his conduct, the Court stated: "The Constitution makes no provision for protecting the citizens of the respective states in their religious liberties; this is left to the state constitutions and laws: nor is there any inhibition imposed by the Constitution of the United States in this respect on the states."[106]

Since the establishment clause was not applicable to the states in the nineteenth century, disestablishment of the Congregational Church in New England came only after years of conflict.[107] The growth of religious pluralism and the importuning of dissenters eventually forced disestablishment in Vermont in 1807, Connecticut in 1818, New Hampshire in 1819, and finally, Massachusetts in 1833. The Reverend Lyman Beecher, one of Connecticut's leading ministers, provides an interesting illustration of changing attitudes towards religious voluntarism and pluralism. Beecher, originally a staunch defender of the state church, was convinced that disestablishment would destroy both church and state. Later, he concluded that it was "the best thing that ever happened to the State of Connecticut" because it threw the churches "wholly on their own resources and on God."[108]

2. The Founders on Religious Liberty

> And let us with caution indulge the supposition that morality can be maintained without religion. Whatever may be conceded to the influence of refined education on minds of peculiar structure, reason and experience both forbid us to expect that national morality can prevail in exclusion of religious principle.
>
> > George Washington,
> > Farewell Address, 1796

In deciding religious liberty issues, the Supreme Court has often referred to the views of the Founding Fathers as expressed in the legislative history of the religion clauses, official acts, proclamations, speeches, and correspondence.[1] Although difficult to define exactly, the term "Founding Fathers" commonly refers to the leaders who forged the nation.[2] It frequently is reserved for those who participated in promulgating one or more of three documents: the Declaration of Independence, the Constitution, and the Bill of Rights. Such criteria, while providing helpful guidance, should not be considered all-inclusive. Jefferson, John Adams, and Samuel Adams made substantial contributions during the nation's formative period, but none was present at the Constitutional Convention. Often used interchangeably with "Founding Fathers," the term "Framers" refers to a narrower category, consisting of those who drafted the nation's fundamental law and its particular guarantees. For example, the Framers of the test oath clause would be limited to the Convention delegates, while the Framers of the First Amendment would include the members of the First Congress, or perhaps only the members of the drafting committee.

It is useful to classify the Founders according to their views on religion and society.[3] Although their sentiments ranged from radical deistic separation to a desire for close cooperation between church and state, at least three major groups may be identified: Enlightenment separationists, political centrists, and pietistic separationists.[4] The views of the Founders fall more on a continuum than in distinct positions, but the categories provide a useful analytical framework.

The Enlightenment Separationists

Those deeply influenced by the Enlightenment, such as Thomas Paine, Jefferson, and to a lesser extent Madison, approached the issue of church and state suspicious of institutional religion and its potential for corrupting government.[5] They were not necessarily irreligious; as adherents of deism, Jefferson and Paine rejected divine revelation, but affirmed the existence of an impersonal Creator, one indifferent to his creation, on the basis of reason and nature. Madison, while circumspect about his religious beliefs, adhered to views closer to traditional Christian doctrine. Although all three saw the necessity of institutional separation, they represented a spectrum of views: from Paine, an extreme separationist, to Madison, who expressed concern for both true piety and government.

Paine, the fiery agitator and pamphleteer during the Revolution, espoused an anticlerical deism, attacked revealed religion as the source for "the most horrid cruelties," and regarded national churches as "human inventions, set up to terrify and enslave mankind, and monopolize power and profit."[6] In *Common Sense* (1776), he emphasized the duty of government to protect all forms of religious profession and asserted that God had intended there to be "a diversity of religious opinions among us." Paine applauded the French Revolution and the Declaration of the Rights of Man and of Citizens (1789), which included a provision recognizing the right to hold religious opinions as inalienable. In *The Rights of Man*, he praised the French for establishing the universal right of conscience, condemning—as he phrased it—the union of church and state as "a sort of mule-animal, capable only of destroying, and not of breeding up."[7]

Jefferson, also deeply influenced by French thought, advocated a more temperate form of separation.[8] An Anglican churchgoer, he denounced Christian doctrine, but adhered to Jesus' moral code as the "most perfect and sublime that has ever been taught by man."[9] As revealed by his epitaph, Jefferson regarded the Declaration of Independence, the founding of the University of Virginia, and the Bill for Establishing Religious Freedom as his greatest achievements—notably omitting his service as President.[10]

Despite its stature, Jefferson's Bill for Establishing Religious Freedom has been overshadowed in constitutional jurisprudence by his reference in a letter to the Danbury Baptist Association in 1802 to "a wall of separation." Emphasizing that "religion is a matter which lies solely between man and his God" and that governmental power can "reach actions only, and not opinions," Jefferson contemplated with "sovereign reverence" the American people's adoption of the religion clauses, "thus building a wall of separation between church and State." The letter closed:

> Adhering to this expression of the supreme will of the nation in behalf of the rights of conscience, I shall see with sincere satisfaction the progress of those sentiments which tend to restore to man all his natural rights, convinced he has no natural right in opposition to his social duties.[11]

Jefferson's wall metaphor has figured prominently in the Supreme Court's decisions on church and state. The Court relied heavily on the metaphor in *Reynolds v. United States* (1879),[12] its first decision under the religion clauses. In *Everson v. Board of Education* (1947),[13] a seminal establishment clause case, it raised the figure of speech to constitutional status, asserting: "The First Amendment has erected a wall between church and state. That wall must be kept high and impregnable."[14] In more recent decisions, the Court has retreated from this position and the Justices are now divided concerning the metaphor's utility.[15] The wall of separation has also generated controversy in the academic community. Scholars supporting the figure of speech argue that it accurately expresses America's constitutional heritage of church-state relations and embodies an ideal towards which American society should strive.[16] Critics of the metaphor stress that constitutional interpretation should focus on the First Amendment's actual wording, rather than on a literary comparison used by one Founder in a personal letter.[17]

Jefferson served as Minister to France from 1785 to 1789, and therefore did not participate in either the Constitutional Convention or the First Congress. Given that he was not a Framer, it is perhaps surprising that the Supreme Court adopted his controversial "wall of separation" metaphor as descriptive of the clauses. While President, Jefferson broke with tradition by refusing to issue religious proclamations because he considered the national government "interdicted by the Constitution from intermeddling with religious institutions, their doctrines, discipline, or exercises."[18] As a state legislator, however, he participated in a comprehensive revision of

Virginia's laws, which included: A Bill for Punishing Disturbers of Religious Worship and Sabbath Breakers; A Bill for Appointing Days of Public Fasting and Thanksgiving; and A Bill Annulling Marriages Prohibited by the Levitical Law, and Appointing the Mode of Solemnizing Lawful Marriage.[19] Perhaps Jefferson's disparate actions on the state and federal levels can be reconciled by reference to the principle of federalism, the belief that the states possessed authority over religious matters not possessed by the federal government.[20]

Although Jefferson was guarded about his religious convictions, certain conclusions emerge from his writings on church and state. First, his deistic world view was tempered by common sense realism and a personal moral code premised in part on theism. Central to this outlook was a confidence that the mind, unfettered by temporal or spiritual coercion, would arrive at truth through reason and experience. Second, Jefferson asserted that institutional religion impeded the quest for truth by diverting the mind to nonessential doctrinal matters derived from revelation. This diversion not only prevented agreement on fundamental truths, it led to division and intolerance among religions. Third, an established church constituted one of the gravest threats to freedom of the mind because it provided the "orthodox" doctrine which civil authorities were to promote through coercive legal means. Finally, Jefferson consistently emphasized, particularly in his writings connected with the Virginia struggle, that man is answerable only to God for the rights of conscience and that governmental authority extends only to regulating external actions injurious to others.

According to Jefferson, at least two social factors operated to preserve religious liberty. First, the presence of numerous sects inhibited the government or a religious majority from attempting to create uniformity in religious matters. Second, the principle of federalism deprived the general government of authority over religion, leaving to the states the power to enact lawful regulations affecting churches and their adherents.

Among the Founders who espoused Enlightenment separation, Madison manifested the most concern for protecting the purity of both government and institutional religion.[21] He differed from Jefferson in deriving religious liberty primarily from divine will rather than political utility.[22] No Founder contributed to the cause of religious liberty more than Madison, considered the chief architect of the Constitution and prime drafter of the Bill of Rights. Although it is often assumed that Madison authored the religion clauses, it should be noted that the evidence for this belief is ambiguous, particularly given the fact that a joint committee produced the present wording.[23] Madison regarded liberty of conscience as the most sacred inalienable right and devoted his greatest efforts to securing its protection. As a Virginia legislator, he insured that the Virginia Declaration of Rights guaranteed the free exercise of religion, not merely toleration, greatly contributed to the defeat of the Assessment Bill with his monumental *Memorial and Remonstrance*, and secured passage of Jefferson's Bill for Establishing Religious Freedom.

On the national level, Madison pressed for a bill of rights in the First Congress and served on the committee that drafted the First Amendment. As President, he demonstrated his commitment to separation of church and state when he vetoed bills incorporating the Episcopal Church in Washington, D.C., and reserving federal land for a Baptist Church.[24] Apparently with some misgivings, however, Madison yielded to the precedent set by Washington and issued three proclamations recommending public humiliation and prayer and one recommending a day of thanksgiving "to Almighty God for His great goodness."[25] In 1822, after his presidency, he wrote that America was teaching the world that "Religion flourishes in greater purity, without than with the aid of Government."[26]

In retirement, Madison argued for complete separation between Christianity and government, asserting that the establishment clause prohibited presidential religious proclamations, as well as congressional and military chaplains.[27] Though distrustful of institutional religion, he remained an Episcopalian throughout his life and maintained strong religious convictions. He wrote in 1825 that "belief in a God All Powerful wise and good, is so essential to the moral order of the World and to the happiness of man, that arguments which enforce it cannot be drawn from too many sources."[28]

Like his friend Jefferson, Madison closely guarded his religious convictions; consequently his views on church and state have been the subject of vigorous debate. Several cardinal themes, however, can be discerned in his writings. First, more so than Jefferson, he derived his convictions from a theistic world view which affirmed liberty of conscience as a God-given right beyond the jurisdiction of government. Second, Madison understood an establishment as an alliance between civil and religious authorities resulting in the coercion of belief and practice to favor a particular church. Such an alliance corrupted both church and state by violating the key principles of religious voluntarism and equality among sects. To preserve the integrity of both government and religion it was therefore necessary to maintain a rigid institutional separation. In a letter written in 1822, Madison asserted that "a perfect separation between ecclesiastical and civil matters" should be maintained because "religion and Government will both exist in greater purity, the less they are mixed together."[29] Third, he believed that religious freedom is most easily guarded in a country with a multiplicity of sects. Finally, Madison agreed with Jefferson that federalism played an essential role in preserving religious liberty by preventing the accumulation of governmental power at the federal level.

The Political Centrists

Although the Supreme Court has stressed the Enlightenment tradition of separation, historical evidence suggests that this tradition was not the predominant position among the Founders. Most, including George Washington, John Adams, the Carrolls of Maryland, John Marshall, and Oliver Ellsworth, believed that religion was an essential cornerstone for morality, civic virtue, and democratic government. While committed to liberty of conscience, they were generally alarmed by the anticlericalism of Enlightenment separationists such as Paine and looked favorably on organized religion as necessary for social cohesion.

Perhaps most representative of this centrist position was Washington, who commanded the greatest respect among the Founders and seemed to embody the popular consensus concerning the interaction of religion and government.[30] He believed "that *Religion* and *Morality* are the essential pillars of Civil society" and affirmed that everyone should be "protected in worshipping the Deity according to the dictates of their consciences."[31] As commander of the Continental Army, Washington ordered soldiers to attend public worship, prohibited "profane cursing," and directed regimental commanders to procure chaplains.[32]

During his presidency, Washington established a precedent by issuing the first thanksgiving day proclamation after the adoption of the Constitution. In promulgating "A National Thanksgiving" in 1789, Washington urged the people to thank that "great and glorious Being . . . for the civil and religious liberty with which we are blessed."[33] He repeatedly acknowledged the Deity in official pronouncements, invoking in his First Inaugural Address the assistance of "that Almighty Being who rules over the universe, who presides in the councils of nations, and whose providential aids can supply every human defect."[34] One of Washington's most famous statements on religious freedom occurred in a reply to the Jewish Congregation of Newport:

It is now no more that toleration is spoken of, as if it was by the indulgence of one class of people, that another enjoyed the exercise of their inherent natural rights. For happily the government of the United States, which gives to bigotry no sanction, to persecution no assistance, requires only that they who live under its protection should demean themselves as good citizens, in giving it on all occasions their effectual support.[35]

In his Farewell Address in 1796, Washington counseled that "reason and experience both forbid us to expect that national morality can prevail in exclusion of religious principle."[36]

The nation's second president, John Adams, stressed theistic natural law and the importance of Christianity in public life.[37] Emphasizing that "we have no government armed with power capable of contending with human passions unbridled by morality and religion," he stated in 1798: "Our Constitution was made only for a moral and religious people. It is wholly inadequate to the government of any other."[38] While influenced by a broadly Puritan upbringing, Adams denounced institutional religion's dogma and intolerance, but defended the Massachusetts Congregational establishment as necessary for social stability. As President, he issued proclamations for two national fast days, urging dependence on God as essential for the "promotion of that morality and piety without which social happiness can not exist nor the blessings of a free government be enjoyed."[39]

In the face of strong anti-Catholic prejudice, the Carroll family of Maryland showed their commitment to the place of religion in the new nation by securing public acceptance of the Roman Catholic Church.[40] Charles Carroll signed the Declaration of Independence, sat in the First Congress, and participated on the committee that drafted the First Amendment. His cousin Daniel signed the Constitution and, as a member of the First Congress, urged a religious freedom guarantee because liberty of conscience was a fundamental right of "peculiar delicacy." John Carroll, Daniel's brother, became America's first Roman Catholic bishop, accommodating the Church to the nation's religious pluralism and counseling toleration towards other Christians.

Two of the most influential Supreme Court Justices in the early years of the nation, Chief Justice John Marshall and Justice Joseph Story, also believed that religion was essential for the survival of the republic.[41] In a letter to the Reverend Jasper Adams in 1833, Marshall stressed the close relationship between Christianity and civil government:

> The American population is entirely Christian, and with us, Christianity and Religion are identified. It would be strange, indeed, if with such a people, our institutions did not presuppose Christianity, and did not often refer to it, and exhibit relations with it. Legislation on the subject is admitted to require great delicacy, because freedom of conscience and respect for our religion both claim our most serious regard.[42]

Story disputed Jefferson's contention that Christianity was not part of the common law, arguing in his *Commentaries on the Constitution* (1833) that the Christian religion provided "the great basis, on which [the republic] must rest for its support and permanence."[43] According to Story, the real object of the religion clauses was "to exclude all rivalry among Christian sects, and to prevent any national ecclesiastical establishment, which should give to an hierarchy the exclusive patronage of the national government."[44]

Oliver Ellsworth of Connecticut, a Framer of the First Amendment and later Chief Justice of the Supreme Court, agreed with political centrists and pietistic separationists on the role of religion in the republic.[45] Defending the federal ban on test oaths, he called religious tests the "parent of hypocrisy" and argued that "government has no business to meddle with the private opinions of the people." According to Ellsworth, the test oath ban was intended to exclude persecution and to secure religious liberty. He conceded, however, that government could interfere in religious matters to "punish gross immoralities and impieties," including "profane swearing, blasphemy, and professed atheism."[46]

The Pietistic Separationists

The third major position among the Founders followed the example of Roger Williams and William Penn in aggressively defending religious liberty as vital to authentic faith and the purity of the church.[47] This theologically grounded stance affirmed that "God has appointed two kinds of government . . . which are distinct in their nature and ought never to be confounded together."[48] This is not to suggest, however, that advocates of pietistic separation conceived of a secular society or even a secular government; rather, they felt that government should foster an environment conducive to voluntary religious faith and practice. The Supreme Court, at least in its earlier decisions, largely overlooked this tradition, perhaps because pietistic separationists generally were members of dissenting religious groups and therefore not well represented at the Convention. Pietists, however, provided essential political support for leaders such as Madison and were well represented in state ratifying conventions.

The leading advocate of this tradition in the revolutionary and early national periods was the Baptist minister Isaac Backus, who rediscovered Williams's thought, expounded a comprehensive theological basis for separation, and worked tirelessly to disestablish Congregationalism in New England.[49] In contrast to either church domination of the state or state domination of the church, both of which were present in New England's history, Backus proposed a third alternative: a government of Christian magistrates who limited themselves to the civil sphere and left the clergy to spiritual functions. Commenting on the role of civil and religious leaders, he remarked, "there may and ought to be a sweet harmony between them; yet as there is a great difference between the nature of their work, they never ought to have *such a union* together" as was found in New England.[50]

Backus's view of pietistic separation can be seen clearly in his political activity. At the request of a delegate to the Massachusetts constitutional convention of 1778, Backus drafted a bill of rights that mirrored the Virginia Declaration of Rights in important respects. The proposed draft differed significantly on freedom of conscience, however, because of his theological presuppositions:

> As God is the only worthy object of all religious worship, and nothing can be true religion but a voluntary obedience unto his revealed will, of which each rational soul has an equal right to judge for itself, every person has an unalienable right to act in all religious affairs according to the full persuasion of his own mind, where others are not injured thereby.[51]

Thus, to Backus religious freedom was a means of ensuring the voluntary worship of God. The state convention did not adopt his draft, deciding instead to protect its establishment by mandating public taxation for the support of the Congregational churches. As a delegate to the Massachusetts ratifying convention of 1788, Backus supported the Federal Constitution, despite Antifederalist convictions, because of the provision in article VI banning religious test oaths. Although an advocate of separation of church and state and a political supporter of Jefferson in the presidential election of 1800, he did not desire the secular state that was envisioned by Jefferson. To the contrary, Backus expressed no opposition to Sabbath laws, teaching Calvinistic doctrine in the public schools, proscribing blasphemy, and conducting official days of fasting and prayer.[52]

Another Founder who championed pietistic separation was John Witherspoon, the only member of the clergy to sign the Declaration of Independence.[53] In his wartime sermon, *The Dominion of Providence over the Passions of Men*, he pointed out: "There is not a single instance in history in which civil liberty was lost, and religious liberty preserved entire."[54] While president of the College of New Jersey, later Princeton University, Witherspoon served as Madison's mentor in law and ethics. In his lectures on moral philosophy, he taught that the civil magistrate should "promote true religion [as] the best and most effectual way of making a virtuous and regular people." Although magistrates should not coerce belief in religion, they ought to "encourage piety by [their] own example," "defend the rights of conscience," and "enact laws for the punishment of acts of profanity and impiety."[55] Witherspoon left an indelible imprint on the political life of the nation, serving as a congressman for six years, a state legislator for two terms, and a delegate to the New Jersey convention that ratified the Federal Constitution.

Evidence also suggests that Roger Sherman of Connecticut was an important advocate of the pietistic tradition.[56] Deeply influenced by the theological views of Jonathan Edwards, Sherman served as a deacon of the evangelical church at New Haven, pastored by Jonathan Edwards, Jr. His commitment to evangelical religion and conviction that the republic rested on Judeo-Christian principles found expression in a distinguished political career. Sherman was not only a Framer of the First Amendment, but one of the few Founders to sign the Declaration of Independence, the Articles of Confederation, and the Constitution. In the Continental Congress, he served on a committee which drafted instructions for a diplomatic mission to Canada in 1776. The committee instructed the delegation to emphasize that if Canada joined the confederation of states, its predominantly Catholic citizens would enjoy the free exercise of religion, "provided, however, that all other denominations of Christians be equally entitled to hold offices and enjoy civil privileges and the free exercise of their religion and be totally exempt from the payment of any tythes or taxes for the support of any religion."[57] During the Constitutional Convention, Sherman seconded Benjamin Franklin's motion to have local clergy open the assembly's deliberations each morning by "imploring the assistance of Heaven."[58] The United States has a separate bill of rights because he persuaded the First Congress to append the amendments rather than to incorporate them into the text of the Constitution, as suggested by Madison.[59]

Summary

The spectrum of views expressed by the Founders on religion and government may be classified for heuristic purposes into three groups: Enlightenment separation, political centrist, and pietistic separation. All three contributed to the historical meaning of the religion clauses, and all three are therefore relevant for constitutional interpretation. Any attempt to reduce the Founders' views to one position or to read the beliefs of certain Founders, no matter how prominent, into the First Amendment is apt to produce indefensible and culturally unacceptable results.

All three traditions were committed to the ideal of religious liberty, but they approached the issue from different perspectives. Both Enlightenment and pietistic separationists worked, often with great zeal, to separate church and state in an institutional sense. Those deeply influenced by the Enlightenment, such as Paine and Jefferson, adhered to anticlerical views and focused on insulating government from religious domination. Madison shared this view somewhat, but tempered it with a concern for protecting the purity of religious belief and practice. Those Founders espousing pietistic separation, most prominently Backus, Witherspoon, and Sherman, inherited the emphasis of Williams and Penn on protecting religion from the corrupting effect of governmental interference. Political centrists such as Washington and John Adams approached the issue of church and state in more pragmatic terms. Less concerned than the separationists with the specific means of attaining religious liberty, they regarded religion as an essential source of personal and social morality and, when in office, repeatedly recognized its importance in the nation's public life. Although the Founders represented a spectrum of views, they were virtually unanimous in the belief that the republic could not survive without religion's moral influence. Consequently, they did not envision a secular society, but rather one receptive to voluntary religious expression.

3. The Supreme Court and Religious Liberty

> The basic purpose of the religion clause of the First Amendment is to promote and assure the fullest possible scope of religious liberty and tolerance for all and to nurture the conditions which secure the best hope of attainment of that end.
>
> Justice Arthur Goldberg,
> *Abington School District v. Schempp*, 1963

After examining the growth of American religious liberty, the framing of the religion clauses, and the views of the Founders, it is appropriate to ask what guidance history affords in construing these provisions. More fundamentally, how useful is history in resolving current issues pertaining to church and state? What values and principles does the American heritage yield to guide modern courts in this area? In addressing these questions, this chapter will discuss the emergence of the Supreme Court as an important institution in determining the relationship between church and state and the Court's resort to history in adjudicating religious freedom issues. We will then consider the historical concept of liberty of conscience in light of the Court's jurisprudence under the religion clauses.

The Court as Constitutional Historian

From the republic's inception to the early decades of the twentieth century, religious liberty emerged largely without the participation of the federal judiciary. Early federal decisions contained language regarding the nation's religious origins and its commitment to religious freedom, but few of these squarely addressed claims arising under the religion clauses. Indeed, the nation had existed for almost a century before the Supreme Court rendered its first decision under the clauses, *Reynolds v. United States* (1879).

The First Amendment originally restricted only the actions of Congress in the realm of religion; as noted in chapter 1, the Supreme Court confirmed this restriction in 1845. The Supreme Court and lower federal courts had the power to review alleged establishment or free exercise violations by Congress under article III, which states that the "judicial Power [of the United States] shall extend to all Cases, in Law and Equity, arising under this Constitution."[1] Thus, suits alleging *congressional* violations under the religion clauses could be resolved by federal courts because they constituted cases arising under the Constitution. Because the clauses limited only Congress, however, the federal courts lacked jurisdiction to review religious liberty claims brought against the state governments. The infrequency of federal cases interpreting the religion clauses between the late eighteenth and early twentieth centuries is thus attributable to at least two factors: the small number of religion-based claims initiated against the national government and the limitations on federal review of state actions involving religion.

The Supreme Court's prominent role in addressing the modern interaction of religion and government derives from the advent in the early twentieth century of a judicial doctrine known as incorporation. Under the incorporation doctrine, the Court extended certain provisions of the Bill of Rights to restrict the scope of state, as well as federal, power. The limited role of the federal judiciary in interpreting the religion clauses changed dramatically in the 1940s when the Court used this doctrine to apply both the establishment and free exercise prohibitions to state and local laws involving religion. The incorporation doctrine, a landmark development in constitutional law, inaugurated a new era of federal judicial supremacy and reshaped the legal landscape for religious liberty issues. On what basis did the Court take this important step?

The Fourteenth Amendment, adopted in 1868, prohibits any state from "depriv[ing] any person of life, liberty, or property, without due process of law."[2] One of the Court's difficult tasks in interpreting this provision, known as the due process clause, was to give content to the broad term "liberty." The Court addressed this task in 1937 in *Palko v. Connecticut*,[3] reasoning that the liberty protected by the due process clause included or "incorporated" those guarantees of the Bill of Rights "implicit in the concept of ordered liberty." Determining whether a guarantee was essential for ordered liberty depended on whether it rested on "a principle of justice so rooted in the traditions and conscience of our people as to be ranked as fundamental."[4] Three years later in *Cantwell v. Connecticut*, a unanimous Court concluded that the liberty protected by the Fourteenth Amendment embraced the free exercise guarantee, making it applicable to laws enacted by the states as well as by Congress.[5] Thus, the Court used the liberty prong of the due process clause to extend the free exercise clause, originally designed to restrict only Congress, to state governmental action. This conclusion sparked little controversy, for the right to exercise one's religion seemed a natural component of any proper conception of liberty.

The more controversial issue was whether the liberty protected by the due process clause encompassed the nonestablishment provision. The Court addressed this question in 1947 in *Everson v. Board of Education*,[6] the seminal decision that sustained a New Jersey law affording reimbursement for the bus fares of parochial school children. The Court stated, without explanation, that the Fourteenth Amendment made the First Amendment guarantees, including the establishment clause, applicable to the states.[7] Prominent legal scholars immediately criticized this conclusion on historical and legal grounds. They argued, for example, that one of the primary purposes of the establishment clause was to preclude federal interference with state religious establishments, and that incorporation therefore turned the clause on its head by transforming it into a vehicle for expansive federal interference in state religious matters.[8] Focusing on the guarantee of liberty in the due process clause, Edward Corwin asserted that "[s]o far as the Fourteenth Amendment is concerned, States are entirely free to establish religions, provided they do not deprive anybody of religious liberty."[9] Paul Freund expressed a similar sentiment: "What does not seem so inevitable is the inclusion within the Fourteenth Amendment of the concept of nonestablishment of religion in the sense of forbidding nondiscriminatory aid to religion, where there is no interference with freedom of religious exercise."[10]

After holding that the establishment clause applied to the states through the Fourteenth Amendment, the *Everson* Court looked to history to determine whether the transportation aid violated the establishment clause. The Court recounted the rise of religious liberty in America, focusing in particular on the campaign in Virginia against Patrick Henry's Assessment Bill and the enactment there of Jefferson's Bill for Establishing Religious Freedom. Invoking Jefferson's wall of separation, Justice Black's majority opinion announced an expansive reading of the establishment clause: "Neither [a state nor the federal government] can pass laws which aid one religion, aid all religions, or prefer one religion over another. . . . No tax in any amount, large or small, can be levied to support any religious activities or institutions. . . ." Relying on a public welfare rationale, however, the Court concluded that the New Jersey bus law did not breach the "high and impregnable" wall between church and state.[11]

In a dissent joined by three colleagues, Justice Rutledge also discussed the Virginia struggle at length and agreed with the majority that the establishment clause erected Jefferson's wall. He thought it clear, however, that the bus law violated the clause, which he read to forbid "any appropriation, large or small, from public funds to aid or support any and all religious exercises."[12] All nine Justices agreed that the establishment clause erected a wall of separation, but the dissenters asserted that the majority had misapplied this principle.

Everson evoked widespread and diverse commentary. In addition to criticizing the incorporation of the establishment clause, scholars challenged the manner in which the Justices employed history and disputed the Court's historical conclusions.[13] Critics asserted that the Court erred in relying solely on Madison and Jefferson and in equating the views that animated the Virginia struggle with those that inspired the religion clauses.[14] They also criticized the Court for failing to analyze the legislative history of the clauses,[15] and for ignoring the theological roots of American religious liberty. On the latter point, Mark DeWolfe Howe maintained that the Court's adoption of the Jeffersonian view of separation caused it to disregard the evangelical tradition of religious freedom espoused by Roger Williams.[16]

Perhaps the most controversial aspect of *Everson* was the Court's broad reading of the establishment clause and its rejection of the nonpreferentialist thesis that the Framers did not intend the clause to ban nondiscriminatory aid to religion in general. Critics maintained that the religion clauses did not foreclose such nondiscriminatory aid;[17] instead, the clauses were intended to prevent establishment of a national church, secure freedom of conscience against invasion by the federal government, and prevent federal interference with state authority in religious matters.[18] Despite heavy criticism, it should be noted that the Black-Rutledge formula of broad separation received support from a number of prominent scholars, including Leonard Levy, Leo Pfeffer, and Milton Konvitz.[19]

The use of history in constitutional interpretation sparked debate in 1985 between then Attorney General Edwin Meese, an advocate of judicial restraint and the originalist position, and Justice William Brennan, a defender of judicial activism and a living Constitution. Criticizing the Court for failing to develop a constitutional jurisprudence premised on the Framers' original intent, Meese asserted that the Court's notion of "strict neutrality between religion and nonreligion would have struck the founding generation as bizarre." Justice Brennan countered by emphasizing that the Constitution is a living document subject to "contemporary ratification," and that the judiciary must interpret the text to promote human dignity in light of society's changing values and needs. Stressing the emergence of issues unforeseen by the Framers, he argued that it was "arrogance cloaked as humility" for anyone "to pretend that from our vantage we can gauge accurately the intent of the Framers on application of principle to specific, contemporary questions."[20]

Several years earlier, in a case involving the constitutionality of Nebraska's legislative chaplaincy, Justice Brennan had stressed that "the Constitution is not a static document whose meaning on every detail is fixed for all time by the life experience of the Framers."[21] Rather, he asserted that proper respect for the Framers demanded that the Court look to "broad purposes, not specific practices."[22]

We are neither as optimistic as Edwin Meese that courts can find detailed answers in the often enigmatic history known as the Framers' intent, nor as pessimistic as Justice Brennan that modern America has changed so markedly that the generating history of the religion clauses and the Framers' beliefs and actions afford only ambiguous guidance.[23] While the Constitution is a living document, a broadly framed plan to guide future generations, it must be interpreted in the context of its history and the traditions and values of the American people. Thus, although history does not supply a detailed blueprint, it does provide an essential framework for resolving modern religious liberty questions. In interpreting the Constitution, one must look to its underlying philosophy and identify the Founders' broad purposes. These animating principles ensure that judges do not read their own ideological views into our fundamental law. At the same time, they are not so outmoded that they prevent the enlightened resolution of twentieth-century problems. What then are the animating principles that inspired the religion clauses? In addressing that question, this chapter will discuss the core value of the clauses, and chapter 4 will consider the historical principles that promote this value.

The Core Value of Religious Liberty

We begin with what may seem a rather obvious proposition—that the Founders intended the establishment and free exercise clauses to be complementary co-guarantors of a single end. As Justice Goldberg observed in *Abington School District v. Schempp*, the "single end" of the clauses is "to promote and assure the fullest possible scope of religious liberty and tolerance for all and to nurture the conditions which secure the best hope of attainment of that end."[24] While this may appear manifest, some scholars assert that the main purpose of the clauses is to effect strict separation between church and state, as if building Jefferson's wall is an end in itself.[25] The separation concept, however, is really a servant of an even greater goal; it is a means, along with concepts such as accommodation and neutrality, to achieve the ideal of religious liberty in a free society.

Modern separationists are mistaken when they equate strict separation of church and state or, more broadly, of religion and society, with religious freedom. Leo Pfeffer asserted, for example, that separation and freedom are synonymous: "[S]eparation guarantees freedom and freedom requires separation. The draftsmen of the [first] amendment regarded freedom of religion and establishment as incompatible. American constitutional history and tradition do not justify an apportionment of values between disestablishment and freedom."[26]

It does not necessarily follow that a society that completely honors the disestablishment principle will be free. While it is true that an established church inhibits the full attainment of religious liberty, it is incorrect to equate disestablishment with liberty, or to infer that the absence of an establishment guarantees freedom. The most disestablished societies in the twentieth century are those governed by totalitarian regimes. On the other hand, countries such as England and Switzerland have nominal establishments, yet afford a degree of religious freedom that compares with that enjoyed in the United States. In short, although the presence of an establishment inhibits the *full* realization of religious liberty, its absence does not itself create a society committed to this liberty. Indeed, a highly regulatory welfare state without an establishment can pose as much, if not more, of a threat to religious freedom than historical establishments. Government today regulates religion in countless ways, presenting the likelihood of interference with ministries such as schools, hospitals, and facilities for the elderly, homeless, or handicapped. In the field of taxation, for example, religious organizations face the possibility of losing their tax-exempt status when they take stances on controversial public issues such as abortion or arms control.

In the struggle for religious freedom, the central ideal from the colonial period of Williams and Penn to the Founders, was not separation of church and state, but liberty of conscience in religious matters. Pietists, Enlightenment separationists, and political centrists uniformly understood this ideal, also referred to as religious liberty, to be an inalienable right encompassing both belief and practice.[27] The Founders differed over the content and means of achieving religious liberty, but they uniformly regarded it as an essential cornerstone of a free society.

Federalists and Antifederalists frequently invoked liberty of conscience when considering the religion clauses; sometimes the term stood alone, at other times it was accompanied with an establishment prohibition and free exercise guarantee. Madison's proposed amendment, introduced on June 8, 1789, referred to the "full and equal rights of conscience" along with nonestablishment and free exercise guarantees.[28] In the House debates held on August 15, 1789, he asserted that the purpose of his proposal was to ensure that Congress could not "infringe the rights of conscience, and establish a national religion."[29] In supporting a religious freedom amendment, Daniel Carroll maintained that "the rights of conscience" need special protection, and Representative Huntington hoped that such an amendment would "secure the rights of conscience, and a free exercise of the rights of religion, but not to patronise those who professed no religion at all."[30] The various proposals for an amendment passed by the House referred to "the rights of conscience."[31]

References to liberty of conscience also occurred in the state assemblies that gathered to consider ratification of the Bill of Rights. The Virginia Senate, for example, protested that the proposed third article, the present First Amendment, did not adequately "prohibit the rights of conscience from being violated or infringed."[32] Between 1776 and 1792, every state that adopted a constitution sought to prevent the infringement of "liberty of conscience," "the dictates of conscience," "the rights of conscience," or the "free exercise of religion."[33]

The Northwest Ordinance of 1787 established a bill of rights for the Northwest Territory in order to extend "the fundamental principles of civil and religious liberty."[34] The emphasis on civil and religious freedom was also evident in the Declaration of the Causes and Necessity of Taking Up Arms, promulgated by the Second Continental Congress in July 1775, three months after the battle of Lexington and Concord. Designed to obtain redress for grievances and restore harmony with Great Britain, the document condemned British colonial policy and referred to the Quebec Act's recognition of Roman Catholicism in Quebec as erecting "a despotism dangerous to our very existence." It approved armed resistance to preserve the liberties of America's forefathers, who "left their native land, to seek on these shores a residence for civil and religious freedom." The document contained numerous references to God, and closed with a prayer for divine assistance: "With an humble confidence in the mercies of the supreme and impartial Judge and Ruler of the Universe, we most devoutly implore his divine goodness to protect us happily through this great conflict. . . ."[35]

While differing over how to attain religious liberty in a free society, advocates of the Enlightenment, pietistic, and political centrist positions agreed that liberty of conscience in religious matters was the central value. Madison regarded this right as inalienable because it entailed a duty towards the Creator that was precedent to the claims of civil society. "Conscience is the most sacred of all property," he asserted in 1792, because, unlike "other property depending in part on positive law, the exercise of [conscience is] a natural and unalienable right."[36] Later in life, he urged those states that retained in their constitutions "any aberration from the sacred principle of religious liberty, by giving to Caesar what belongs to God, or joining together what God has put asunder," to purify their systems "in what relates to the freedom of the mind and its allegiance to its maker, as in what belongs to the legitimate objects of political and civil institutions."[37] In A Bill for Establishing Religious Freedom, Jefferson emphasized that "Almighty God hath created the mind free" and that governmental compulsion in religious matters was "a dangerous Fallacy, which at once destroys all religious liberty."[38] His famous Danbury letter, the source of the controversial wall metaphor, indicated that the religion clauses expressed "the supreme will of the nation in behalf of the rights of conscience."[39]

In his two extensive, sometimes impenetrable, treatises on church and state, Williams disputed the prevailing justifications for governmental force in matters of conscience. In the first treatise, *The Bloudy Tenent, of Persecution, for Cause of Conscience* (1644), he rejected the Puritan view, advanced forcefully by the Reverend John Cotton,[40] that the civil magistrate should suppress dissent, coerce conscience to promote orthodoxy, and watch over the church to ensure its purity. Governmental coercion of conscience violated God's command that "the most pagan, Jewish, Turkish, or anti-Christian consciences and worships, be granted to all men in all nations and countries."[41] In an even longer work, *The Bloody Tenent Yet More Bloody* (1652), Williams asserted that two opinions "bewitched the nations": "First, that a national church or state, is of Christ's appointing. Secondly, that such a national church or state must be maintained pure by the power of the sword."[42] Rhode Island, of course, reflected Williams's commitment to religious liberty at an early date. In 1640, representatives of the town of Providence agreed "as formerly hath been the liberties of the town, so still, to hold forth liberty of conscience."[43]

Nowhere does the centrality of religious liberty emerge more clearly among the pietists than in Penn's tract, *The Great Case of Liberty of Conscience*. The colonial leader understood well the consequences of living under a government insensitive to the religious needs of its citizens. During his early years as a Quaker activist in England, the authorities jailed him on at least four occasions for doing nothing more than practicing his religion. Written from crowded Newgate prison in 1671, the tract espoused a broad understanding of liberty of conscience that became part of America's heritage:

> First, by liberty of conscience, we understand not only a mere liberty of the mind, in believing or disbelieving . . . , but the exercise of ourselves in a visible way of worship, upon our believing it to be indispensably required at our hands, that if we neglect it for fear or favor of any mortal man, we sin, and incur divine wrath.[44]

If religious liberty is the core value of the religion clauses, then the Supreme Court's rigid dichotomy between the establishment and free exercise clauses, without reference to this unifying value, would appear to be flawed historically.[45] The dichotomy generates unnecessary tension between the clauses and fosters inconsistent precedent in an area already fraught with confusion.[46] As Chief Justice Burger conceded in *Walz v. Tax Commission*, "[t]he Court has struggled to find a neutral course between the two Religion Clauses, . . . either of which, if expanded to a logical extreme, would tend to clash with the other."[47]

The tension between the clauses is illustrated by modern litigation, which often places them in opposition to one another. Thus, attempts under the free exercise clause to secure exemptions from laws affecting religious practice are invariably opposed on establishment grounds. In *Sherbert v. Verner*,[48] for example, the Court held that the free exercise clause compelled South Carolina to grant unemployment benefits to a

Seventh-Day Adventist unable to find employment because she refused to work on her Sabbath. It concluded that affording such benefits "plainly" did not establish the Seventh-Day Adventist religion, but that the benefits in fact promoted governmental neutrality between Sabbatarians and Sunday worshippers.[49] Subsequent free exercise cases involving unemployment compensation have summarily rejected the establishment clause contention.[50]

But the *Sherbert* Court's dismissal of the tension between the religion clauses "papered over" a deep-seated jurisprudential problem. Constitutional scholar Jesse Choper recently asserted, for example, that it is not at all plain that the benefits compelled in *Sherbert* were consistent with the establishment clause. Indeed, he maintained that *Sherbert* was "doubly wrong": "Not only was South Carolina's denial of unemployment compensation to Sherbert not a violation of the free exercise clause, it was a violation of the establishment clause for the Court to require the State to grant it to her."[51]

The Court's struggle to find a neutral course between the clauses has provoked a large body of commentary aimed at reconciling the tension between nonestablishment and free exercise values. The predominant school of thought asserts that establishment clause values such as no governmental aid to religion and separation of church and state should yield to free exercise claims because the "establishment clause is largely designed to implement the free exercise clause."[52] Under a related view, the free exercise clause would be interpreted broadly to protect religious minorities, while the establishment clause would be construed narrowly to permit cultural expressions of majority religions.[53] Those advocating separation between church and state, however, resolve the tension in favor of the establishment clause.[54] Conceiving of religion as a "private" matter, they generally concede that individual accommodations for religious practice are permissible, but assert that the establishment clause strictly forbids any governmental solicitude for organized religion, particularly when the "public" arena is involved.

Doctrinal confusion stemming from the Court's distinct tests for the establishment and free exercise clauses is heightened by the absence of workable principles for determining under which clause a case falls. In *Widmar v. Vincent*,[55] for example, a student religious group challenged a University of Missouri regulation prohibiting the use of school buildings or grounds for religious meetings. The district court not only sustained the regulation but concluded that it was compelled by the establishment clause.

The court of appeals reversed this decision on the ground that the exclusionary policy violated the general rule under the free speech clause that the government cannot discriminate against speech based on its content. The Supreme Court affirmed, agreeing that the case fell under the free speech clause rather than the establishment clause. Thus, the outcome of a religious liberty case may depend on whether the Court characterizes it as falling under the establishment clause, free exercise clause or, as in a growing number of cases, the free speech clause.[56] The Court has failed, however, to develop neutral principles to govern this determination. Consequently, characterizing a controversy may depend on analogizing it to prior cases or, more disturbingly, on what result the Justices desire to reach.

4. The Animating Principles of the Religion Clauses

> [C]oercive measures about religion also tend to provoke
> emulation, wrath, and contention, and who can describe all the
> mischiefs of this nature that such measures have produced in our
> land! But where each person and each [religious] society are
> equally protected from being injured by others, all enjoying
> equal liberty to attend and support the worship which they
> believe is right, . . . how happy are its effects in civil society?
>
> Isaac Backus,
> *An Appeal to the Public for Religious Liberty*, 1773

Chapter 3 examined the incorporation doctrine and the Supreme Court's emergence in the last half-century as a key institution in directing the interaction of religion and government in American society. After discussing the use of history by the *Everson* Court, it was proposed that the core value of the religion clauses is religious liberty and that the Court's rigid dichotomy between nonestablishment and free exercise has generated doctrinal tension and inconsistent precedent. In criticizing this dichotomy, it is not suggested that the clauses are coextensive and lack independent vitality. The Framers made a textual distinction between the two, and history supports the view that the nonestablishment and free exercise guarantees play different, although mutually supportive, roles in protecting religious liberty. These roles will become more apparent in the discussion of four historical principles animating the religion clauses: federalism, institutional separation, accommodation, and benevolent neutrality.[1]

The Principle of Federalism

To the Puritans, the prosperity of society rested on the proposition "that our churches and civil state have been planted, and grown up (like two twins) together."[2] In his debates with Williams, John Cotton stressed the importance of the established church in maintaining civil order, asking at one point: "And can the Church then break up, into pieces, and dissolve into nothing, and yet the peace and welfare of the city, not in the least measure [be] impaired or disturbed?"[3] This question poses one of the principal challenges faced by the Founders: to create a republic free of an established church and committed to religious liberty, yet open to religion as a necessary and cohesive moral force in society. They were well aware of the intolerance and persecution characteristic of Old World and colonial establishments, but they generally agreed with Washington: "Of all the dispositions and habits which lead to political prosperity, religion and morality are indispensable supports. In vain would that man claim the tribute of patriotism who should labor to subvert these great pillars of human happiness—these firmest props of the duties of men and citizens."[4] How then did the Founders go about creating a republic premised on civil and religious liberty?

Deeply influenced by political theorists such as Locke and Montesquieu, the Founders believed that the "accumulation of all powers, legislative, executive, and judiciary, in the same hands, whether of one, a few, or many, and whether hereditary, self-appointed, or elective, may justly be pronounced the very definition of tyranny."[5] To prevent the centralization of political authority at the national level, they created a tripartite federal government that was to exercise only enumerated powers. Under the Tenth Amendment, any powers not delegated to the federal government by the Constitution, "nor prohibited by it to the States, [were] reserved to the States respectively, or to the people."[6] The Bill of Rights, added largely at the insistence of the public and the state ratifying conventions, explicitly circumscribed the power of Congress in religious matters.

Legislative history suggests that a variety of convictions inspired the religion clauses, including a belief that religious exercise was a fragile and inalienable right needing special protection;[7] that authority over religion, to the extent it could be exercised, was a state matter;[8] and that, unless prevented, Congress would pose a dangerous threat to religious liberty or would interfere with existing state establishments. Underlying these convictions was a principle of federalism premised on the political philosophy of the Framers and their fear of centralized authority. The preservation of religious liberty depended in part on this principle, which marked the boundaries between federal and state authority. History reveals at least three reasons why the religion clauses were directed only against Congress.

First, while Madison and others recognized that existing state estab-lishments threatened religious liberty,[9] the Framers appeared united in the belief that a national church, patterned after the English model, posed the greatest threat to this liberty. Thus, Madison's proposed amendment of June 8, 1789, read, "nor shall any national religion be established,"[10] and the Senate's version adopted on September 9 provided that "Congress shall make no law establishing articles of faith or a mode of worship."[11] An alliance of church and state at the national level would result in the "ac-cumulation" of religious and civil power in "the same hands," the very essence of tyranny. This accounts for the "deeply rooted" fear of an Amer-ican episcopacy, as Edwin Gaustad points out: "Throughout much of the eighteenth century, colonists were haunted by a fear of *episcopacy*—i.e., a fear that Anglican bishops would sail to America, there to exercise spiritual *and* temporal powers—powers made the more fearful because no proper distinction between them was made."[12] The colonists expressed similar concerns over the Quebec Act, a British law enacted in May 1774 that recognized Roman Catholicism in Quebec and extended the province's boundaries as far south as the Ohio Valley. In his *Remarks on the "Quebec Bill"* (1775), Alexander Hamilton defined establishment in terms of gov-ernmental protection and support for a religion and alleged that the mea-sure established the "Church of Rome" in Canada.[13] The Declaration and Resolves of the First Continental Congress, adopted in October 1774, denounced as one of Parliament's "Intolerable Acts" the statute "estab-lishing the Roman Catholic religion, in the province of Quebec . . . to the great danger" of the colonies.[14]

Second, as a corollary to their apprehension of a national establishment, the Founders generally believed that civil authority in religious matters, to the extent it could be exercised, was a state function. According to Jeffer-son, the "power to prescribe any religious exercise, or to assume authority in religious discipline," rested not with the federal government, but with the states, "as far as it [could] be in any human authority." In explaining why he did not follow precedent and proclaim national days of fasting and prayer, he asserted: "I have ever believed, that the example of State exec-utives led to the assumption of that authority by the General Government, without due examination, which would have discovered that what might be a right in a State government, was a violation of that right when assumed by another."[15] Under the constitutional plan of limited and enu-merated congressional powers, the states exercised the general health and welfare authority, retaining control over most governmental matters affecting citizens. This division of political authority derived in part from a view that the national and state governments would check each other from usurping the liberties of the people, and in part from the notion that the states would act as a shield between federal power and individual liberty. Hamilton, the chief proponent of a strong national government, conveyed the latter notion in *The Federalist Papers*: "It may safely be received as an axiom in our political system, that the State governments will, in all possible contingencies, afford complete security against invasions of the public liberty by the national authority."[16]

The religion clauses, at least originally, embodied the jurisdictional concern of federalism; civil authority in religious affairs resided with the states, not the national government. The Constitution nowhere granted Congress explicit authority in such matters. Many Framers, primarily the Federalists, therefore thought that an express limitation on congressional power over religion was unnecessary, and perhaps dangerous, because it would suggest that Congress possessed such authority.[17] While Federalists and Antifederalists debated the need for a bill of rights, they appeared to agree that redress for religious grievances should be left primarily, if not exclusively, to the states;[18] to give Congress authority over such matters would intrude on the states and create a centralized threat to religious freedom. Such an approach was not unenlightened, for a majority of the states had disestablished their preferred churches and, in those states retaining establishments, forces were at work steadily increasing the freedom of dissenters.

Third, the recognition that civil authority in religious affairs was a state rather than a federal matter accounts for the view that some Framers intended the establishment clause to prevent congressional interference with existing state establishments.[19] Congress arguably could have interfered either by establishing a national church to displace state-preferred churches or by enacting laws that favored or burdened all or some state religious establishments. Indeed, some of the Framers feared that Congress would intrude in religious matters under its authority to "make all Laws which shall be necessary and proper" to carry out its enumerated powers.[20] The Framers' anxiety regarding noninterference may explain the use of the word "respecting" in the establishment clause: an amendment that read "nor shall any national religion be established"[21] would still permit Congress to attempt, perhaps under the "necessary and proper" clause, to meddle with state establishments. By prohibiting Congress from making any law "respecting" an establishment of religion, the proposed amendment would satisfy both concerns and gain the support of those Founders seeking to protect established state churches.

It should be stressed that this explanation does not preclude the use of the word "respecting" as a means of satisfying those Founders who sought to secure religious liberty by limiting congressional power. The final choice of wording may have resulted from a coalition of Founders influenced by different motivations—one faction stressing the danger to religious liberty posed by an alliance between ecclesiastical and civil authority at the national level, and another faction desiring to limit Congress in order to preserve existing state establishments.

In addition to dividing state and federal authority, the Founders sought to ensure a free society by affording constitutional protection, at both levels, to "mediating" institutions such as the family, churches, the press, business, and voluntary associations. These institutions not only serve as buffers between the individual and the government, but often represent different interests in the public arena. While liberty inevitably produces conflicting factions that threaten civil unity, Madison argued in *Federalist No. 10* that the method of "curing the mischiefs of faction" was not to remove its causes,[22] but to control its effects through a properly structured and extended republican government: "A religious sect may degenerate into a political faction in a part of the Confederacy; but the variety of sects dispersed over the entire face of it must secure the national councils against any danger from that source."[23] Madison reiterated this theme in *Federalist No. 51*: "In a free government the security for civil rights must be the same as that for religious rights. It consists in the one case in the multiplicity of interests, and in the other in the multiplicity of sects."[24]

In evaluating the current relevance of the federalism principle, it must be remembered that the Court's use of the Fourteenth Amendment to apply the religion clauses to the states reshaped the legal landscape for religious liberty issues. In his dissent in *Abington School District v. Schempp*, Justice Stewart accepted the incorporation of the establishment clause, but noted that "it is not without irony that a constitutional provision evidently designed to leave the States free to go their own way should now have become a restriction upon their autonomy."[25] Since *Everson*, the issue has continued to spark heated scholarly debate.[26] Whatever the conceptual and historical difficulties with the incorporation of the establishment clause, it must be recognized, as one federal judge recently learned, that the Court now considers the matter closed.[27] While scholars undoubtedly will persist in debating the matter, lawyers and judges must continue to confront the question, "when is the right to be free from establishment violated?"[28]

The starting point in addressing this question is the recognition that the Fourteenth Amendment absorbs "the Establishment Clause as a co-guarantor, with the Free Exercise Clause, of religious liberty."[29] To the extent the establishment clause is understood to perform this role, rather than the mistaken function of effecting strict separation between church and state, the conceptual and historical difficulties with incorporation are minimized. Interpreted in the light of history, the establishment clause should prohibit only those governmental actions threatening religious liberty in a manner analogous to traditional establishments.

Recognizing the change created by incorporation of the religion clauses, what can be learned from the Founders' political philosophy and the principle of federalism? The Founders would likely be surprised and perhaps even alarmed by the size and power of today's government. Such concentration of authority, particularly at the federal level, inevitably poses a threat to religious liberty. This threat is particularly acute in areas such as church labor relations[30] and the administration of the federal tax exemption for religious organizations.[31] In the latter area, governmental agencies and courts face delicate tasks: ensuring that entities are "organized and operated exclusively" for religious purposes; defining "church," "religious purposes," and related terms; determining whether a religious group is substantially engaged in political action; gauging whether net earnings illegally benefit private individuals; and ascertaining whether a particular group meets public policy criteria.[32]

Accompanying the expansive growth of the regulatory state is a prevailing paternalistic belief that government must meet the primary needs of its citizens, and a notion derived from strict separation that virtually all avenues for discourse and resolution are in a public arena shut off to religion by virtue of the establishment clause. Consequently, functions formerly regarded as familial or religious, such as child care, social services, and education, are now carried out by government and viewed by many as secular. Those holding such beliefs might be surprised to learn that John Stuart Mill, the most prominent spokesman for classical liberalism in the nineteenth century, regarded state control of education as a principal threat to liberty:

A general State education is a mere contrivance for moulding people to be exactly like one another: and as the mould in which it casts them is that which pleases the predominant power in the government, whether this be a monarch, a priesthood, an aristocracy, or the majority of the existing generation; in proportion as it is efficient and successful, it establishes a despotism over the mind, leading by natural tendency to one over the body.[33]

The monopolistic trend of government has contributed to a subtle but steady "privatization" of religion, based on the belief that religious conviction and influence are not only unwelcome in the public sphere, but are in fact constitutionally excluded from it. Thus, one scholar has made the rather startling and ahistorical suggestion that the establishment clause may preclude public officials from even thinking in religious terms when discharging governmental duties.[34]

The growth of government and the expanded role of the Court are not the only forces leading to the secularization of society and the privatization of religion. These developments occurred along with the emergence of an increasingly mobile and heterogeneous population captivated by consumer capitalism. In modern advertising media, religion is invariably excluded so as not to offend potential consumers, hence reinforcing the irrelevance of spiritual values to public life. The dominance of consumerism is best illustrated by the appropriation of Christmas, a sacred day commemorating the birth of Jesus, as a national holiday of materialism, symbolized by Santa Claus.

Given the increased privatization of religion and the pervasiveness of government in our lives, the Founders' political philosophy and the concepts underlying federalism take on added significance. First, the federal judiciary should pause in contemplating the enormous task it inherited, somewhat suddenly, as a result of the incorporation of the establishment clause. This action nationalized issues of church and state that had been resolved by democratic processes or under state constitutional provisions and laws for over 150 years. It placed in the hands of the federal judiciary expansive power in formulating the role of religion in society. In view of the religious foundations of American culture, judges should approach this task with diffidence and avoid the temptation to impose their personal preferences. Without the guidance of history and tradition, judicial decision making in this sensitive field is fundamentally antidemocratic. In discussing the limits of judicial review, Learned Hand stressed that judges should not act as social engineers or "Platonic Guardians": "[I]t certainly does not accord with the underlying presuppositions of popular government to vest in a chamber, unaccountable to anyone but itself, the power to suppress social experiments which it does not approve."[35] By failing to heed this advice, the courts have undertaken a long and hard journey into the area of church and state, one that often has aroused the passions and disdain of the people. Guided by personal predilections or questionable history, judicial construction of the religion clauses too often constitutes a tyranny of the few.

That personal predilections or distorted history can lead to decisions with enormous social consequences is illustrated by the 1985 decision in *Aguilar v. Felton*. In a five-four decision, the Court invalidated a New York program under which public school employees conducted remedial reading, mathematics, and guidance programs in parochial schools. The services, limited to educationally deprived children from low-income families, were also provided to children in public and nonreligious private schools. Despite the program's noted success and the absence of even one instance of religious indoctrination in its nineteen-year history, the Court invoked its strict separationist rhetoric in concluding that the remedial program violated the establishment clause because it *might* lead to excessive entanglement between church and state.[36]

Second, the principle of federalism compels recognition that mediating structures, "those institutions standing between the individual in his private life and the large institutions of public life,"[37] are essential to the preservation of civil and religious freedom. Prompted by their fear of centralized authority, the Founders created a constitutional system under which state and local governments, as well as other social institutions, are positional between the citizen and the national government. Institutions such as the family, voluntary associations, the press, universities, and particularly churches, are essential sources for the values necessary to sustain a free society. Because they are more accessible and responsive to the needs of people than large governmental and corporate bureaucracies, these mediating structures empower citizens to speak effectively and to challenge questionable government activities.

The advent of a regulatory state of leviathan proportions and the nationalization of constitutional issues through incorporation has led mediating structures to play a critical role in at least two respects: on a personal level, they provide meaning in an increasingly alienating culture and, in the public realm, they facilitate the independent articulation of alternative perspectives. The latter function may be traced to the political philosophy of the Founders, who believed that liberty is most easily secured in a society characterized by the interaction of competing interests, and who sought to prevent tyranny by dispersing governmental power. While moral authority must be exercised prudently, religious organizations have performed a unique and vital function as mediating structures by appealing to transcendent values.

The Principle of Institutional Separation

Any use of the word "separation" in the context of church and state must be guarded. The term has become talismanic to the public and media and provokes confusion, particularly when associated with words such as "complete," "strict," and "wall." The poet Robert Frost may have defined the problem: "Before I built a wall I'd ask to know / What I was walling in or walling out. . . ."[38] While the separation principle is a means of achieving liberty of conscience, the principle must be understood in the context of the American heritage of religious liberty. Two misconceptions have obscured the meaning of separation: that it requires a secular society, and that it demands the exclusion of religion from political discourse.

First, the Founders conceived of separation in institutional rather than cultural terms. The principal evil they sought to avoid was an alliance of civil and ecclesiastical power that would threaten religious liberty; that religion and society should be separated was a notion that would have met with uniform disapproval. The centrist position that predominated among the Founders recognized that religion was a great teacher of morality and an essential pillar of civil society. This view was expressed in article III of the Northwest Ordinance and in Washington's Farewell Address.

History also provides numerous instances in which early American governments sanctioned religious involvement in society. The same Congress that framed the religion clauses requested President Washington to proclaim a day of public thanksgiving and approved legislative chaplains.[39] In 1791, Congress established a military chaplaincy for the nation. Presidents Washington, Adams, and Madison issued proclamations for days of thanksgiving that repeatedly invoked the Deity. Presidents Washington, Jefferson, Monroe, John Quincy Adams, Jackson, and Van Buren entered into treaties with various Indian tribes authorizing the use of federal funds for religious purposes.[40] In short, the Founders affirmed the importance of religion to the new republic and would have rejected the use of the establishment clause to eradicate the religious leaven from public life.[41] Instead, while recognizing the dangers posed by establishments, they would agree that government may acknowledge the importance of religion to many citizens. The Founders undoubtedly would have concurred with the Court's observation in *Zorach v. Clauson*: "We are a religious people whose institutions presuppose a Supreme Being."[42]

Second, separation of church and state does not mean separation of religion and politics. In this respect, it is probably a mistake, both as a matter of history and constitutional principle, to assert that the religion clauses command "mutual abstention—keeping politics out of religion and religion out of politics."[43] From politically active ministers such as Samuel Davies and John Witherspoon during the Revolution to Reinhold Niebuhr and Martin Luther King, Jr., in modern times, American history is replete with examples of religious leaders entering the political arena and influencing social policy.[44] The participation of religious groups in public issues such as the abolition of slavery, school prayer, civil rights, the reduction of nuclear arms, and abortion is evidence of a free society. In *Walz v. Tax Commission*, which sustained New York's tax exemption for church property, the Court noted: "Of course, churches as much as secular bodies and private citizens have that right [to speak to public issues]. No perfect or absolute separation is really possible; the very existence of the Religion Clauses is an involvement of sorts—one that seeks to mark boundaries to avoid excessive entanglement."[45]

The nation's religious groups come largely from traditions that reject the Enlightenment tenet that they are subservient to government. Instead, they view both church and state as God-ordained institutions entrusted with the public welfare.[46] To assert the absolute supremacy of the state over religious institutions and over the individual conscience is to take a step toward totalitarianism. In a century that has witnessed brutal savagery, churches understandably realize the important prophetic role they must play. Referring to Pastor Dietrich Bonhoeffer, killed by the Nazis in April 1945, American theologian Reinhold Niebuhr stated that his example "will have enabled people to learn to overcome the one disastrous mistake of German Protestantism: that is, the complete separation of faith from political life."[47] Having affirmed the right, indeed the responsibility, of religious groups to speak on public issues, it should be stressed that merely because one has a right to speak does not mean it is always prudent to do so. When religious leaders enter the political arena, they expose themselves to competing views and often harsh rhetoric and risk losing sight of their spiritual calling.[48]

Strict separationists, who draw support from a wide spectrum of organizations, would appear to have a valid point when they warn that religion can become a disruptive and sometimes oppressive force in society. The danger of persecution can occur especially in homogeneous regions, underscoring Madison's concern that majoritarian oppression poses one of the principal threats to the republic. While the public square can develop into a field of conflict between religious views and symbols, religious differences, like political discord, are not an evil per se; indeed, if expressed in a tolerant manner, they manifest a healthy democracy. In contrast to the separationists who would resolve this problem by excluding religion altogether, the solution most consistent with our historical commitment to religious liberty and free speech is to welcome religious expression. Only when such expression disrupts the civil peace in an overt and coercive manner or erupts into violence does the speech begin to approach unconstitutionality. The threat posed by sectarian conflicts may be real, but the greater dangers to religious liberty stem from excessive governmental interference, hostile secularism, materialism, and the decline of civic virtue.

In considering the separation principle embodied in the religion clauses, one must recognize that all three traditions informed the principle's meaning. We have already considered the influence of the political centrist position in rejecting the view that the First Amendment mandates a secular society or the exclusion of religion from politics. To an extent, the religion clauses also embody the Enlightenment and pietistic traditions of separation, and constitutional interpretation must reckon with them as well. These traditions look in two directions: to prevent governmental alliances with religion analogous to those in historical establishments and to protect churches and their adherents from governmental interference in religious matters.

The Enlightenment separationists contributed to the meaning of the establishment clause by recognizing that state-preferred churches corrupted governmental functions and inhibited the full attainment of religious liberty. To America's settlers and the Founders, the paradigm in understanding an establishment of religion was the Church of England. Historically, this Church received the exclusive support and protection of the sovereign, who exercised control over both the "Lords Spiritual and

Temporal" and over "all manner of jurisdictions, privileges and preeminences, in any wise touching or concerning any spiritual or ecclesiastical jurisdiction."[49] Civil and religious leaders were required to take an oath of supremacy recognizing the monarch as head of the Anglican Church, and the "Lords Spiritual"—bishops and archbishops—sat in the House of Lords. Parliament dictated the content and use of the Book of Common Prayer, as well as the "sacraments, rites, and ceremonies" of the Church. It passed laws to insure the purity of the Church, provide public support for the establishment, compel attendance at religious services, enforce conformity to orthodox doctrine, and suppress heresy, dissent, and blasphemy.[50]

When the Puritans settled in Massachusetts, they rejected the concept of ecclesiastical courts and distinguished between civil and religious functions. They emphasized, however, that magistrates and clergy should "stand together and flourish, the one being helpful to the other, in their distinct and due administrations."[51] In 1648, a synod of Congregational churches in New England expressed its understanding of an establishment in *The Cambridge Platform*, an ecclesiastical constitution that endured as the standard for the established Congregational Church until 1780. The document directed the magistrate to raise public support for ministers if private contributions proved inadequate and to use the civil sword "for helping in and furthering" the Congregational churches. It urged the civil authority to restrain and punish "idolatry, blasphemy, heresy, venting corrupt and pernicious opinions, that destroy the foundation, open contempt of the word preached, profanation of the Lord's day, disturbing the peaceable administration and exercise of the worship and holy things of God, and the like."[52]

In arguing that the Congregational Church in New England was a "state church," Williams maintained that it resembled the Church of England in that there was only one "religion and worship [which] is commanded or permitted."[53] He stressed that the Congregational Church exhibited the five principal characteristics of an establishment. First, civil authorities required attendance at common worship and holy days, compelled contributions to clergy, and prohibited dissenting faiths. Second, the civil power performed the function of overseeing "the conforming and reforming of the Church, the truth or falsehood of the churches, ministries or ministrations, ordinances, doctrine." Third, the magistrates punished "the heretic, blasphemer, [and] seducer" by death or banishment. Fourth, the state used its power to enforce public "maintenance of the worship, priests and officers." Finally, as with state or national churches, the representatives of the Congregational churches assembled in synods and councils.[54]

When one considers the English establishment and the colonial adaptations of this model, the essential characteristic was support for a preferred church through governmental compulsion. Thus, civil authorities imposed harsh penalties for heresy, blasphemy, and dissenting views, and compelled church attendance, conformity to orthodox doctrine, and contributions to the preferred church. Perhaps the most powerful weapon for maintaining an establishment was the religious test oath, which proved effective in detecting dissenters and compelling allegiance to orthodoxy.

The prohibition against government compulsion or coercion in religious matters emerges repeatedly in American history. The Maryland Act Concerning Religion (1649) guaranteed that Christians could not be in "any way compelled to the belief or exercise of any other religion."[55] A repudiation of governmental coercion of conscience animated the works of Williams, Clarke, and Penn.[56] The Pennsylvania Frame of Government (1682) protected theists from being "compelled, at any time, to frequent or maintain any religious worship, place or ministry whatever," and the Charter of Privileges (1701) contained a similar provision.[57] Many of the early state constitutions prohibited compulsory attendance at or support of worship,[58] and dissenters often remonstrated that liberty of conscience meant freedom from governmental compulsion in religious matters, particularly from taxation for established churches.[59] Madison's *Memorial and Remonstrance* and Jefferson's Bill for Establishing Religious Freedom denounced governmental attempts to compel citizens to attend or support any church.[60] In the legislative history of the religion clauses, Madison emphasized that if Congress established a church, it might then enact laws compelling religious conformity.[61]

The historical record demonstrates that when a state sought to establish a church it did so by using the civil sword to compel beliefs and conduct supportive of that church. The essence of an establishment, therefore, was governmental coercion of conscience. In this respect, history lends support to the views of Michael McConnell and Jesse Choper, who advocate the adoption of an establishment clause test premised on coercion. Choper, for example, proposed that "[g]overnment action should be held to violate the establishment clause if it meets two criteria: first, if its purpose is to aid religion; and second, if it significantly endangers religious liberty in some way by coercing, compromising, or influencing religious beliefs."[62]

Despite the historical centrality of coercion, the Supreme Court has not taken account of this element in its establishment clause jurisprudence, resorting instead to the somewhat amorphous formula announced in *Lemon v. Kurtzman* (1971).[63] Under this formula, premised on an ahistorical separation of church and state, a litigant need not show that government action coerces religious choice to make out an establishment clause claim. According to the *Lemon* test, an action violates the clause if it lacks a secular purpose, has a primary effect that either advances or inhibits religion, or fosters excessive entanglement between church and state. The Court's adherence to an establishment clause test stressing rigid separation rather than governmental coercion of conscience is a primary cause for a confusing jurisprudence under the religion clauses.

Although pietistic separationists contributed to establishment clause jurisprudence by campaigning vigorously for disestablishment, their more important legacy was the defense of values that animate the free exercise clause. Historically, the free exercise of religion encompassed both institutional and individual components; it included the right of churches to exist free from governmental interference and the right of persons to practice their religions in accordance with individual conscience. In contrast to Enlightenment rationalists, Roger Williams and others in the pietistic tradition built a wall of separation "not to prevent the state from becoming an instrument of 'priestcraft,' but in order to keep the holy and pure religion of Jesus Christ from contamination by the slightest taint of earthly support."[64] They fought for institutional separation because the colonial establishments, patterned in many respects after the Church of England, threatened "not only the purity but also the very life and being of religion."[65] Civil magistrates who coerced conscience, the mediator between man and the Creator, invaded a realm belonging to God alone; such usurpation of authority produced hypocrisy, weakened virtue, and threatened the peace, prosperity, and unity of society.

The pietists' condemnation of governmental force in religious matters stemmed from a theological conviction that God had ordained church and state to carry out essentially distinct, although complementary, functions, and that the confounding of these two functions violated the divine order. The church was armed with truth and light to persuade, edify, and serve, while the state was armed with the sword to preserve the peace by regulating society and punishing immoral conduct. This two-kingdoms view rested on a jurisdictional notion that there is a realm of religious belief and experience beyond the power of government; state intrusion into this realm threatened authentic faith and, in extreme cases, justified civil disobedience, for as the pietists stressed, ultimate allegiance belonged to God.[66]

It bears emphasis that, in their struggle to keep the hands of the state off the church, pietistic separationists did not advocate the absolute supremacy of the individual conscience, even if religiously motivated, over the legitimate concerns of civil government. One of the strongest strains in their thought was respect for temporal authority, for as the Apostle Paul stated: "Let every soul be subject unto the higher powers. For there is no power but of God: the powers that be are ordained of God."[67] Without government and social order, there could be no civil or religious liberty. In the preface to his Frame of Government, Penn quoted Paul's injunction in asserting that government, although lower in dignity than the heavenly kingdom, was "a part of religion itself, a thing sacred in its institution and end." In contrasting the two kingdoms, Penn stressed that religion removed the cause of evil, whereas government crushed its effects, and "that the one is more free and mental, the other more corporal and compulsive in its operations."[68]

While serving as governor of Rhode Island, Williams explored the interaction of religious conscience and civil duties in his famous letter to the town of Providence. Prompted by Baptists and Quakers who had objected on religious grounds to serving in the city's militia, Williams wrote that liberty of conscience did not mandate excusal from social duties connected with the common good. Employing a favorite simile, he compared society to a ship at sea, with all aboard, Catholic, Protestant, Jew, and Moslem alike, embarked on a journey. Williams pleaded for a liberty of conscience under which none of those aboard would "be forced to come to the ship's prayers or worship, nor compelled from their own particular prayers or worship, if they practice any." The ship's commander, however, retained authority to ensure the peace and safety of the vessel, specifically to "compel and punish" those who refused "to help, in person or purse, toward the common charges or defence," who disobeyed his orders concerning the "common peace or preservation," or who mutinied or taught "that there ought to be no commanders."[69] This letter discloses that Williams basically adhered to the Puritan view of governmental authority to enforce temporal civility and morality.[70]

Even with similar theological convictions, pietistic separationists differed among themselves concerning the scope and interaction of the two kingdoms. To what extent, if at all, should believers be involved in government? To what extent should the church provide moral support for government? When should it play a prophetic role and stand in judgment of the civil order? What conduct prohibited by the Ten Commandments should the temporal authorities punish? At what point does conflict between the two kingdoms justify civil disobedience?

Williams, Penn, and Backus diverged on these issues. At one end of the spectrum, Williams approached the issue of Christian involvement in government cautiously, asserting that the magistrates had no authority to enforce the first table of the Decalogue, which consisted of the four spiritual commandments against idolatry, image worship, blaspheming God's name, and breaking the Sabbath.[71] He therefore opposed test oaths, Sabbath laws, and the punishment of blasphemy, stating that it contradicted Christian principles for the state "to impose upon the souls of the people, a religion, a worship, a ministry, oaths (in religious and civil affairs), tithes, times, days, marryings and buryings in holy ground." Instead, the magistrates' principal duty with respect to religion was to remove legal obstructions to religious exercise and foster an environment conducive to the "free and absolute permission of the consciences of all men, in what is merely spiritual."[72] At the other end of the spectrum, Penn urged Christian involvement in government and, while granting broad religious freedom in his colony, thought that the state should encourage Christianity through test oaths, Sabbath laws, and the punishment of blasphemy and wild and loose behavior. Backus stood between Williams and Penn. He vigorously opposed test oaths and espoused a broader view of separation than Penn, but like Penn, he encouraged Christians to become magistrates and supported Sabbath laws, the punishment of blasphemy, and the proclamation of days of thanksgiving.

The Principle of Accommodation

The special place accorded religious freedom by the Founders is illustrated by the concept of accommodation, a free exercise doctrine that may be defined as an area of allowable and, in some cases, compelled governmental deference to the religious needs of people holding a variety of beliefs.[73] Generally implicated when tension arises between civil duties and religious conviction, accommodation calls for a delicate balance between government's duty to promote the cohesiveness necessary for an ordered society and its responsibility to honor the religious practices of citizens by refraining from unnecessary or burdensome regulation. Before considering the historical roots of accommodation, it may be helpful to illustrate the social importance of the concept and discuss its use by the Supreme Court.

Accommodation takes on added significance in a society characterized by expansive government and religious pluralism because, accompanying such growth, there is an increase in the tension between governmental power and diverse convictions. The task of resolving this tension has fallen primarily to the courts, which have considered numerous cases involving religious groups or individuals seeking exemptions from laws prohibiting conduct deemed inconsistent with the public welfare or from laws impos- ing social and civic duties.[74] In the category of laws prohibiting conduct, for example, courts have wrestled with religious defenses to prosecutions for disruptive public behavior, Sunday business or labor, commercial fortune-telling, handling poisonous snakes, mail fraud, the practice of medicine without a license, and the use of illegal substances such as peyote.[75] In the category of social and civic duties, courts have entertained religious claims to be excused from legally required jury duty, military service, vaccination and other medical procedures, military science courses in colleges, the flag salute and pledge of allegiance in public schools, naturalization oaths, social security coverage, and parental care for children in meeting educational and medical needs.[76]

In resolving cases in both categories, courts in the nineteenth and early twentieth centuries generally applied a concept known as the secular reg- ulation rule, which provided that there is "no constitutional right to ex- emption on religious grounds from the compulsion of a general regulation dealing with non-religious matters."[77] In 1879, the Court adopted this approach in the criminal law context in *Reynolds v. United States*. It con- cluded that the free exercise clause did not confer a right on "those who make polygamy a part of their religion" to be "excepted from the operation of [antipolygamy laws]." The Court stressed that to do so would introduce "a new element into criminal law"—those practicing polygamy because of religious conviction would be acquitted, while all other polygamists would be punished.[78] It should be emphasized that *Reynolds* rested on the con- viction that monogamy was an indispensable institution for the survival of American culture.

These early cases were decided primarily under state constitutional pro- visions before the advent of the incorporation doctrine and the welfare state. In addition, they often involved requests for religious accommoda- tion at a time when courts generally exercised great restraint in assessing the constitutionality of general welfare measures. Rather than being asked to carve out religiously based exemptions, courts today are increasingly called upon to determine the constitutionality of accommodations granted by the legislative branch. Although the Supreme Court has largely abandoned the secular regulation rule in favor of a balancing of interests approach, the rule's principal rationale—that religious groups and citizens stand before the law on equal terms with other groups and citizens— continues to influence the jurisprudence of the religion clauses. This policy of equality or fairness has figured prominently in the Court's search for a coherent theory to interpret the religion clauses, posing a fundamental and recurring theme under the free exercise clause: whether the Constitution permits government, at least in some instances, to afford special treatment to religious groups and citizens. In other words, does religion enjoy a special constitutional status in American culture? The constitutional text, the rise of religious liberty in America, the views of the Founders, and the generating history of the religion clauses clearly support an affirmative answer to this question.

While one might disagree with particular applications of the principle, the Supreme Court has recognized that the free exercise clause sometimes compels and, at other times, counsels accommodation of religious belief and practice. At least three categories have emerged in this regard. One line of cases, following the 1972 decision in *Wisconsin v. Yoder*,[79] holds that the clause sometimes affirmatively compels governmental accommodation of religion. In *Yoder*, Amish parents sent their children to school through the eighth grade, but declined to enroll them in high school because the worldly values prevalent in secondary education contravened their faith. The Court concluded that the free exercise clause mandated the exemption of the Amish children from that part of Wisconsin's compulsory education law requiring high school attendance.

A second group of cases involves situations in which accommodation is neither compelled by the free exercise clause nor forbidden by the establishment clause. This category generally presents judicial review of governmental measures designed to recognize citizens' religious needs. In *Zorach v. Clauson*,[80] for example, the Court sustained a New York City program that allowed public schools to excuse students to receive religious instruction off school premises for one hour each week. Other accommodations falling in the "permissible zone" between the clauses include the tax exemption for religious property[81] and the conscientious objector exemption.[82]

A third category involves statutory accommodations that transgress the establishment clause. This occurred in *Estate of Thornton v. Caldor, Inc.*, in which the Court concluded that a Connecticut statute attempting to accommodate religious worship by providing "Sabbath observers with an absolute and unqualified right not to work on their Sabbath" impermissibly advanced religion.[83]

History does not yield the nuanced approach to accommodation prevalent in current cases, for the colonists lived in a more homogeneous culture and adhered to a concept of limited government. Even in the seventeenth century, however, sufficient pluralism existed among Christian groups for the colonists to appreciate the nature of the problem. The Maryland Act Concerning Religion reflected this pluralism in banning the offensive use of names such as "heretic, schismatic, idolater, Puritan, Independent, Presbyterian, popish priest, Jesuit, Jesuited papist, Lutheran, Calvinist, Anabaptist, Brownist, Antinomian, Barrowist, Roundhead, Separatist, or any other [religious] name or term in a reproachful manner."[84] Williams addressed the issue of conscientious objection to military service as early as 1655. In his letter to Providence, he asserted that the Quakers and Baptists in question could not claim a right, divine or otherwise, to exemption from militia service. Williams did not state, however, that it would be inappropriate for government to accommodate conscientious objectors. His insistence that every qualified male serve in the militia probably resulted from the turmoil in the colony, the impending threat of Indian raids, and friction with the neighboring colony of Massachusetts Bay.

The concept of accommodation finds support in the thought and actions of the Founders, who were well aware of potential conflicts between religious conviction and social duties. In 1793, just two years after the states ratified the Bill of Rights, an interesting accommodation case arose in Pennsylvania involving a Jew named Jonas Phillips.[85] The court fined Phillips for refusing to testify on his Sabbath, but later remitted the fine when the defendant waived the benefit of his testimony. Unfortunately, the reporter only summarized the case and did not record the court's justification for imposing the fine. Although this early court did not accommodate Phillips's religious needs, the Founders manifested a sensitivity to religious practice in the free exercise clause, in article VI of the Federal Constitution, and in state constitutional oath provisions and exemptions for conscientious objectors.

One of the clearest illustrations of the Founders' accommodation of religious belief came in the loyalty requirement of article VI. Certain minority religious groups, most notably the Quakers, refused on Biblical grounds to take oaths, but were willing to make affirmations. In recognition of this, the Framers drafted article VI to require federal and state officials to be "bound by Oath *or Affirmation*, to support this Constitution."[86] Legislative history confirms that the choice of wording was deliberate. Prior to August 30, 1787, the various loyalty proposals considered by the Convention referred to officials being bound only by an oath.[87] Both the Convention journal and Madison's notes reveal that on August 30 the body arrived at what is now article VI by adding the words "or affirmation" and Pinckney's clause banning a federal test oath.[88] Joseph Story further confirmed the Framers' specific intent to accommodate religion in the article, indicating in his *Commentaries on the Constitution* that it "permitted a solemn affirmation to be made instead of an oath" because some denominations were "conscientiously scrupulous of taking oaths."[89]

The accommodation in article VI undoubtedly was derived from the state constitutions, which contained numerous provisions permitting Quakers and others to meet civil obligations through affirmations rather than oaths. Prior to the Federal Constitutional Convention, every state except Massachusetts, North Carolina, and Virginia showed such a sensitivity to religious belief in their first constitutions. The Maryland Constitution of 1776 allowed Quakers, Dunkers, and Mennonites to make a "solemn affirmation" and required oaths to be administered to a person in a manner deemed by that person's faith to be "the most effectual confirmation, by the attestation of the Divine Being."[90] The Delaware Constitution of 1776 required an officeholder to take a loyalty "oath, or affirmation, if conscientiously scrupulous of taking an oath."[91] Pennsylvania and New Hampshire incorporated similar provisions in their first constitutions.[92] Legislators in New Jersey took an "oath or affirmation" under which they "solemnly declare[d]" to discharge their duties faithfully.[93] Under the New York Constitution of 1777, electors could be required to "take an oath, or, if of the people called Quakers, an affirmation, of allegiance to the State."[94] Electors in Georgia subscribed to an "oath or affirmation" of allegiance, and those in South Carolina could be compelled to "take an oath or affirmation of qualification."[95] South Carolina also permitted a citizen, "when called to make an appeal to God as a witness of truth," to do so in the manner "which is most agreeable to the dictates of his own conscience."[96]

In addition to the accommodations in article VI and the state constitutional oath provisions, the Founders demonstrated their solicitude towards religious practice in the area of conscientious objection to military service. In 1775, the First Continental Congress granted an exemption from military service to those religiously opposed to bearing arms "in any case," stating that it "intend[ed] no violence to their consciences, but liberally recommend[ed] it to them, to contribute liberally . . . and to do all other services . . . which they can consistently with their religious principles."[97] When Madison proposed his constitutional amendments in the First Congress, he included a provision that "no person religiously scrupulous of bearing arms shall be compelled to render military service in person."[98] Like the accommodation in article VI, this proposal mirrored provisions in the state constitutions. A provision in the Pennsylvania Constitution of 1776, adopted in substantially similar form by Delaware, New Hampshire, and Vermont, read: "Nor can any man who is conscientiously scrupulous of bearing arms, be justly compelled thereto, if he will pay such equivalent. . . ."[99] The New York Constitution of 1777 excused Quakers "averse to the bearing of arms" on the condition that they pay an equivalent "in lieu of their personal service."[100] Perhaps the First Congress did not adopt Madison's proposal because it regarded the issue of conscientious objection as a state matter.

The House debates on the exemption, however, are instructive concerning the Framers' views on accommodation. On August 17, 1789, it considered a derivative of Madison's clause that read, "but no person religiously scrupulous shall be compelled to bear arms." Representative Gerry feared that those in power would use this provision to destroy the Constitution. By broadly construing the exemption, they could weaken the state militias and open the way for a standing army, a dangerous threat to liberty. Gerry desired to narrow the exemption by confining it "to persons belonging to a religious sect scrupulous of bearing arms." Representative Jackson "was willing to accommodate," but only if those exempted paid an equivalent for a substitute. Noting that the exemption probably would not influence many to become "Quakers or Moravians," he stressed the injustice of exempting some men without obligation while most others defended their country. Roger Sherman doubted that those religiously opposed to bearing arms would be willing to get substitutes or pay an equivalent. He argued that the clause was not essential, emphasizing that the states controlled the militias, and that American government was not "arbitrary." In addition, Sherman thought it unwise to exempt a whole sect, because some Quakers, for example, might be willing to defend their country irrespective of the doctrines of their sect. Representative Vining opposed the suggestion "to compel a man to find a substitute," agreeing with the proposal as it stood.

Representative Benson closed the debate by moving to strike the exemption. Maintaining that no citizen could "claim this indulgence" as a natural right, he asserted that it would be impossible to state the exemption unambiguously, and that the matter should therefore be left to the "benevolence of the Legislature." Benson stressed that the exemption would transfer the entire matter to the judiciary, and that the legislatures would be sensitive to the needs of citizens. The House defeated Benson's motion to strike the provision by a vote of 24 to 22, thereby upholding the proposed exemption.[101]

In the House debates on August 20, Representative Scott objected to the conscientious objector exemption because, although he did not mean to deprive religious citizens of "any indulgence the law affords," he feared that those of no religion would take advantage of the exemption. Noting that some believed religion to be on the decline, Scott reasoned that "when the time comes that religion shall be discarded, the generality of persons will have recourse to these pretexts to get excused from bearing arms." Arguing in favor of the exemption, Representative Boudinot asked, "what justice can there be in compelling [conscientious objectors] to bear arms, when, according to their religious principles, they would rather die than use them?" Furthermore, they would not contribute significantly to forming an "effectual" militia. Boudinot hoped that "in establishing this Government, we may show the world that proper care is taken that the Government may not interfere with the religious sentiments of any person." The House then adopted a provision that "[n]o person religiously scrupulous shall be compelled to bear arms in person."[102]

These interchanges disclose that the Framers not only appreciated the delicate nature of accommodation, but placed a high value on religious conviction, even when it conflicted with a fundamental social duty. All of them appeared to agree that legislatures possessed the authority constitutionally or statutorily to exempt conscientious objectors. Indeed, most agreed with Benson that the legislatures should "possess humanity enough to indulge [conscientious objectors] in a matter they are so desirous of."[103] The more troublesome issue was whether the exemption should be provided in the nation's fundamental law. The Framers appeared to understand the problems attending such an accommodation, issues such as delineating federal and state authority, defining and applying the exemption, determining the proper role of the judiciary, and recognizing the social impact of the provision and the need for fairness. But they also recognized that accommodation must occur if religious liberty was to flourish, particularly in a society characterized by pluralism and expansive government. It deserves emphasis that the Founders accorded religious exercise a special status in the Constitution[104] and that, given the changes in the social and legal landscapes, the preservation of this status necessitates a broad view of accommodation.[105]

The Principle of Benevolent Neutrality

The principle of neutrality, like that of separation, can be a source of great confusion if uprooted from the generating history of the religion clauses. As Justice Harlan observed, neutrality is "a coat of many colors,"[106] depending for content on the context and nature of its use. In the framework of history, religious neutrality derives specific meaning from the nation's commitment to the ideals of equality and voluntarism. The first of these found classic expression in the Declaration of Independence, which affirmed that individuals, while perhaps not equal in ability, intelligence, or other criteria, are equal as moral agents before God and the law.[107] In light of traditional establishments, the Founders conceived of religious equality primarily in terms of a government neither endorsing nor preferring any religious group over any other; in principle, all religions stood on an equal footing legally.[108] Voluntarism, the antithesis of compulsion, rests largely on the conviction that government should be neutral in religious matters because "both religion and society will be strengthened if spiritual and ideological claims seek recognition on the basis of their intrinsic merit."[109] When a state uses its coercive power to favor an establishment, it infringes on the freedom of churches, established and dissenting alike, and on the right of their adherents to act voluntarily in accordance with conscience.

With these general observations in mind, it may be helpful to review the Supreme Court's concept of neutrality and then to consider scholarly proposals concerning the principle. When the Court invalidated state-sponsored Bible reading in public schools, it did so under a "strict neutrality" approach embodying what are now the first two prongs of its tripartite establishment clause test: "[T]o withstand the strictures of the Establishment Clause there must be a secular legislative purpose and a primary effect that neither advances nor inhibits religion."[110] The Bible-reading exercise, it concluded, violated the command that "the Government maintain strict neutrality, neither aiding nor opposing religion."[111] Five years later, in 1968, the Court employed the neutrality principle and its two-prong test to strike down an Arkansas statute that prohibited teaching evolution in public schools. The decision, which did not refer to "strict" neutrality, defined the concept as follows:

> Government in our democracy, state and national, must be neutral in matters of religious theory, doctrine, and practice. It may not be hostile to any religion or to the advocacy of no-religion; and it may not aid, foster, or promote one religion or religious theory against another or even against the militant opposite. The First Amendment mandates governmental neutrality between religion and religion, and between religion and nonreligion.[112]

Two years later the Court explicitly abandoned strict neutrality. Confronted with a choice between a rigid judicial test of recent vintage and tax exemptions for church property, which are embedded in American history and culture, the Court in *Walz v. Tax Commission* had little difficulty choosing the latter. To pose the dilemma was to resolve it. Tempering the neutrality concept with accommodation values, the *Walz* Court stressed that constitutional neutrality "cannot be an absolutely straight line; rigidity could well defeat the basic purpose of [the religion clauses], which is to insure that no religion be sponsored or favored, none commanded, and none inhibited." In announcing the concept of benevolent neutrality, it concluded that between the clauses there was "room for play in the joints productive of a benevolent neutrality which will permit religious exercise to exist without sponsorship and without interference."[113]

The Court's definition of neutrality under the establishment clause contains two very different propositions: government must be neutral between religions, and it must be neutral between religion and nonreligion. The first proposition, that government may not prefer one religion over any other, receives overwhelming support in the American tradition of church and state.[114] In the legislative history of the religion clauses, Madison noted that the prevailing fear was that one or two sects "might obtain a pre-eminence" and create an establishment.[115] When New York ratified the Constitution in July 1788, it enumerated the rights deemed consistent with the Constitution. Included among these was that "the people have an equal, natural, and unalienable right freely and peaceably to exercise their religion, according to the dictates of conscience; and that no religious sect or society ought to be favored or established by law in preference to others."[116] Rhode Island, the state affording the greatest degree of religious liberty, placed a similar provision in its ratification document.[117]

The early constitutions of ten of the first thirteen states contained provisions prohibiting governmental preference among religions or among Christian sects. The Delaware Constitution of 1776 declared that "[t]here shall be no establishment of any one religious sect in this State in preference to another."[118] Georgia, New Jersey, North Carolina, and Pennsylvania included substantially similar provisions in early constitutions.[119] The New York Constitution of 1777 guaranteed "the free exercise and enjoyment of religious profession and worship, without discrimination or preference"; South Carolina included an identical provision in its constitution of 1790.[120] Massachusetts and New Hampshire, which maintained Congregational establishments well into the nineteenth century, guaranteed equal protection of the law for Christian denominations and provided that "no subordination of any one sect or denomination to another shall ever be established by law."[121] When Congregationalism was disestablished in Connecticut in 1818, the state included a provision in its first constitution that read, "No preference shall be given by law to any Christian sect or mode of worship."[122]

The theme of equal treatment also recurs in the writings of the Founders, particularly in those of Madison among the Enlightenment separationists and Backus among the pietistic separationists. In the *Memorial and Remonstrance*, Madison opposed Patrick Henry's Assessment Bill because it violated "that equality which ought to be the basis of every law." Later in the document, he explained that "[a just] Government will be best supported by protecting every Citizen in the enjoyment of his Religion with the same equal hand which protects his person and his property; by neither invading the equal rights of any Sect, nor suffering any Sect to invade those of another."[123] In *An Appeal to the Public for Religious Liberty*, Backus opposed the tax exemption system in Massachusetts because it required dissenting churches to obtain annual certificates of exemption from the established Congregational Church, thereby implying "an acknowledgement that the civil power has a right to set one religious sect up above another." He condemned "coercive measures about religion," which occur "when temporal advantages are annexed to one persuasion and disadvantages laid upon another," concluding: "But where each person and each [religious] society are equally protected from being injured by others, all enjoying equal liberty to attend and support the worship which they believe is right, . . . how happy are its effects in civil society?"[124]

In light of the historical record, the Court correctly observed that "[t]he clearest command of the Establishment Clause is that one religious denomination cannot be officially preferred over another."[125] Influenced by strict separationist rhetoric in early opinions, however, the Court has gone further by asserting that neutrality proscribes not only governmental preference among religions but also every form of nondiscriminatory aid to religion in general.[126] This expansive view of neutrality has proven controversial. While scholars appear to agree that the establishment clause prohibits preferential treatment for a religion, they sharply disagree over whether it also proscribes nonpreferential aid to religion.[127]

The debate may well turn on how one defines forbidden "aid" and, at any rate, may be directed at the wrong issue. A broad definition that would preclude accommodation of religion in any way, whether involving public funds[128] or other forms of governmental solicitude for religious practice, finds little support in American history. There is no evidence, for example, that when the Founders accommodated Quakerism and other minority sects in the areas of loyalty oaths and conscientious objection, they believed they were impermissibly aiding religion or preferring such sects over other religions. Indeed, some of the early state constitutions that prohibited governmental preference for one religion over others also granted loyalty oath and conscientious objector accommodations. Properly understood, these accommodations show a sensitivity to the core value of religious liberty and, in a sense, may reflect a concern to place all denominations on an equal footing in terms of the interaction of civil obligation and religious conviction. Thus, Quakers could fulfill their civil duty of declaring loyalty without compromising their convictions, thereby placing them on the same level as adherents of religious groups not opposed to taking oaths.

In any case, the debate over nonpreferential aid may be cast in incorrect terms because it focuses on the issue of "no-aid" rather than on that of "coercion." Even assuming that Madison's *Memorial and Remonstrance* occupies a special place in interpreting the religion clauses, separationists and most in the strict neutrality camp have invoked the document to support the proposition that government cannot give even "three pence" to religion.[129] This interpretation does not account adequately for a consistent understanding in American history that the central feature of an establishment was governmental coercion of conscience.[130] Madison's three-pence argument reflects this understanding: "Who does not see . . . that the same authority which can *force* a citizen to contribute three pence only of his property for the support of any one establishment, may *force* him to *conform* to any other establishment in all cases whatsoever?"[131]

Other references to coercion or its opposite, voluntarism, occur in the *Memorial and Remonstrance*. Thus, Madison quoted article 16 of the Virginia Declaration of Rights in objecting to governmental use of "force and violence" to direct religious conviction; referred to the belief of "Quakers and Menonists" that "compulsive support" of their religions was unnecessary; commended the Church prior to Constantine because religious teachers "depended on the voluntary rewards of their flocks"; argued that the "proposed establishment" degrades some citizens "whose opinions in Religion do not bend to those of the Legislative authority"; condemned governmental attempts "to extinguish Religious discord, by proscribing all difference in Religious opinion"; asserted the ineffectual nature of "attempts to enforce by legal sanctions, acts obnoxious to so great a proportion of the Citizens"; and maintained that a measure of such "singular magnitude and delicacy ought not to be imposed."[132] These passages demonstrate that Madison opposed the Assessment Bill as an impermissible establishment not because public funds would go to religion, but because the secular arm would use its coercive power to compel citizens to contribute.

The element of coercion not only provides a unifying thread to Madison's views on church and state,[133] it largely accounts for the numerous practices of the Founders recognizing the importance of religion to the republic.[134] These practices are a source of embarrassment to separationists, who are required to advance the untenable thesis that, shortly after enacting an establishment clause intended to proscribe federal aid to religion and religious involvement in society, the Founders violated it in countless ways.[135] When faced with an interpretive approach that fails to elucidate the historical meaning of a text, the solution is not to distort the text or denigrate its history, but to abandon the approach. In short, the Framers intended the establishment clause to forbid discriminatory aid among religions and those forms of nondiscriminatory aid to religion that exert a coercive influence on religious choice; they did not intend the clause broadly to proscribe aid to religion per se. Affording evenhanded and noncoercive aid in a religiously pluralistic society may be a difficult and sensitive task, but that has to do with the principle's implementation, not with its historical soundness.

The Court's second proposition, that government maintain neutrality between religion and nonreligion, is problematic from the standpoint of history and semantics. First, the principal, if not exclusive, emphasis on government neutrality in the colonial and early republican periods was government action that favored one or more religions over all others; there is little stress on comparing religious rights to practices or beliefs that are not religious. One reads the historical record impressed, however, with the sacrifices made and the creative energy expended on behalf of religious freedom by individuals such as the Lords Baltimore, Williams, Clarke, Penn, and Backus, and by colonial Catholics, Jews, Quakers, Baptists, and other dissenters. Religious conviction and a desire for religious freedom drove these people as few secular forces would. The issue of church and state thus posed a unique problem deserving special attention. The Founders responded by specifically protecting religion in the early state constitutions and in the First Amendment, thereby according religious practice and belief a status not accorded to secular activities.

A second difficulty arises in the Court's use of the term "nonreligion," which literally means "that which is not religion" or the absence of religion.[136] A neutrality between religion and "everything that is not religion" defies definition and leads to results difficult to explain. Countless human activities, such as golf, carpentry, driving, eating, sleeping, and hiking, to name a few, fall into the category of nonreligion. But it does not follow that government must be neutral between such activities and those motivated by religion. Although a dedicated adherent to strict neutrality might answer yes, our heritage of religious liberty and the presence of the religion clauses in the First Amendment dictate otherwise. The historical principle of accommodation, for example, cannot be explained satisfactorily in terms of strict neutrality, but it makes sense if one recognizes that the protection of voluntary religious expression occupies a special place in the constitutional hierarchy.

The Court's use of nonreligion is more properly understood as connoting the right of an individual to believe or not to believe in religious matters. This definition not only reduces the neutrality principle's comparative universe, it embodies the central historical concern with governmental coercion of conscience to compel adherence to "orthodox" doctrine. Pietistic separationists, particularly Williams and Penn, affirmed one's right to believe or not to believe free from the corrupting hand of government. In condemning the "straining of men's c[o]nsciences by civil power," Williams asserted that "[t]his binding and rebinding of conscience, contrary or without its own persuasion, so weakens and defiles it, that it (as all other faculties) loses its strength, and the very nature of a common honest conscience."[137] The essence of Penn's thought was a belief that a person's "religious life was authentic only when he willingly and spontaneously granted his allegiance to God on the basis of understanding and conviction and without the base motives introduced by coercion."[138] While the religion clauses properly encompass a right not to believe and therefore compel neutrality between belief and unbelief, they do not protect actions stemming from secular value systems occasioned by unbelief. The Constitution extends protection only to the free exercise of religion and therefore does not require neutrality between actions premised on religious belief and those premised on moral codes not rooted in religion.[139]

Given the core value of religious liberty, the special status accorded religious exercise by the Founders, and the values underlying accommodation, the Constitution does not compel a strict neutrality that is blind to the religious needs of American citizens. Philip Kurland's much debated "equal protection" interpretation of the religion clauses therefore does not appear to take adequate account of fundamental historical values. Under his standard, essentially a reformulation of the secular regulation rule, the clauses would "be read as a single precept that government cannot utilize religion as a standard for action or inaction because these clauses prohibit classification in terms of religion either to confer a benefit or to impose a burden."[140] His standard, however, would appear to ignore the text of the First Amendment, which itself uses religion as a standard for governmental "action or inaction." In addition, implementation of Kurland's standard would entail heavy costs to religious liberty, because it rejects explicit accommodations. Instead of a religion-blind approach, history supports the *Walz* Court's concept of benevolent neutrality and Wilbur Katz's view of "neutralizing aids." Recognizing that religious liberty is the basic value of the clauses, Katz correctly asserts that the neutrality compelled by the establishment clause permits special provisions for religion "designed to counteract or neutralize the restrictions of religious freedom that would otherwise result from government's secular activities."[141]

Summary

The core value of the religion clauses is liberty of conscience in religious matters, an ideal that recurs throughout American history from early colonial times to the early national period. All three traditions of church and state—Enlightenment, pietistic, and political centrist—regarded religious liberty as an essential cornerstone of a free society and as an inalienable right encompassing both belief and action. The establishment and free exercise clauses are complementary means to attain this liberty, and are given content by the animating principles of federalism, institutional separation, accommodation, and benevolent neutrality.

In creating a republic premised on civil and religious liberty, yet receptive to religion as a cohesive moral force, the Founders looked largely to prevailing political philosophy and the principle of federalism. Fearful of centralized authority, they sought to preserve religious freedom and other fundamental rights by dividing civil power within the federal government and between the federal and state governments. The religion clauses reflect the concerns of federalism, in particular the Framers' beliefs that a national church posed the greatest danger to liberty of conscience, that the exercise of civil authority in religious matters should be left to the states, and that the establishment clause prevented congressional infringement of religious liberty, as well as interference with existing state establishments. The Framers also sought to ensure a free society by affording constitutional protection to mediating institutions such as the family, churches, the press, business, and voluntary associations. The Court's use of the Fourteenth Amendment to incorporate the establishment clause created historical and conceptual difficulties which can be minimized by recognizing that the clause prohibits only those governmental actions threatening religious liberty in a manner analogous to traditional establishments. The principle of federalism counsels the judiciary to exercise restraint in formulating the role of religion in society, and reinforces the view that mediating institutions are essential to the preservation of civil and religious freedom.

Institutional separation requires neither a secular society nor the exclusion of religion from the public arena. The Founders, particularly the political centrists, acknowledged that the republic rested largely on moral principles derived from religion. Those who contributed most in the struggle for religious liberty, such as Williams, Clarke, Penn, Jefferson, Madison, and Backus, uniformly regarded governmental coercion of conscience as the essence of an establishment. The Enlightenment tradition of separation contributed to the meaning of the establishment clause by stressing that state-preferred churches corrupted the civil power and prevented the full achievement of religious liberty. The pietistic separationists campaigned primarily for values that animate the free exercise clause; they worked to protect the integrity of religious exercise, both in individual and institutional terms, from governmental interference.

The special status accorded religion by the Founders is manifested by the principle of accommodation, a free exercise concept which encourages and sometimes compels governmental deference to the religious needs of citizens in a pluralistic society. That religion enjoys a special constitutional status in American culture is also evident from the constitutional text, the historical growth of religious freedom, the beliefs of the Founders, and the legislative history of the religion clauses. Accommodation can be traced to the Founders, who manifested a sensitivity to religious practice in the free exercise clause, in the "Oath or Affirmation" requirement in article VI of the Federal Constitution, in state constitutional oath provisions, and in exemptions for conscientious objectors. In a society characterized by expansive governmental power and regulation, accommodation of religion becomes increasingly important as a means for fostering religious liberty.

Benevolent neutrality derives specific meaning from the nation's historical commitment to the ideals of equality and voluntarism. Government preference for one religious group over others not only violates the ideal of equality, but undermines the principle that each group should be left to grow or decline on the basis of the voluntary actions of its adherents. While history supports the view that the establishment clause requires governmental neutrality among religions, it provides little evidence for the concept that government must maintain strict neutrality between religion and nonreligion. The religion clauses do not compel a neutrality that is blind to the spiritual needs of citizens. Instead, they promote religious liberty through a benevolent neutrality that permits government to foster a society committed to voluntary religious belief and practice. In the final analysis, the special constitutional status enjoyed by religion rests on a conviction that in America "the spirits of religion and of freedom . . . [are] intimately linked together in joint reign over the same land."[142]

5. Religious Liberty in Contemporary America

> Religion, which never intervenes directly in the government of American society, should therefore be considered as the first of their political institutions, for although it did not give them the taste for liberty, it singularly facilitates their use thereof.
>
> Alexis De Tocqueville,
> *Democracy in America*, 1835

Since their incorporation through the Fourteenth Amendment, the religion clauses have been widely applied. On the social landscape, the activities of government have increased dramatically with the rise of the welfare state, creating myriad points of contact between government and religious organizations and citizens. Recent cases illustrate the increasing interaction of religion and government. Courts have grappled, for example, with such sensitive issues as the scope of the clergy-penitent privilege;[1] the permissibility of tort actions against churches for administering discipline or for alleged "clergy malpractice;"[2] the assertions of parents that public school textbooks unconstitutionally advance the religion of secular humanism;[3] the prosecution of church sanctuary workers for violating immigration laws;[4] and the extent of an employer's statutory obligation to accommodate religion in the workplace.[5]

In resolving contemporary conflicts under the clauses, courts should look to the basic value of religious liberty and its implementing principles of federalism, institutional separation, accommodation, and benevolent neutrality. These principles, however, should not be regarded as a test or formula to be applied woodenly to current issues. The purpose of the discussion in chapters 3 and 4 was not to suggest a specific judicial test, but to identify those principles that should govern the revision of existing tests or the formulation of new ones.

The animating principles represent a distillation of historical values derived from the American heritage of religious liberty. In discerning the founding generation's ideals in this regard, the state constitutions preceding the Bill of Rights are an important, although often overlooked, source. The official actions of the Founders, and to a lesser extent their personal views, provide helpful guidance, but they should not be regarded as decisive. Thus, the historical principles endure, but their application may differ as society changes.[6]

Since modern America poses situations unforeseen by the Founders, the animating principles necessarily must be extended to meet these new developments. In this regard, the emergence of widespread public education, the rise of the welfare state, and the proliferation of religious groups present a cultural milieu quite different from that of 1789. Specific historical practices and views become less analogous and consequently less helpful, but the importance of fundamental principles derived from history endures. To illustrate this proposition, this chapter will apply the animating principles to three current issues: equal access for student religious groups in public high schools; religious symbols and ceremonies in public life, particularly in light of the concept of "civil religion"; and the constitutional definition of religion.

The Equal-Access Controversy

One of the most volatile religious issues in this decade concerns the right of student religious groups to meet on the same basis as other student groups in public high schools. This equal-access controversy[7] arises in the broader context of the role that public education has played in American culture. With the growth of compulsory education in the mid-nineteenth century, a function traditionally performed by parents and private religious and nonreligious schools was entrusted largely to the state. The public school proved to be a critical institution for inculcating and maintaining democratic ideals; during successive waves of immigration, it performed the task of assimilating diverse peoples into our society. Prominent educators such as John Dewey even asserted that in teaching civic virtue the public schools were "performing an infinitely significant religious work."[8]

Whether or not one agrees with this role, the fact remains that public schools have transmitted values, not merely knowledge, and increasingly have been called on to prepare children for productive involvement in society. Given this fact and the large amount of time education consumes in the lives of children, it is understandable that parents and religious organizations have expressed concern over such matters as the place of objective instruction about religion in the curriculum, the character of school employees, the values and manners taught, the content of textbooks, and the activities sponsored. Some parents have alleged, for example, that the public school curriculum and modern textbooks contain few references to the historical influence of religion and that public education is impermissibly advancing the religion of secular humanism.[9] The first allegation receives significant support from educators and other professionals,[10] who attribute the exclusion primarily to a fear that materials on religion will provoke controversy and breach the wall between church and state. Thus, the wall metaphor not only has generated confusing judicial precedent, it has exerted a chilling effect on educational efforts to present knowledge in a balanced and accurate manner; it has transformed the Pilgrims from religious dissenters into international travelers.

If these assessments are correct, then Justice Goldberg may well have been prophetic when he warned in 1963 that an "untutored devotion to the concept of neutrality" in religious matters could lead to a "brooding and pervasive devotion to the secular and a passive, or even active, hostility to the religious."[11] In this regard, Charles Malik, distinguished Lebanese educator and former President of the United Nations, concluded in 1980 that the "enormity of what is happening is beyond words." What can the church and family do, he asked, "if the children spend between fifteen and twenty years of their life, and indeed the most formative period of their life, in school and college in an atmosphere of formal denial of any relevance of God and spirit and soul and faith to the formation of their mind?"[12] To the extent it holds the rudder that steers children morally and socially, public education exercises, in the words of John Stuart Mill, a dangerous power to mold "people to be exactly like one another."[13] To prevent such an outcome, he proposed a system of competing state and private schools that would give objective examinations on essential areas of knowledge, including religion. While the state should not "bias the conclusions of its citizens," he concluded that it properly could examine a student, even an atheist, on religious matters "provided he is not required to profess a belief in them."[14]

The value-laden role of public education, the task of presenting knowledge in a responsible and accurate manner, and concerns regarding the exclusion of religion from the curriculum lead to a question that undergirds the equal-access controversy and virtually every other legal issue involving religion and public education: is the public school a fundamentally secular institution? If by secular one means that it may not inculcate religious beliefs, then it properly may be understood as a secular institution. From all indications, however, this is not the definition of secular one encounters today. Instead, the untutored understanding is that secular means the absence of all things religious, so that public schools should excise all references, objective or otherwise, to religion. If used in this sense, the public school should not be regarded as a secular institution. To assert otherwise would place educators in the difficult position of providing a complete and balanced education without referring to one of the most dynamic forces in mankind's history. As Justice Jackson observed, an attempt to eliminate the objective study of religion from the public schools is neither constitutionally compelled nor educationally wise: "Music without sacred music, architecture minus the cathedral, or painting without the scriptural themes would be eccentric and incomplete, even from a secular point of view."[15]

In light of the confusion engendered by the term "secular," it perhaps would be more appropriate to view the public school as a pluralistic institution dedicated to neutrality in religious matters. Achieving this neutrality in a society characterized by a high degree of pluralism constitutes an imposing challenge, one that increases the growing number of cases involving religion and public education. With the erosion of the broad moral consensus of prior generations, public schools can no longer appeal to particular premises for morality but must think in terms of presenting various value systems in a balanced manner. A key question becomes whether religious perspectives can be included in this endeavor on equal terms with nonreligious views and influences. Recent cases offer one answer; history and tradition afford another.

When the federal courts first considered the equal-access issue, they uniformly answered no to the above question.[16] Armed with a judicial heritage of strict separation, they rejected the contention that the free exercise and free speech clauses compel public schools to treat student religious groups the same as other groups.[17] Indeed, the courts reasoned that even if school boards wanted to treat religious groups equally, they could not do so because the establishment clause prohibited such an "endorsement" of religion. Prompted by such cases and a conviction that discrimination against student religious speech was widespread, Congress enacted the Equal Access Act in 1984 by an overwhelming margin.[18] In an effort to end such discrimination, the Act prohibits a public high school with a forum for noncurriculum student groups "to deny equal access" to groups desiring to meet for "religious, political, philosophical, or other [speech purposes]."[19]

The equal-access controversy is illustrated by *Bender v. Williamsport Area School District*,[20] initiated before passage of the Equal Access Act. In *Bender*, a student religious group called Petros sought permission to meet during the regularly scheduled activity period of a public high school. During this period, pupils were free to participate in student clubs or to pursue personal interests on the school premises. Over forty groups had been allowed to meet through the years, including Student Government, Band, and the Chess, Poetry, Audubon, Photography, Speech, Drama, and Ski Clubs.[21] Although no request to organize a club had ever been denied, the school board rejected Petros's application because it concluded that religious activities on the school premises would violate the establishment clause.

Members of Petros filed suit, alleging that the school board had violated their rights under the free speech and free exercise clauses. The district court rejected the students' free exercise claim, but sustained their free speech claim. Finding that the activity period constituted an open forum, the court held that the school board had impermissibly excluded the religious club because of the content of its speech. It dismissed the argument that the establishment clause justified such content-based discrimination and ordered the school to permit Petros to meet.

A divided court of appeals reversed. It conceded that the school had created a "limited forum" and that the free speech clause afforded protection to the members of Petros. The majority found, however, that the students' free speech rights were outweighed by establishment clause interests, particularly the prohibition against endorsement: "the presence of religious groups within the school during the curricular day has the effect of advancing religion, in that it communicates a message of government endorsement of such activity."[22] Adopting the view that religion is a "private" matter, the court concluded that "prayer in the public schools segregates students along religious lines."[23]

Emphasizing the critical difference between voluntary and state-sponsored religious activity, the dissent criticized the majority's endorsement approach and asserted that the student body was far more likely to read the selective exclusion of Petros as "a manifestation of official hostility towards religion."[24] Nor did the establishment clause justify the school board's content-based discrimination against the speech of Petros's members. Relying on the Supreme Court's decision in *Widmar v. Vincent*,[25] which held that the free speech clause compelled the University of Missouri to permit a student religious group to meet on campus, the dissent reasoned that the difference between the maturity of high school and college students was insufficient to justify a distinction of constitutional import.

The Supreme Court set aside the judgment of the court of appeals on procedural grounds, thereby reinstating the district court's decision recognizing the right of Petros to meet. Four Justices dissented on the procedural issue and would have addressed the equal-access question. Chief Justice Burger, joined by Justices White and Rehnquist, emphasized that the establishment clause mandates "state neutrality, not hostility, toward religion" and concluded that granting equal access to Petros was "wholly consistent with the Constitution." Justice Powell largely agreed with the Chief Justice but wrote separately to state that the case was controlled by *Widmar*.[26]

The *Bender* Court's failure to resolve this volatile issue, coupled with enactment of the Equal Access Act, portends continued litigation. Perhaps the Court will provide guidance when it reviews a recent federal decision concluding that a student Bible study club is entitled under the First Amendment and the Act to meet in a public high school on the same basis as other noncurriculum student groups.[27] In any case, litigation over the equal-access issue could have been avoided, for the controversy and the resulting tension between constitutional values—establishment interests versus free exercise and free speech interests—is a dilemma of the judiciary's own making. Proceeding from a strict separation position and the corollaries of "privatized" religion and a secular society, the courts that ruled on equal access viewed religious expression suspiciously and employed the establishment clause as a means of excluding such expression from the public schools. If the courts had proceeded under the principles that we have discussed, they would have recognized that the establishment clause is a co-guarantor of religious liberty, not a device to defeat other constitutional rights. Properly framed, the issue becomes whether equal access for student religious groups advances religious liberty, the core value of the religion clauses. A related question is whether the selective exclusion of such groups violates this value. Understood in light of its implementing principles of federalism, institutional separation, accommodation, and benevolent neutrality, religious liberty not only would seem to permit but would require equal access for student religious groups.

Principles of federalism counsel that the judiciary should interfere with mediating structures only when important constitutional values are clearly at stake. The public high school is a mediating institution that performs a task of the highest order—educating and preparing children for productive involvement in a democratic society. When high schools selectively exclude influences such as religion, however, it becomes necessary for the courts to intervene. The justification for intervention gains greater credence in light of the Equal Access Act, which constitutes Congress's considered judgment that widespread discrimination against religion has occurred in public education. Passage of the Act sends a signal that the legislative branch desires student religious groups to be treated on the same basis as other student groups.

The principal error of the court of appeals in *Bender*, pointed out by the dissent, arose because of its adherence to strict rather than institutional separation. Viewing religious influences as a divisive rather than a healthy manifestation of pluralism, the majority failed to grasp a critical distinction in applying the concept of governmental endorsement of religion—the difference between governmental and private speech. The identity of the speaker, not the location of the speech, should be the focus of the inquiry. No reasonable constitutional objection, for example, could be made against a Jewish student sharing a religious experience as part of a public school exercise. No reasonable school employee, parent, or student would conclude that the state "symbolically" endorses this student's views simply because the speech takes place in a public school. In the same setting, however, serious establishment clause concerns would arise if a public school teacher used a classroom as a forum for sharing his or her religious views. The student groups in *Bender* are analogous to the former example; they were engaged in private speech in a context in which not even an appearance of endorsement is present. To assert otherwise leads to the dubious proposition that the school board implicitly endorses all speech that occurs during the activity period, including that of the Student Government, Band, and Ski Club, as well as that of Petros.[28]

When the establishment clause is interpreted in terms of the historical element of coercion, it becomes plain that allowing Petros to meet along with other student groups does not violate institutional separation. No impermissible alliance between the school board and religion exists that threatens to coerce or influence the voluntary formation of religious belief. Students initiate and operate the various clubs with little or no assistance from school officials. During the activity period, they may choose to attend any one of the clubs or pursue personal interests on their own. No concern arises under the pietistic tradition of separation because the school board, from all indications, would interfere with Petros only if the club creates a disturbance. In any case, it is unlikely that such interference would entangle the school board with the religious views of Petros and its members.

Allowing Petros to meet would accord with the Founders' solicitude for voluntary religious expression and promote the free exercise values underlying the principle of accommodation, particularly in light of the considerable amount of time that compulsory education occupies in the lives of children. During the school year, most children between the formative ages of five and sixteen spend about one third of their waking hours in public schools. Given that many schools have discriminated against religious speech, it is understandable that some parents are concerned and expect the accommodation of voluntary religious expression in the school setting.

Under the accommodation principle, equal access is at least constitutionally permissible and, in terms of educational policy, appears commendable in terms of free exercise values. Under the principle of benevolent neutrality, equal access is not only constitutionally permissible, but compelled. The selective exclusion of religious groups clearly violates strict neutrality for, under Kurland's religion-blind view, it uses religion as a classification for determining governmental action and, under the view of other scholars, such as Douglas Laycock, it treats religious speech differently from other private speech.[29] With respect to religion, however, the Constitution demands not strict but benevolent neutrality. It was because voluntary religious expression needed special protection that the Founders granted it a status not given to other expression.

Refusing Petros permission to meet, while granting it to all other groups, constitutes official hostility towards religion in violation of benevolent neutrality. What message does such selective exclusion *by the state* send to high school students—that religious matters are somehow less worthy of consideration than chess, drama, art, skiing, and home economics? The message that public schools should send, given this nation's tradition of religious liberty, is that religion plays an integral part in the lives of many students. The animating principles of the clauses, particularly in a compulsory setting like the public schools, support Petros's right to meet on the same basis as other student groups.

Finally, equal access teaches students the valuable civic lesson of toleration for the beliefs and practices of others. As the dissent pointed out in

Bender: "Our country's continued progress in [avoiding religious strife] ultimately depends on the individual citizen's tolerance and respect for religious diversity. When the schools can teach such tolerance to our young citizens without impermissibly sponsoring religion, I believe the Constitution and the Nation are the better for it."[30]

Religious Symbolism in Public Life

The influence exerted by religion in the development of American culture and institutions manifests itself in the contemporary religious symbolism that pervades our society. Communities throughout the nation have recognized this influence in monuments, murals, seals, names, and ceremonies. Public parks contain statues commemorating Roger Williams, William Penn, Isaac Backus, Lord Baltimore, and Martin Luther King, Jr.; city halls and courthouses display monuments inscribed with the Ten Commandments; public buildings are etched with Biblical verses; and public funds are expended to restore famous religious landmarks, to erect crosses as war memorials, and to provide grave monuments with religious symbols for veterans. Our cities bear names such as St. Paul, St. Augustine, Zion, Corpus Christi, and San Francisco, and their boards and councils often open sessions with invocations. Quite symbolic in terms of the judiciary is the relief of "Moses the Lawgiver" above the Supreme Court's bench.

Religious symbols in American society are not, as the secular philosopher Sidney Hook contends, "vestigial remains of a once strongly religious culture."[31] Even though confronted with competing ideologies such as materialism, hedonism, and moral relativism, religion remains a vital force in the lives of many citizens. What De Tocqueville observed over a century and a half ago with respect to Christianity in America is true today with respect to religion: "Christianity and liberty are so completely mingled that it is almost impossible to get [Americans] to conceive of the one without the other; it is not a question with them of sterile beliefs bequeathed by the past and vegetating rather than living in the depths of the soul."[32]

American culture can thus be seen as a tapestry, with religion as its warp threads. According to anthropologist Clifford Geertz, cultural and religious symbols synthesize "what is known about the way the world is, the quality of the emotional life it supports, and the way one ought to behave while in it." Symbols identify "fact with value at the most fundamental level, [giving] what is otherwise merely actual, a comprehensive normative import." Symbols are universal among cultures and, Geertz added, are essential: "[T]hough in theory we might think that a people could construct a wholly autonomous value system independent of any metaphysical referent, an ethics without ontology, we do not in fact seem to have found such a people."[33]

Theologian Paul Tillich contended that "[r]eligion as ultimate concern is the meaning-giving substance of culture, and culture is the totality of forms in which the basic concern of religion expresses itself." In brief, this suggests that "religion is the substance of culture, culture is the form of religion."[34] If these scholars are correct, then to eradicate religious symbols from public life would tear at the fabric of our cultural tapestry.

The analysis of these scholars indicates that when the judiciary considers constitutional challenges to religious symbols, it should proceed cautiously, recognizing the broader cultural role of symbolism. In contrast to many of the secular symbols occupying our attention, religious symbols perform unique and significant functions: teaching historical values and traditions, providing social cohesion at a fundamental level, and reminding us that there are transcendent values and moral standards higher than the state. To remove religious symbols from public life would change the substance of American culture. This may or may not be a valid goal, but in a democratic society such a change must be wrought by the people, not compelled by one branch of government. That, at least, is the lesson that the principle of federalism would teach.

The Supreme Court recognized the importance of public religious ceremonies in *Marsh v. Chambers* (1983),[35] when it eschewed its much criticized establishment clause test announced in *Lemon* and sustained legislative prayers and chaplaincies on the basis of a history dating to the Framers. The decision was correct in its conclusion that history provides a compelling basis for sustaining such practices and in its underlying premise that the Framers had a far more intrusive kind of religious sponsorship in mind when they provided for nonestablishment. While legislative chaplaincies are constitutional in principle, however, the particular chaplaincy considered in *Marsh* may have violated the establishment clause because it favored one religion over others, thereby failing the standard of benevolent neutrality.[36]

More recently, in *Stein v. Plainwell Community Schools*,[37] a federal court of appeals considered the constitutionality of including prayers in high school commencement ceremonies. The court posed the question: "[W]hat kind of invocations and benedictions, if any, does the Establishment Clause of the First Amendment permit the public schools to conduct at their annual commencement exercises?"[38] The plaintiffs, parents of school children, challenged the inclusion of prayers in the commencement ceremonies of two Michigan high schools. They argued that the prayers "invoke[d] the image of a God or Supreme Being" and thus violated the First Amendment values of "liberty of conscience, state neutrality and noninterference with religion."[39] Attendance at the commencement ceremonies was voluntary, and failure to attend did not affect the receipt of a diploma. Students supervised the ceremonies; in one school they delivered the prayers themselves, at the other they selected various local clergy to pray.

Judge Merritt concluded in his majority opinion that the religion clauses, taken together, guarantee "equal liberty of conscience," erecting "a neutral state designed to foster the most extensive liberty of conscience compatible with a similar or equal liberty for others."[40] Treating benedictions and invocations as analogous to legislative prayers, the court concluded that *Marsh* governed the case, permitting some accommodation to the nation's religious traditions. According to the court, *Marsh* required public prayers to be framed in terms of "the American civil religion":

> So long as the invocation or benediction on these public occasions does not go beyond "the American civil religion," so long as it preserves the substance of the principle of equal liberty of conscience, no violation of the Establishment Clause occurs under the reasoning of *Marsh*.[41]

In sustaining commencement prayers generally, the court emphasized that, unlike classroom prayer, they presented little danger of religious coercion or indoctrination. The court, however, found the prayers in question unacceptable because they were so overtly Christian that they connoted a symbolic governmental endorsement of Christianity. Thus, the prayers failed to qualify as permissible invocations and benedictions under the concept of American civil religion.[42]

In dissent, Judge Wellford objected to the majority's focus on the content of the commencement prayers. He stressed that content was immaterial to the issue of governmental sponsorship of religion, because school officials played no part in composing the prayers, or even in choosing who would give them. He criticized the majority for casting the issue in terms of content, especially since the plaintiffs' complaint objected not to "sectarian or denominational" prayers, but to "*any* reference to a Deity."[43] According to Judge Wellford, the majority misread *Marsh*, for the Supreme Court there specifically declined "to embark on a sensitive evaluation or to parse the content of a particular prayer."[44] Considering the "whole context" in which the activity took place, he would have sustained the invocations and benedictions in question: "Here there is, at most, a kind of acknowledgment of religion in a brief part of an annual commencement ceremony, which takes place outside of any classroom setting, and is not directed towards influencing young children at a formative period."[45]

The general approach in *Stein*, particularly of the dissent, represents a departure from the strict separation rhetoric pervading numerous other decisions. Evaluated in light of the animating principles discussed earlier, the *Stein* court correctly recognized that liberty of conscience in religious matters stands at the core of the religion clauses, and that this value should be fostered to the maximum extent consistent with public order and the rights of others. In addition, in sustaining commencement prayers generally, *Stein* accords with the Founders' intent to create a society receptive to voluntary religious expression and with their belief that religion is an essential source of personal and public virtue.

By adhering to the emphasis in *Marsh* on the nation's tradition of public prayer, the *Stein* court placed the case in historical context, recognizing that it should invalidate ceremonies embedded in tradition only if clearly compelled to do so by the Constitution. Thus, the decision followed the principle of federalism and evidenced an understanding of the judiciary's role in a free society. The Constitution, the nation's fundamental law, cannot legitimately be construed to afford redress to every citizen who takes offense at public expressions, whether religious or secular in content. Although the establishment clause forbids the state from sponsoring religiously coercive symbols and practices, it does not require the state to excise public symbols and practices merely because they may be offensive to some. The screening and complete elimination of objectionable views and practices from public life is a characteristic of totalitarian regimes, not democratic states. The privilege of living in a free society, characterized by robust debate in a marketplace of ideas, entails exposure to conflicting and sometimes disagreeable views. To propose that the Constitution should shield citizens from such views may be seen as an undemocratic notion.[46] This principle does not minimize the fact that some individuals may be offended, but emphasizes instead the nature of the Constitution and the proper role of the judiciary. As Benjamin Cardozo asserted in *The Nature of the Judicial Process*, a judge "is not a knight-errant roaming at will in pursuit of his own ideal of beauty or of goodness." Rather than yield to "unregulated benevolence," he should "exercise a discretion informed by tradition, methodized by analogy, disciplined by system, and subordinated to 'the primordial necessity of order in the social life.'"[47]

It is under the principle of institutional separation that the decision in *Stein* encounters the greatest difficulty. In finding that invocations and benedictions pose little danger of religious indoctrination, the majority discerned the importance of coercion to establishment clause analysis. Unlike the dissent, however, the majority did not perceive that judicial examination of the prayers in question might violate the religion clauses. This error was compounded when the court did not distinguish between governmental and private speech and when it essentially established "the American civil religion."

Like the court of appeals in *Bender*, the *Stein* court focused its symbolic endorsement analysis on the location of the activity rather than the identity of the actor. There is an important distinction between public prayers that are state-sponsored and those that are offered voluntarily by individual citizens. The former implicate establishment clause concerns, while the latter pose no significant threat, "symbolic" or otherwise. The commencement prayers in *Stein* were delivered by students or local clergy, once a year, in an environment in which they spoke as private citizens, not as representatives of the school board. By requiring commencement invocations and benedictions to conform to the American civil religion, *Stein* may have transformed private prayers into governmentally controlled prayers, making them official endorsements of the new civil religion.

The majority may have misread the *Marsh* opinion regarding judicial examination of the content of prayers. In any case, it should be cause for concern if the civil power, whether through judges, legislators, or executive officials, is seen as telling citizens how they should pray in public or in private. The pietistic tradition of institutional separation rests on the notion that government officials exceed their authority when they interfere in religious matters by compelling conformity to acceptable or "orthodox" views. Apart from thrusting judges into the business of composing prayers and into a theological quagmire, the *Stein* court's precedent of reviewing particular commencement prayers to ensure acceptability under the American civil religion may create excessive governmental interference with religion.[48]

Stein appears to be the first explicit recognition of American civil religion as a juridical concept. Judicial recognition of such a religion is somewhat questionable, as the scholars who formulated the concept now regard its utility as limited. Sociologist Robert Bellah, one of the early proponents of the concept, later stated that the "American civil religion is an empty and broken shell."[49] Its cultural vitality aside, the notion of a civil religion by which to assess the constitutionality of time-honored religious practices is troubling in several respects.

First, constitutionally establishing a religion, civil or otherwise, is antithetical to the establishment clause. Troubled by the sectarian nature of some public religious expressions, the *Stein* court essentially posited an orthodox religion by which to judge these expressions. If the establishment clause means anything, it means that government cannot adopt and apply standards of religious orthodoxy. Second, the concept imposes another definitional task—in addition to defining religion under the First Amendment, the judiciary must now define the contours of an amorphous religion with no recognizable adherents, clergy, ruling body, ritual, history, tradition, or sacred work. The first definitional task is difficult, the second almost impossible. Certainly civil religion must be given content if it is to serve as the comparative paradigm for assessing the acceptability of "authentic" religious symbols and ceremonies in public life. This fact poses the question of where the courts are to look for guidance.

Third, in defining the civil religion the courts run the risk of favoring traditional and majority religions, thereby giving them a preferred constitutional status. Fourth, as noted above, implementation of the concept conflicts with the pietistic tradition by creating an unacceptable degree of interference in religious matters and by threatening authentic faith. Finally, raising the American civil religion to constitutional status gives government, through the courts, a tool to justify and reinforce its own policies. As the standard for acceptability, the civil religion would enjoy a preferred status that could be used to exclude prophetic voices from the public arena.

While the principle of accommodation does not compel invocations and benedictions at commencement ceremonies, it permits their inclusion as an acknowledgment of religion's important place in public life. Having said this, the principle of benevolent neutrality requires that the opportunity for offering commencement prayers be open to students and clergy of various faiths. A consistent pattern of prayers by ministers or students of the same denomination might signal that the public school is preferring one religion over others.[50]

In many respects, the Supreme Court has admirably discharged the difficult and often thankless task of interpreting the religion clauses. If the Justices decide, however, to embark on a course of excising the religious leaven from the nation's public life, they will undertake a difficult journey, likely to bring disfavor from the coequal branches as well as the American people. Moreover, they cannot do so legitimately in the name of the historic First Amendment. Rather, the Justices will have to look elsewhere for legitimation, perhaps to their own predilections or to brooding forces such as materialism or secularism, which seem to be pressing in on the culture from many directions. If they choose this course and create a public square devoid of religion, they might regret the result.[51]

The Constitutional Definition of Religion

One of the more troubling constitutional issues today is that of deciding whether a belief system constitutes a religion under the First Amendment.[52] Judicial definitions of religion have great impact, for if a set of beliefs does not constitute a religion, then its adherents are not afforded protection under the clauses. The proliferation of government programs and regulations in our society has heightened conflicts between facially neutral statutes and individual beliefs, pushing to the forefront the issue of which of these beliefs falls under the mantle of the clauses. Cases involving new sects or unfamiliar beliefs generally present situations in which an individual must choose between deeply held convictions, on the one hand, and state entitlements, property interests, or liberty, on the other. Adherents of unfamiliar beliefs often seek relief from state burdens on free exercise grounds, thereby requiring the courts to determine whether the beliefs are in fact religious. Because this definitional issue was largely unforeseen by the Founders, the animating principles enumerated earlier can provide guidance only in the broadest sense.

In 1982, a federal court of appeals addressed the sensitive task of defining religion under the First Amendment in *Africa v. Commonwealth of Pennsylvania*.[53] A prisoner named Frank Africa asserted that he was a member of a religion known as MOVE, which required a special diet of uncooked fruits and vegetables. He claimed that the prison was violating his free exercise rights by denying him this diet. The district court held that MOVE was not a religion. The court of appeals affirmed, employing a definition-by-analogy approach consisting of three indicia:

First, a religion addresses fundamental and ultimate questions having to do
with deep and imponderable matters. Second, a religion is comprehensive in
nature; it consists of a belief-system as opposed to an isolated teaching.
Third, a religion often can be recognized by the presence of certain formal
and external signs.[54]

In examining MOVE's beliefs, the court noted that the group rejected
contemporary society and was committed to a natural, unadulterated lifestyle. Central to this lifestyle was a diet provided by God, which prohibited
the consumption of processed or cooked food. Ingestion of such food
constituted deviation from the "direct, straight, and true" and would result
in "confusion and disease."[55]

In applying the three-pronged definitional test, the court found that
MOVE's tenets failed to meet the "ultimate" ideas criterion. Unlike recognized religions, MOVE referred to "no transcendental or all-controlling
force" and did not address matters of morality, mortality, or the meaning
of life.[56] Its rejection of society appeared to be a product of a secular
philosophy rather than religious conviction. In this, the members of
MOVE resembled Henry David Thoreau, whose isolation at Walden Pond
resulted from philosophical choices, rather than religious belief. The court
emphasized that "the free exercise clause does not protect all deeply held
beliefs, however 'ultimate' their ends or all-consuming their means."[57]

Second, MOVE espoused a single governing idea, best described as a
philosophical naturalism, rather than a comprehensive world view. It resembled single-faceted ideologies such as economic determinism or social
Darwinism more than any recognized religion. Third, MOVE did not
exhibit the "external signs" of a religion—it had no clergy, no services, no
holy days, and no scripture. The absence of these signs, while not con-
trolling, strengthened the conclusion that MOVE was not a religion.

The Supreme Court has not defined religion for constitutional purposes, but decisions in other contexts reveal the steady expansion of the
term to meet needs arising in an increasingly complex and pluralistic society. Although older cases defined religion in theistic terms as one's
relation to a Supreme Being, a Court stated in 1961 that "[a]mong religions
. . . which do not teach what would generally be considered a belief in the
existence of God are Buddhism, Taoism, Ethical Culture, Secular Humanism and others."[58] During the Vietnam War, the Court held in *United
States v. Seeger* that religious belief for draft exemption purposes connoted
any sincere and meaningful conviction that occupied "a place in the life of

its possessor parallel to that filled by the orthodox belief in God of [a theist]."[59] In more recent cases, the Court appears to have retreated from *Seeger*. In *Wisconsin v. Yoder*, it emphasized that religion did not encompass purely secular value systems such as Thoreau's; his "choice was philosophical and personal rather than religious, and such belief does not rise to the demands of the Religion Clauses."[60] In 1981, the Court stated cryptically that some claims may be "so bizarre" as to be "clearly nonreligious in motivation."[61]

As *Africa* and Supreme Court precedent illustrate, the proliferation of new sects and belief systems has confronted courts with a task largely unforeseen by the Founders. Nothing in the historical record suggests that they thought it necessary to define religion in the First Amendment, and from every indication, they appeared to regard the term as almost self-evident. While some pluralism existed in the colonies, the religious groups were virtually all theistic and followed the Judeo-Christian model. As evident from the Virginia Declaration of Rights, Madison, Mason, Henry, Washington, Marshall, and others in Virginia uniformly appeared to regard religion as "the duty which we owe to our Creator, and the manner of discharging it."[62]

Jefferson entertained a somewhat broader view, stating that his Bill for Establishing Religious Freedom was "meant to comprehend, within the mantle of it's protection, the Jew and the Gentile, the Christian and Mahometan, the Hindoo, and infidel of every denomination."[63] Among the pietistic separationists, Roger Williams espoused a definition, remarkable for its time, that included pagan, Jewish, Islamic, and anti-Christian worship.[64] These views assist modern courts only insofar as they evidence an intent to construe liberally the scope of religious freedom. In brief, the colonists and Founders lived in a more homogeneous society where religion was understood in a Judeo-Christian framework and where governmental contact with religion was arguably less extensive.

Unless one believes that the Framers drafted the Constitution as a static document, incapable of adaptation to meet new challenges, the definitional task is an area where original intent affords no complete solution. The Founders' theistic understanding of religion proves inadequate in twentieth-century America because it is underinclusive, failing to account for nontheistic religions such as Buddhism and Taoism. Consequently, in contrast to issues such as equal access and religious symbolism, the animating principles identified earlier can provide courts with only limited guidance in defining religion. These principles, however, yield at least three observations that may inform endeavors in this area: the necessity of defining religion, the cautionary ideal of noninterference, and the need for a unitary constitutional definition of religion.

First, courts must continue to distinguish religion from nonreligion. The task is compelled by our fundamental law, for special protection is granted religion in the constitutional text. The Framers did not define the term, but they did earmark the free exercise of religion for protection not accorded other conduct. Not every idea, belief, moral code, or philosophy can be regarded as religious. If it were otherwise, all deeply held beliefs that conflicted with civil duties would implicate the free exercise clause, requiring accommodation unless the government advanced a compelling interest. This would create a chaotic situation, particularly in a culture in which so many entitlements and consequences attach to a determination of religious purpose or conduct.

The historical principles of accommodation and benevolent neutrality rest on the premise that the Founders granted religion a special status in the Constitution. This status derived from a conviction that religious exercise, as opposed to other personal and social forces, needed and deserved unique treatment. Although the Framers did not define religion for constitutional purposes, they clearly did not envision special protection for every deeply held moral code, ideology, or set of beliefs.[65]

Second, the recognition that judges must distinguish between religion and nonreligion leads to a cautionary observation derived from the pietistic separationists. In shaping the principle of institutional separation that informs our heritage, they stressed the fragile nature of conscience and the destructive effect of governmental interference with religion. Their focus on noninterference counsels a recognition that the definitional task is a delicate one and that judges, not well equipped to deal with such matters, should approach this task only if all other means of resolution are foreclosed. Consider, for example, the adherent of an unfamiliar belief system who invokes a free exercise claim when the state is advancing a compelling interest. The court should consider avoiding the definitional issue by holding that, even if the individual's claim was religiously motivated, he or she would not prevail. Similarly, if the factual record appears incomplete, the court should consider remanding the case before addressing the definitional issue; perhaps the case will be resolved on remand. In addition, courts should fashion and apply definitional tests with a view towards minimizing inquiry into the content and meaning of avowed religions.

Third, religion would seem to have the same meaning under both the establishment and free exercise clauses.[66] Nothing in the text or history of the clauses or their generating history suggests a dual meaning. The view that religion should be more broadly construed for free exercise than for establishment purposes is of recent vintage, arising primarily because of problems generated by the Court's sweeping definition of the establishment clause in *Everson* and its progeny. With the Court's early adherence to strict separation and the no-aid principle, commentators feared that an expansive definition of religion under the establishment clause would result in the invalidation of numerous governmental programs with arguably religious premises or effects. These fears were perhaps unfounded, but the dilemma stems primarily from a misunderstanding of the term "establishment," not from a broad definition of religion. No dilemma exists if the establishment clause is understood in its historical sense as a prohibition against those institutional alliances of church and state that threaten to coerce or influence religious choice. With this understanding, both "free exercise" and "religion" can be given broad content without fear of infringing the nonestablishment guarantee.

Defining religion for constitutional purposes has proven to be a controversial task, one characterized by developing and shifting analysis. To return briefly to the *Africa* case, for example, critics have asserted that its three-part definitional test favors Western models of religion, and that MOVE may have functioned as a religion in Frank Africa's life.[67] It may be that MOVE was central to Africa's life, but the centrality of an idea or belief system does not necessarily transform it into a religion. Under current judicial definitions, not every deeply held conviction that guides an individual is recognized as religious. Adoption of an expansive view would provide constitutional protection to a wide variety of philosophies that motivate individuals. People are devoted to a remarkable range of beliefs and activities: some are materialists and seek to accumulate wealth; others are hedonists, building their lives around the pursuit of pleasure; still others center their interests on secret societies or fraternal organizations. A definition that recognized as religious every central influence in the lives of people would undermine the fundamental nature of the Bill of Rights, generate further confusion in First Amendment jurisprudence, and render it difficult to create any sense of social cohesion.

Admittedly, the process of defining religion by analogy is a difficult one. Bias for traditional religions, the standard references for such an approach, may result in the exclusion of legitimate, although unconventional, religions. That is why the analysis does not inquire whether a belief system includes a God, a messiah, an afterworld, or a concept of sin. The analogy is drawn at the more general level of whether the belief system addresses ultimate concerns, the meaning of life, humanity's place in the universe, and a comprehensive range of moral concerns. Thus, the approach would encompass religions different from those in the Judeo-Christian tradition, such as Taoism, Hinduism, and Buddhism, but would exclude belief systems like Epicureanism, nihilism, solipsism, and materialism, which arguably may take the place of religion in the lives of some but certainly do not resemble religion in their essence or purpose. While communism might prove more troublesome to assess, under *Africa*'s definitional test it would not appear to address "fundamental and ultimate questions" at a level similar to that in traditional religions. Communism, a system of social order based on common ownership of the means of production, is more in the nature of a single-faceted political philosophy than a comprehensive world view. In any case, communists themselves do not regard their system as religious.

Conclusion

Studying the history of law and ideas, as Sir Frederic Maitland admonished, is a difficult task.[1] It is a necessary task, however, for history provides an essential framework for resolving contemporary religious freedom issues. Those in the legal profession must look to the traditions and values of the American people as more than vague generalities to introduce the resolution of difficult cases. In order for the judiciary to use history properly, however, it is necessary for historians to take a more active role in addressing the historical aspects of emerging legal issues.

The Founders drew on rich and diverse ideas in formulating their views on church and state. They looked to the Protestant Reformers, Catholic humanists, Puritans, Quakers, Baptists and other dissenters, Whig political theorists, natural law philosophers, and British jurists. From their experiences under the colonial establishments, the Founders learned that governmental coercion of conscience threatened the purity of religion and the peace of the state. Those in the Enlightenment, pietistic, and political centrist traditions approached the issue of church and state somewhat differently, but they agreed that religion was an indispensable source of public and private morality, and that the stability of the republic depended on fostering voluntary religious expression.

The principles animating the religion clauses can be discovered by examining colonial and early national antecedents on religious freedom, the legislative history of the clauses, and the Founders' beliefs and practices concerning religion and government. Historically, the establishment and free exercise clauses are best understood as co-guarantors of the core value of liberty of conscience in religious matters. The Founders implemented this concept through the principles of federalism, institutional separation, accommodation, and benevolent neutrality. These principles provide important, although somewhat varying, degrees of guidance for the resolution of contemporary religious freedom issues. Their usefulness ranges from the assessment of historical precedent approved by the Framers, such

as legislative chaplains, to relatively unforeseen problems, such as the proliferation of religious groups and the resulting need to define religion for
constitutional purposes. Between these extremes lies a large middle
ground, where one finds issues such as equal access for religious student
groups and the presence of religious symbols and ceremonies in public life.
It is in this middle area that the animating principles can provide significant
guidance.

A more fundamental question concerns the place of religion in contemporary American society. Does it occupy the same place today as it did
in previous generations? One commentator recently suggested, for example, that "the free exercise clause is an anachronism." Asserting that the
First Amendment was primarily a product of Enlightenment philosophy,
he remarked that religion may no longer merit a preferred constitutional
status because American society has become largely secular.[2] This assessment, we believe, fails to take adequate account of the dynamic role played
by religion in history and in contemporary America. The religion clauses
owe as much, if not more, to the pietistic and political centrist positions as
to the Enlightenment. While it is true that secularization has occurred,
religion remains a vital force in the nation and in the lives of citizens.
Indeed, many of the current religious liberty issues, such as the problem of
accommodation, have arisen precisely because we are a religious people.

The philosophy underlying the Constitution, as John Mansfield ob-
serves, is not necessarily secular. With respect to the religion clauses, it
affirmatively recognizes the "spiritual element in man" and addresses "fundamental questions regarding human nature, human destiny and other
such realities."[3] Thus, the American heritage of religious liberty not only
yields animating principles useful in deciding particular issues, it also discloses "general truths" about mankind. This heritage affirms that religion
has a special constitutional status because it occupies an essential place in
shaping public and private virtue; it provides transcendent values and a
degree of moral legitimacy not supplied by other social forces; it shapes
and holds people together through the most trying of times; it recognizes
a domain for the conscience beyond the control of the state; and it stands,
along with other mediating institutions, as a check on governmental
power. Indeed, the Founders' political philosophy and distrust of centralized authority stemmed from a skeptical view of human nature derived
largely from religious principles. They established the republic on a premise
articulated by John Adams in 1798: "Our constitution was made only for
a moral and religious people. It is wholly inadequate to the government of

any other."[4] Whether the Constitution can endure in the absence of a moral and religious milieu remains to be seen.

Roger Williams, Mr. Cottons Letter Lately Printed, Examined and Answered, 1644[1]

First, the faithful labors of many witnesses of Jesus Christ, extant to the world, abundantly proving, that the Church of the Jews under the Old Testament in the type, and the Church of the Christians under the New Testament in the antitype, were both separate from the world; and that when they have opened a gap in the hedge or wall of separation between the garden of the Church and the wilderness of the world, God hath ever broke down the wall itself, removed the candlestick, etc., and made his garden a wilderness, as at this day. And that therefore if he will ever please to restore his garden and paradise again, it must of necessity be walled in peculiarly unto himself from the world, and that all that shall be saved out of the world are to be transplanted out of the wilderness of the world, and added unto his Church or garden.

Roger Williams, The Bloudy Tenent, of Persecution, for Cause of Conscience, 1644[2]

First, that the blood of so many hundred thousand souls of Protestants and Papists, spilt in the wars of present and former ages, for their respective consciences, is not required nor accepted by Jesus Christ, the Prince of Peace.

Secondly, pregnant Scriptures and arguments are throughout the work proposed against the doctrine of persecution for cause of conscience.

Thirdly, satisfactory answers are given to Scriptures, and objections produced by Mr. Calvin, Beza, Mr. Cotton, and the ministers of the New English Churches and others former and later, tending to prove the doctrine of persecution for cause of conscience.

Fourthly, the doctrine of persecution for cause of conscience, is proved guilty of all the blood of the souls crying for vengeance under the altar.

Fifthly, all civil states with their officers of justice in their respective constitutions and administrations are proved essentially civil, and therefore not judges, governors, or defenders of the spiritual or Christian state and worship.

Sixthly, it is the will and command of God, that (since the coming of his Son the Lord Jesus) a permission of the most pagan, Jewish, Turkish, or anti-Christian consciences and worships, be granted to all men in all nations and countries, and they are only to be fought against with that sword which is only (in soul matters) able to conquer, to wit, the sword of God's Spirit, the Word of God.

Seventhly, the state of the land of Israel, the kings and people thereof in peace and war, is proved figurative and ceremonial, and no pattern nor precedent for any kingdom or civil state in the world to follow.

Eighthly, God requires not an uniformity of religion to be enacted and enforced in any civil state; which enforced uniformity (sooner or later) is the greatest occasion of civil war, ravishing of conscience, persecution of Christ Jesus in his servants, and of the hypocrisy and destruction of millions of souls.

Ninthly, in holding an enforced uniformity of religion in a civil state, we must necessarily disclaim our desires and hopes of the Jews' conversion to Christ.

Tenthly, an enforced uniformity of religion throughout a nation or civil state, confounds the civil and religious, denies the principles of Christianity and civility, and that Jesus Christ is come in the flesh.

Eleventhly, the permission of other consciences and worships than a state professes, only can (according to God) procure a firm and lasting peace (good assurance being taken according to the wisdom of the civil state for uniformity of civil obedience from all sorts).

Twelfthly, lastly, true civility and Christianity may both flourish in a state or kingdom, notwithstanding the permission of diverse and contrary consciences, either of Jew or Gentile.

Roger Williams, Letter to the Town of Providence, 1655[3]

That ever I should speak or write a tittle, that tends to such an infinite liberty of conscience, is a mistake, and which I have ever disclaimed and abhorred. To prevent such mistakes, I shall at present only propose this case: There goes many a ship to sea, with many hundred souls in one ship, whose weal and woe is common, and is a true picture of a commonwealth, or a human combination or society. It hath fallen out sometimes, that both Papists and Protestants, Jews and Turks, may be embarked in one ship; upon which supposal I affirm, that all the liberty of conscience, that ever I pleaded for, turns upon these two hinges—that none of the Papists, Protestants, Jews or Turks, be forced to come to the ship's prayers or worship, nor compelled from their own particular prayers or worship, if they practice any. I further add, that I never denied, that notwithstanding this liberty, the commander of this ship ought to command the ship's course, yea, and also command that justice, peace and sobriety, be kept and practiced, both among the seamen and all the passengers. If any of the seamen refuse to perform their services, or passengers to pay their freight; if any refuse to help, in person or purse, toward the common charges or defence; if any refuse to obey the common laws and orders of the ship, concerning their common peace or preservation; if any shall mutiny and rise up against their commanders and officers; if any should preach or write that there ought to be no commanders or officers, because all are equal in Christ, therefore no masters nor officers, no laws nor orders, nor corrections nor punishments;—I say, I never denied, but in such cases, whatever is pretended, the commander or commanders may judge, resist, compel and punish such transgressors, according to their deserts and merits. This, if seriously and honestly minded, may, if it so please the Father of lights, let in some light to such as willingly shut not their eyes.

I remain studious of your common peace and liberty. . . .

William Penn, The Great Case of Liberty of Conscience, 1671[4]

THE PREFACE

WERE some as Christian, as they boast themselves to be, it would save us all the labor we bestow in rendering persecution so unchristian, as it most truly is. Nay, were they those men of reason they character themselves, and what the civil law styles good citizens, it had been needless for us to tell them, that neither can any external coercive power convince the understanding of the poorest idiot, nor fines and prisons be judged fit and adequate penalties for faults purely intellectual; as well as that they are destructive of all civil government. . . .

[S]uch earnest persecutors [do not consider] that the enaction of such laws as restrain persons from the free exercise of their consciences in matters of religion, is but a knotting whipcord to lash their own posterity; whom they can never promise to be conformed to a national religion. Nay, since mankind is subject to such mutability, they cannot ensure themselves from being taken by some persuasions that are esteemed heterodox, and consequently catch themselves in snares of their own providing. And for men thus liable to change, (and no ways certain of their own belief to be the most infallible) as by their multiplied concessions may appear, to enact any religion, or prohibit persons from the free exercise of theirs, sounds harsh in the ears of all modest and unbiased men. . . .

CHAPTER I

. . . .

The Terms explained, and the Question stated.

First, by liberty of conscience, we understand not only a mere liberty of the mind, in believing or disbelieving this or that principle or doctrine, but the exercise of ourselves in a visible way of worship, upon our believing it to be indispensably required at our hands, that if we neglect it for fear or favor of any mortal man, we sin, and incur divine wrath. Yet we would be so understood to extend and justify the lawfulness of our so meeting to worship God, as not to contrive, or abet any contrivance destructive of the government and laws of the land, tending to matters of an external nature, directly, or indirectly; but so far only, as it may refer to religious matters, and a life to come, and consequently wholly independent of the secular affairs of this, wherein we are supposed to transgress.

Secondly, by imposition, restraint, and persecution, we do not only mean, the strict requiring of us to believe this to be true, or that to be false, and upon refusal, to incur the penalties enacted in such cases; but by those terms we mean thus much, any coercive let or hindrance to us, from meeting together to perform those religious exercises which are according to our faith and persuasion.

The Question stated.

For proof of the aforesaid terms thus given, we singly state the question thus,

Whether imposition, restraint, and persecution, upon persons for exercising such a liberty of conscience . . . be not to impeach the honor of God, the meekness of the Christian religion, the authority of Scripture, the privilege of nature, the principles of common reason, the well being of government, and apprehensions of the greatest persons of former and latter ages.

[W]e say that imposition, restraint, and persecution, for matters relating to conscience directly invade the divine prerogative, and divest the Almighty of a due, proper to none besides himself. And this we prove by these five particulars.

First, if we do allow the honor of our creation, due to God only, . . . then whosoever shall interpose their authority to enact faith and worship, in a way that seems not to us congruous with what he has discovered to us to be faith and worship (whose alone property it is to do it) or to restrain us from what we are persuaded is our indispensable duty, they evidently usurp this authority and invade his incommunicable right of government over conscience. . . .

Secondly, such magisterial determinations carry an evident claim to that infallibility, which Protestants have been hitherto so jealous of owning, that to avoid the Papists, they have denied it to all but God himself. . . .

Thirdly, it enthrones man as king over conscience, the alone just claim and privilege of his Creator, whose thoughts are not as men's thoughts, but has reserved to himself that empire from all the Caesars on earth; for if men in reference to souls, and bodies, things appertaining to this and the other world, shall be subject to their fellow creatures, what follows, but that Caesar (however he got it) has all, God's share, and his own too. And being Lord of both, both are Caesar's and not God's.

Fourthly, it defeats God's work of grace, and the invisible operation of his eternal Spirit, which can alone beget faith, and is only to be obeyed, in and about religion and worship, and attributes men's conformity to outward force and corporal punishments. A faith subject to as many revolutions as the powers that enact it.

Fifthly and lastly, such persons assume the judgment of the great tribunal unto themselves; for to whomsoever men are imposedly or restrictively subject and accountable in matters of faith, worship, and conscience, in them alone must the power of judgment reside; but it is equally true that God shall judge all by Jesus Christ, and that no man is so accountable to his fellow creatures, as to be imposed upon, restrained, or persecuted for any matter of conscience whatever.

Thus and in many more particulars are men accustomed to entrench upon divine property, to gratify particular interests in the world (and at best) through a misguided apprehension to imagine they do God good service, that where they cannot give faith, they will use force, which kind of sacrifice is nothing less unreasonable than the other is abominable. God will not give his honor to another, and to him only that searches the heart and tries the reins, it is our duty to ascribe the gifts of understanding and faith, without which none can please God.

Isaac Backus, An Appeal to the Public for Religious Liberty, 1773[5]

INTRODUCTION

. . . .

The true liberty of man is to know, obey, and enjoy his Creator and to do all the good unto, and enjoy all the happiness with and in, his fellow creatures that he is capable of. . . .

SECTION I

. . . [T]he true difference and exact limits between ecclesiastical and civil government is this, That the church is armed with *light and truth* to pull down the strongholds of iniquity and to gain souls to Christ and into his Church to be governed by his rules therein, and again to exclude such from their communion, who will not be so governed, while the state is armed with the *sword* to guard the peace and the civil rights of all persons and societies and to punish those who violate the same. And where these two kinds of government, and the weapons which belong to them are well distinguished and improved according to the true nature and end of their institution, the effects are happy, and they do not at all interfere with each other. But where they have been confounded together no tongue nor pen can fully describe the mischiefs that have ensued. . . .

SECTION II

. . . We view it to be our incumbent duty to render unto Caesar the things that are his but also that it is of as much importance not to render unto him anything that belongs only to God, who is to be obeyed rather than any man. And as it is evident to us that God always claimed it as his sole prerogative to determine by his own laws what his worship shall be, who shall minister in it, and how they shall be supported, so it is evident that this prerogative has been, and still is, encroached upon in our land. . . .

. . . .

These evils [religious imposition and persecution] cleaved so close to the first fathers of the Massachusetts as to move them to imprison, whip, and banish men only for denying infant baptism and refusing to join in worship that was supported by violent methods. Yet they were so much blinded as to declare that there was this *vast difference* between these proceedings and the coercive measures which were taken against themselves in England, viz., We compel men to "God's institutions," they in England compelled to "men's inventions." . . .

SECTION III

. . . .

. . . And we freely confess that we can find no more warrant from divine truth for any people on earth to constitute any men their representatives to make laws, to impose religious taxes than they have to appoint Peter or the Virgin Mary to represent them before the throne above. We are therefore brought to a stop about paying so much regard to such laws as to give in annual certificates to the other denomination [i.e., the Congregational or Standing Churches] as we have formerly done.

1. Because the very nature of such a practice implies an acknowledgement that the civil power has a right to set one religious sect up above another, else why need we give certificates to them any more than they to us? It is a tacit allowance that they have a right to make laws about such things which we believe in our consciences they have not. For,

2. [H]ow came a civil community by any ecclesiastical power? How came the kingdoms of *this world* to have a right to govern in Christ's kingdom which is *not of this world*! . . .

4. The scheme we oppose evidently tends to destroy the purity and life of religion, for the inspired apostle assures us that the church is *espoused as a chaste virgin to Christ* and is obliged to be *subject to him in everything* as a true wife to her husband. . . . But for a woman to admit the highest ruler in a nation into her husband's place would be *adultery* or *whoredom*. . . .

5. The custom which they want us to countenance is very hurtful to civil society, for by the law of Christ *every man* is not only allowed but also required to judge for himself concerning the circumstantials as well as the essentials of religion. . . . What a temptation then does it lay for men to contract such guilt when temporal advantages are annexed to one persuasion and disadvantages laid upon another? i.e., in plain terms, how does it tend to hypocrisy and lying? than which, what can be worse to human society! Not only so, but coercive measures about religion also tend to provoke emulation, wrath, and contention, and who can describe all the mischiefs of this nature that such measures have produced in our land! But where each person and each society [i.e., religious congregation] are

equally protected from being injured by others, all enjoying equal liberty to attend and support the worship which they believe is right, . . . how happy are its effects in civil society? . . .

James Madison, Memorial and Remonstrance Against Religious Assessments, 1785[6]

To the Honorable the General Assembly of the
Commonwealth of Virginia
A Memorial and Remonstrance

We the subscribers, citizens of the said Commonwealth, having taken into serious consideration, a Bill printed by order of the last Session of General Assembly, entitled "A Bill establishing a provision for Teachers of the Christian Religion," and conceiving that the same if finally armed with the sanctions of a law, will be a dangerous abuse of power, are bound as faithful members of a free State to remonstrate against it, and to declare the reasons by which we are determined. We remonstrate against the said Bill,

1. Because we hold it for a fundamental and undeniable truth, "that Religion or the duty which we owe to our Creator and the manner of discharging it, can be directed only by reason and conviction, not by force or violence."* The Religion then of every man must be left to the conviction and conscience of every man; and it is the right of every man to exercise it as these may dictate. This right is in its nature an unalienable right. It is unalienable, because the opinions of men, depending only on the evidence contemplated by their own minds cannot follow the dictates of other men: It is unalienable also, because what is here a right towards men, is a duty towards the Creator. It is the duty of every man to render to the Creator such homage and such only as he believes to be acceptable to him. This duty is precedent, both in order of time and in degree of obligation, to the claims of Civil Society. Before any man can be considered as a member of Civil Society, he must be considered as a subject of the Governour of the Universe: And if a member of Civil Society, who enters into any subordinate Association, must always do it with a reservation of

---

*In the margin, Madison identified the source for this quotation as article 16 of the Virginia Declaration of Rights.

his duty to the General Authority; much more must every man who becomes a member of any particular Civil Society, do it with a saving of his allegiance to the Universal Sovereign. We maintain therefore that in matters of Religion, no mans right is abridged by the institution of Civil Society and that Religion is wholly exempt from its cognizance. True it is, that no other rule exists, by which any question which may divide a Society, can be ultimately determined, but the will of the majority; but it is also true that the majority may trespass on the rights of the minority.

2. Because if Religion be exempt from the authority of the Society at large, still less can it be subject to that of the Legislative Body. The latter are but the creatures and vicegerents [*sic*] of the former. Their jurisdiction is both derivative and limited: it is limited with regard to the co-ordinate departments, more necessarily is it limited with regard to the constituents. The preservation of a free Government requires not merely, that the metes and bounds which separate each department of power be invariably maintained; but more especially that neither of them be suffered to overleap the great Barrier which defends the rights of the people. The Rulers who are guilty of such an encroachment, exceed the commission from which they derive their authority, and are Tyrants. The People who submit to it are governed by laws made neither by themselves nor by an authority derived from them, and are slaves.

3. Because it is proper to take alarm at the first experiment on our liberties. We hold this prudent jealousy to be the first duty of Citizens, and one of the noblest characteristics of the late Revolution. The free men of America did not wait till usurped power had strengthened itself by exercise, and entangled the question in precedents. They saw all the consequences in the principle, and they avoided the consequences by denying the principle. We revere this lesson too much soon to forget it. Who does not see that the same authority which can establish Christianity, in exclusion of all other Religions, may establish with the same ease any particular sect of Christians, in exclusion of all other Sects? that the same authority which can force a citizen to contribute three pence only of his property for the support of any one establishment, may force him to conform to any other establishment in all cases whatsoever?

4. Because the Bill violates that equality which ought to be the basis of every law, and which is more indispensable, in proportion as the validity or expediency of any law is more liable to be impeached. If "all men are by

nature equally free and independent,"* all men are to be considered as entering into Society on equal conditions; as relinquishing no more, and therefore retaining no less, one than another, of their natural rights. Above all are they to be considered as retaining an *"equal* title to the free exercise of Religion according to the dictates of Conscience."** Whilst we assert for ourselves a freedom to embrace, to profess and to observe the Religion which we believe to be of divine origin, we cannot deny an equal freedom to those whose minds have not yet yielded to the evidence which has convinced us. If this freedom be abused, it is an offence against God, not against man: To God, therefore, not to man, must an account of it be rendered. As the Bill violates equality by subjecting some to peculiar burdens, so it violates the same principle, by granting to others peculiar exemptions. Are the Quakers and Menonists the only sects who think a compulsive support of their Religions unnecessary and unwarrantable? Can their piety alone be entrusted with the care of public worship? Ought their Religions to be endowed above all others with extraordinary privileges by which proselytes may be enticed from all others? We think too favorably of the justice and good sense of these denominations to believe that they either covet pre-eminences over their fellow citizens or that they will be seduced by them from the common opposition to the measure.

5. Because the Bill implies either that the Civil Magistrate is a competent Judge of Religious Truth; or that he may employ Religion as an engine of Civil policy. The first is an arrogant pretension falsified by the contradictory opinions of Rulers in all ages, and throughout the world: the second an unhallowed perversion of the means of salvation.

6. Because the establishment proposed by the Bill is not requisite for the support of the Christian Religion. To say that it is, is a contradiction to the Christian Religion itself, for every page of it disavows a dependence on the powers of this world: it is a contradiction to fact; for it is known that this Religion both existed and flourished, not only without the support of human laws, but in spite of every opposition from them, and not only during the period of miraculous aid, but long after it had been left to its own evidence and the ordinary care of Providence. Nay, it is a contradiction in terms; for a Religion not invented by human policy, must have

*In the margin, Madison identified the source for this quotation as article 1 of the Virginia Delcaration of Rights.
**In the margin, Madison identified the source for this quotation as article 16 of the Virginia Declaration of Rights.

pre-existed and been supported, before it was established by human policy. It is moreover to weaken in those who profess this Religion a pious confidence in its innate excellence and the patronage of its Author; and to foster in those who still reject it, a suspicion that its friends are too conscious of its fallacies to trust it to its own merits.

7. Because experience witnesseth that ecclesiastical establishments, instead of maintaining the purity and efficacy of Religion, have had a contrary operation. During almost fifteen centuries has the legal establishment of Christianity been on trial. What have been its fruits? More or less in all places, pride and indolence in the Clergy, ignorance and servility in the laity, in both, superstition, bigotry and persecution. Enquire of the Teachers of Christianity for the ages in which it appeared in its greatest lustre; those of every sect, point to the ages prior to its incorporation with Civil policy. Propose a restoration of this primitive State in which its Teachers depended on the voluntary rewards of their flocks, many of them predict its downfall. On which Side ought their testimony to have greatest weight, when for or when against their interest?

8. Because the establishment in question is not necessary for the support of Civil Government. If it be urged as necessary for the support of Civil Government only as it is a means of supporting Religion, and it be not necessary for the latter purpose, it cannot be necessary for the former. If Religion be not within the cognizance of Civil Government how can its legal establishment be necessary to Civil Government? What influence in fact have ecclesiastical establishments had on Civil Society? In some instances they have been seen to erect a spiritual tyranny on the ruins of the Civil authority; in many instances they have been seen upholding the thrones of political tyranny: in no instance have they been seen the guardians of the liberties of the people. Rulers who wished to subvert the public liberty, may have found an established Clergy convenient auxiliaries. A just Government instituted to secure and perpetuate it needs them not. Such a Government will be best supported by protecting every Citizen in the enjoyment of his Religion with the same equal hand which protects his person and his property; by neither invading the equal rights of any Sect, nor suffering any Sect to invade those of another.

9. Because the proposed establishment is a departure from that generous policy, which, offering an Asylum to the persecuted and oppressed of every Nation and Religion, promised a lustre to our country, and an accession to the number of its citizens. What a melancholy mark is the Bill of sudden degeneracy? Instead of holding forth an Asylum to the persecuted, it is

itself a signal of persecution. It degrades from the equal rank of Citizens all those whose opinions in Religion do not bend to those of the Legislative authority. Distant as it may be in its present form from the Inquisition, it differs from it only in degree. The one is the first step, the other the last in the career of intolerance. The magnanimous sufferer under this cruel scourge in foreign Regions, must view the Bill as a Beacon on our Coast, warning him to seek some other haven, where liberty and philanthrophy in their due extent, may offer a more certain repose from his Troubles.

10. Because it will have a like tendency to banish our Citizens. The allurements presented by other situations are every day thinning their number. To superadd a fresh motive to emigration by revoking the liberty which they now enjoy, would be the same species of folly which has dishonoured and depopulated flourishing kingdoms.

11. Because it will destroy that moderation and harmony which the forbearance of our laws to intermeddle with Religion has produced among its several sects. Torrents of blood have been spilt in the old world, by vain attempts of the secular arm, to extinguish Religious discord, by proscribing all difference in Religious opinion. Time has at length revealed the true remedy. Every relaxation of narrow and rigorous policy, wherever it has been tried, has been found to assuage the disease. The American Theatre has exhibited proofs that equal and compleat liberty, if it does not wholly eradicate it, sufficiently destroys its malignant influence on the health and prosperity of the State. If with the salutary effects of this system under our own eyes, we begin to contract the bounds of Religious freedom, we know no name that will too severely reproach our folly. At least let warning be taken at the first fruits of the threatened innovation. The very appearance of the Bill has transformed "that Christian forbearance, love and charity,"* which of late mutually prevailed, into animosities and jealousies, which may not soon be appeased. What mischiefs may not be dreaded, should this enemy to the public quiet be armed with the force of a law?

12. Because the policy of the Bill is adverse to the diffusion of the light of Christianity. The first wish of those who enjoy this precious gift ought to be that it may be imparted to the whole race of mankind. Compare the number of those who have as yet received it with the number still remaining under the dominion of false Religions; and how small is the former! Does the policy of the Bill tend to lessen the disproportion? No; it at once

*In the margin, Madison identified the source for this quotation as article 16 of the Virginia Declaration of Rights.

discourages those who are strangers to the light of revelation from coming into the Region of it; and countenances by example the nations who continue in darkness, in shutting out those who might convey it to them. Instead of Levelling as far as possible, every obstacle to the victorious progress of Truth, the Bill with an ignoble and unchristian timidity would circumscribe it with a wall of defence against the encroachments of error.

13. Because attempts to enforce by legal sanctions, acts obnoxious to so great a proportion of Citizens, tend to enervate the laws in general, and to slacken the bands of Society. If it be difficult to execute any law which is not generally deemed necessary or salutary, what must be the case, where it is deemed invalid and dangerous? And what may be the effect of so striking an example of impotency in the Government, on its general authority?

14. Because a measure of such singular magnitude and delicacy ought not to be imposed, without the clearest evidence that it is called for by a majority of citizens, and no satisfactory method is yet proposed by which the voice of the majority in this case may be determined, or its influence secured. "The people of the respective counties are indeed requested to signify their opinion respecting the adoption of the Bill to the next Session of Assembly." But the representation must be made equal, before the voice either of the Representatives or of the Counties will be that of the people. Our hope is that neither of the former will, after due consideration, espouse the dangerous principle of the Bill. Should the event disappoint us, it will still leave us in full confidence, that a fair appeal to the latter will reverse the sentence against our liberties.

15. Because finally, "the equal right of every citizen to the free exercise of his Religion according to the dictates of conscience" is held by the same tenure with all our other rights. If we recur to its origin, it is equally the gift of nature; if we weigh its importance, it cannot be less dear to us; if we consult the "Declaration of those rights which pertain to the good people of Virginia, as the basis and foundation of Government,"* it is enumerated with equal solemnity, or rather studied emphasis. Either then, we must say, that the Will of the Legislature is the only measure of their authority; and that in the plenitude of this authority, they may sweep away all our fundamental rights; or, that they are bound to leave this particular right untouched and sacred: Either we must say, that they may controul

*In the margin, Madison identified the source for this quotation as the title of the Virginia Declaration of Rights.

the freedom of the press, may abolish the Trial by Jury, may swallow up the Executive and Judiciary Powers of the State; nay that they may despoil us of our very right of suffrage, and erect themselves into an independent and hereditary Assembly or, we must say, that they have no authority to enact into law the Bill under consideration. We the Subscribers say, that the General Assembly of this Commonwealth have no such authority: And that no effort may be omitted on our part against so dangerous an usurpation, we oppose to it, this remonstrance; earnestly praying, as we are in duty bound, that the Supreme Lawgiver of the Universe, by illuminating those to whom it is addressed, may on the one hand, turn their Councils from every act which would affront his holy prerogative, or violate the trust committed to them: and on the other, guide them into every measure which may be worthy of his [blessing, may re]dound to their own praise, and may establish more firmly the liberties, the prosperity and the happiness of the Commonwealth.

Thomas Jefferson, A Bill for Establishing Religious Freedom, 1785[7]

[*Well aware that the opinions and belief of men depend not on their own will, but follow involuntarily the evidence proposed to their minds, that*]

I. WHEREAS Almighty God hath created the mind free [, *and manifested his supreme will that free it shall remain, by making it altogether insusceptible of restraint*]; that all attempts to influence it by temporal punishments or burthens, or by civil incapacitations, tend only to beget habits of hypocrisy and meanness, and are a departure from the plan of the Holy author of our religion, who being Lord both of body and mind, yet chose not to propagate it by coercions on either, as was in his Almighty power to do [, *but to extend it by its influence on reason alone*]; that the impious presumption of legislators and rulers, civil as well as ecclesiastical, who being themselves but fallible and uninspired men, have assumed dominion over the faith of others, setting up their own opinions and modes of thinking as the only true and infallible, and as such endeavouring to impose them on others, hath established and maintained false religions over the greatest part of the world, and through all time; that to compel a man to furnish contributions of money for the propagation of opinions which he disbelieves, [*and abhors,*] is sinful and tyrannical; that even the forcing him to support this or that teacher of his own religious persuasion, is depriving him of the comfortable liberty of giving his contributions to the particular pastor, whose morals he would make his pattern, and whose powers he feels most persuasive to righteousness, and is withdrawing from the ministry those temporary rewards, which proceeding from an approbation of their personal conduct, are an additional incitement to earnest and unremitting labours for the instruction of mankind; that our civil rights have no dependence on our religious opinions, any more than our opinions in physics or geometry; that therefore the proscribing any citizen as unworthy the public confidence by laying upon him an incapacity of being called to offices of trust and emolument, unless he profess or renounce this or that religious opinion, is depriving him injuriously of those privileges and advantages to which in common with his fellow-citizens he has a natural right; that it tends only [*also*] to corrupt the principles of that [*very*] religion it is meant to encourage, by bribing with a monopoly of worldly honours and emoluments, those who will externally profess and conform to it; that though indeed these are criminal who do not withstand such temptation, yet neither are those innocent who lay the bait in their way; [*that the opinions of men are not the object of civil government, nor under its jurisdiction;*] that to suffer the civil magistrate to intrude his powers into the field of opinion, and to restrain the profession or propagation of principles on supposition of their ill tendency, is a dangerous fallacy, which at once destroys all religious liberty, because he being of course judge of that tendency will make his opinions the rule of judgment, and approve or condemn the sentiments of others only as they shall square with or differ from his own; that it is time enough for the rightful purposes of civil government, for its officers to interfere when principles break out into overt acts against peace and good order; and finally, that truth is great and will prevail if left to herself, that she is the proper and sufficient antagonist to error, and has nothing to fear from the conflict, unless by human interposition disarmed of her natural weapons, free argument and debate, errors ceasing to be dangerous when it is permitted freely to contradict them:

II. *Be it enacted by the General Assembly,* [*We the General Assembly of Virginia do enact,*] That no man shall be compelled to frequent or support any religious worship, place, or ministry whatsoever, nor shall be enforced, restrained, molested, or burthened in his body or goods, nor shall otherwise suffer on account of his religious opinions or belief; but that all men shall be free to profess, and by argument to maintain, their opinion in matters of religion, and that the same shall in no wise diminish, enlarge, or affect their civil capacities.

III. And though we well know that this assembly elected by the people for the ordinary purposes of legislation only, have no power to restrain the acts of succeeding assemblies, constituted with powers equal to our own, and that therefore to declare this act to be irrevocable would be of no effect in law; yet we are free to declare, and do declare, that the rights hereby asserted are of the natural rights of mankind, and that if any act shall be hereafter passed to repeal the present, or to narrow its operation, such act will be an infringement of natural right.

Thomas Jefferson, Reply to the Danbury Baptist Association, 1802[8]

MESSRS. NEHEMIAH DODGE, EPHRAIM ROBBINS, AND STEPHEN S. NELSON, A COMMITTEE OF THE DANBURY BAPTIST ASSOCIATION, IN THE STATE OF CONNECTICUT.

January 1, 1802.

GENTLEMEN,—The affectionate sentiments of esteem and approbation which you are so good as to express towards me, on behalf of the Danbury Baptist Association, give me the highest satisfaction. My duties dictate a faithful and zealous pursuit of the interests of my constituents, and in proportion as they are persuaded of my fidelity to those duties, the discharge of them becomes more and more pleasing.

Believing with you that religion is a matter which lies solely between man and his God, that he owes account to none other for his faith or his worship, that the legislative powers of government reach actions only, and not opinions, I contemplate with sovereign reverence that act of the whole American people which declared that their legislature should "make no law respecting an establishment of religion, or prohibiting the free exercise thereof," thus building a wall of separation between church and State. Adhering to this expression of the supreme will of the nation in behalf of the rights of conscience, I shall see with sincere satisfaction the progress of those sentiments which tend to restore to man all his natural rights, convinced he has no natural right in opposition to his social duties.

I reciprocate your kind prayers for the protection and blessing of the common Father and Creator of man, and tender you for yourselves and your religious association, assurances of my high respect and esteem.

George Washington, Proclamation: A National Thanksgiving, 1789[9]

Whereas it is the duty of all nations to acknowledge the providence of Almighty God, to obey His will, to be grateful for His benefits, and humbly to implore His protection and favor; and

Whereas both Houses of Congress have, by their joint committee, requested me "to recommend to the people of the United States a day of public thanksgiving and prayer, to be observed by acknowledging with grateful hearts the many and signal favors of Almighty God, especially by affording them an opportunity peaceably to establish a form of government for their safety and happiness:"

Now, therefore, I do recommend and assign Thursday, the 26th day of November next, to be devoted by the people of these States to the service of that great and glorious Being who is the beneficent author of all the good that was, that is, or that will be; that we may then all unite in rendering unto Him our sincere and humble thanks for His kind care and protection of the people of this country previous to their becoming a nation; for the signal and manifold mercies and the favorable interpositions of His providence in the course and conclusion of the late war; for the great degree of tranquility, union, and plenty which we have since enjoyed; for the peaceable and rational manner in which we have been enabled to establish constitutions of government for our safety and happiness, and particularly the national one now lately instituted; for the civil and religious liberty with which we are blessed, and the means we have of acquiring and diffusing useful knowledge; and, in general, for all the great and various favors which He has been pleased to confer upon us.

And also that we may then unite in most humbly offering our prayers and supplications to the great Lord and Ruler of Nations, and beseech Him to pardon our national and other transgressions; to enable us all, whether in public or private stations, to perform our several and relative duties properly and punctually; to render our National Government a blessing to all the people by constantly being a Government of wise, just, and constitutional laws, discreetly and faithfully executed and obeyed; to protect and guide all sovereigns and nations (especially such as have shown

kindness to us), and to bless them with good governments, peace, and
concord; to promote the knowledge and practice of true religion and
virtue, and the increase of science among them and us; and, generally, to
grant unto all mankind such a degree of temporal prosperity as He alone
knows to be best.

Given under my hand, at the city of New York, the 3d day of October,
A.D. 1789.

George Washington, Farewell Address, 1796[10]

. . . .

Of all the dispositions and habits which lead to political prosperity,
religion and morality are indispensable supports. In vain would that man
claim the tribute of patriotism who should labor to subvert these great
pillars of human happiness—these firmest props of the duties of men and
citizens. The mere politician, equally with the pious man, ought to respect
and to cherish them. A volume could not trace all their connections with
private and public felicity. Let it simply be asked, Where is the security for
property, for reputation, for life, if the sense of religious obligation *desert*
the oaths which are the instruments of investigation in courts of justice?
And let us with caution indulge the supposition that morality can be
maintained without religion. Whatever may be conceded to the influence
of refined education on minds of peculiar structure, reason and experience
both forbid us to expect that national morality can prevail in exclusion of
religious principle.

It is substantially true that virtue or morality is a necessary spring of
popular government. The rule indeed extends with more or less force to
every species of free government. Who that is a sincere friend to it can look
with indifference upon attempts to shake the foundation of the fabric?
Promote, then, as an object of primary importance, institutions for the
general diffusion of knowledge. In proportion as the structure of a government gives force to public opinion, it is essential that public opinion
should be enlightened. . . .

Appendix Two
Early Declarations and Constitutional Provisions on Religion

The Declaration of Independence, 1776[11]

WHEN in the Course of human events, it becomes necessary for one people to dissolve the political bands which have connected them with another, and to assume among the Powers of the earth, the separate and equal station to which the Laws of Nature and of Nature's God entitle them, a decent respect to the opinions of mankind requires that they should declare the causes which impel them to the separation.

We hold these truths to be self-evident, that all men are created equal, that they are endowed by their Creator with certain unalienable Rights, that among these are Life, Liberty and the pursuit of happiness. That to secure these rights, Governments are instituted among Men, deriving their just powers from the consent of the governed, That whenever any Form of Government becomes destructive of these ends, it is the Right of the People to alter or to abolish it, and to institute new Government, laying its foundation on such principles and organizing its powers in such form, as to them shall seem most likely to effect their Safety and Happiness. . . .

We, therefore, the Representatives of the united States of America, in General Congress, Assembled, appealing to the Supreme Judge of the world for the rectitude of our intentions, do, in the Name, and by Authority of the good People of these Colonies, solemnly publish and declare, That these United Colonies are, and of right ought to be Free and Independent States; that they are Absolved from all Allegiance to the British Crown. . . . And for the support of this Declaration, with a firm reliance on the Protection of Divine Providence, we mutually pledge to each other our Lives, our Fortunes and our sacred Honor.

State Constitutional Provisions Before the Federal Constitution[12]

CONSTITUTION OF VIRGINIA, JUNE 12, 1776

Declaration of Rights[13]

ART. 16. That religion, or the duty which we owe to our Creator, and the manner of discharging it, can be directed only by reason and conviction, not by force or violence; and therefore all men are equally entitled to the free exercise of religion, according to the dictates of conscience; and that it is the mutual duty of all to practise Christian forbearance, love, and charity towards each other.

CONSTITUTION OF NEW JERSEY, JULY 3, 1776

XVIII. That no person shall ever, within this Colony, be deprived of the inestimable privilege of worshipping Almighty God in a manner agreeable to the dictates of his own conscience; nor, under any pretence whatever, be compelled to attend any place of worship, contrary to his own faith and judgment; nor shall any person, within this Colony, ever be obliged to pay tithes, taxes, or any other rates, for the purpose of building or repairing any other church or churches, place or places of worship, or for the mainte- nance of any minister or ministry, contrary to what he believes to be right, or has deliberately or voluntarily engaged himself to perform.

XIX. That there shall be no establishment of any one religious sect in this Province, in preference to another; and that no Protestant inhabitant of this Colony shall be denied the enjoyment of any civil right, merely on account of his religious principles. . . .

DELAWARE DECLARATION OF RIGHTS, SEPTEMBER 11, 1776[14]

SECT. 2. That all men have a natural and unalienable right to worship Almighty God according to the dictates of their own consciences and understandings; and that no man ought or of right can be compelled to attend any religious worship or maintain any ministry contrary to or against his own free will and consent, and that no authority can or ought to be vested in, or assumed by any power whatever that shall in any case interfere with, or in any manner controul the right of conscience in the free exercise of religious worship.

SECT. 3. That all persons professing the Christian religion ought forever to enjoy equal rights and privileges in this state, unless under colour of religion, any man disturb the peace, the happiness or safety of society.

CONSTITUTION OF PENNSYLVANIA, SEPTEMBER 28, 1776

Declaration of Rights

II. That all men have a natural and unalienable right to worship Al- mighty God according to the dictates of their own consciences and understanding: And that no man ought or of right can be compelled to attend any religious worship, or erect or support any place of worship, or maintain any ministry, contrary to, or against, his own free will and consent: Nor can any man, who acknowledges the being of a God, be justly deprived or abridged of any civil right as a citizen, on account of his religious sentiments or peculiar mode of religious worship: And that no authority can or ought to be vested in, or assumed by any power whatever, that shall in any case interfere with, or in any manner controul, the right of conscience in the free exercise of religious worship.

CONSTITUTION OF MARYLAND, NOVEMBER 11, 1776

Declaration of Rights
XXXIII. That, as it is the duty of every man to worship God in such manner as he thinks most acceptable to him; all persons, professing the Christian religion, are equally entitled to protection in their religious liberty; wherefore no person ought by any law to be molested in his person or estate on account of his religious persuasion or profession, or for his religious practice; unless, under colour of religion, any man shall disturb the good order, peace or safety of the State, or shall infringe the laws of morality, or injure others, in their natural, civil, or religious rights; nor ought any person to be compelled to frequent or maintain, or contribute, unless on contract, to maintain any particular place of worship, or any particular ministry; yet the Legislature may, in their discretion, lay a general and equal tax, for the support of the Christian religion; leaving to each individual the power of appointing the payment over of the money, collected from him, to the support of any particular place of worship or minister, or for the benefit of the poor of his own denomination, or the poor in general of any particular county. . . .

CONSTITUTION OF NORTH CAROLINA, DECEMBER 18, 1776

Declaration of Rights
XIX. That all men have a natural and unalienable right to worship Almighty God according to the dictates of their own consciences.

CONSTITUTION OF GEORGIA, FEBRUARY 5, 1777

Art. LVI. All persons whatever shall have the free exercise of their religion; provided it be not repugnant to the peace and safety of the State;

and shall not, unless by consent, support any teacher or teachers except those of their own profession.

CONSTITUTION OF NEW YORK, APRIL 20, 1777

XXXVIII. And whereas we are required, by the benevolent principles of rational liberty, not only to expel civil tyranny, but also to guard against that spiritual oppression and intolerance wherewith the bigotry and ambition of weak and wicked priests and princes have scourged mankind, this convention doth further, in the name and by the authority of the good people of this State, ordain, determine, and declare, that the free exercise and enjoyment of religious profession and worship, without discrimination or preference, shall forever hereafter be allowed, within this State, to all mankind: *Provided*, That the liberty of conscience, hereby granted, shall not be so construed as to excuse acts of licentiousness, or justify practices inconsistent with the peace or safety of this State.

CONSTITUTION OF SOUTH CAROLINA, MARCH 19, 1778[15]

XXXVIII. That all persons and religious societies who acknowledge that there is one God, and a future state of rewards and punishments, and that God is publicly to be worshipped, shall be freely tolerated. The Christian Protestant religion shall be deemed, and is hereby constituted and declared to be, the established religion of this State. That all denominations of Christian Protestants in this State, demeaning themselves peaceably and faithfully, shall enjoy equal religious and civil privileges. . . . And that whenever fifteen or more male persons, not under twenty-one years of age, professing the Christian Protestant religion, and agreeing to unite themselves in a society for the purposes of religious worship, they shall . . . be constituted a church, and be esteemed and regarded in law as of the established religion of the State, and on a petition to the legislature shall be entitled to be incorporated and to enjoy equal privileges. . . . [E]ach society so petitioning shall have agreed to and subscribe in a book the following five articles . . . :

1st. That there is one eternal God, and a future state of rewards and punishments.

2d. That God is publicly to be worshipped.

3d. That the Christian religion is the true religion.

4th. That the holy scriptures of the Old and New Testaments are of divine inspiration, and are the rule of faith and practice.

5th. That it is lawful and the duty of every man being thereunto called
by those that govern, to bear witness to the truth.

. . . No person shall, by law, be obliged to pay towards the maintenance
and support of a religious worship that he does not freely join in, or has
not voluntarily engaged to support. . . .

CONSTITUTION OF MASSACHUSETTS, OCTOBER 25, 1780

Declaration of Rights

II. It is the right as well as the duty of all men in society, publicly, and
at stated seasons, to worship the SUPREME BEING, the great Creator, and
Preserver of the universe. And no subject shall be hurt, molested, or
restrained, in his person, liberty, or estate, for worshipping GOD in the
manner and season most agreeable to the dictates of his own conscience;
or for his religious profession of sentiments; provided he doth not disturb
the public peace, or obstruct others in their religious worship.

III. As the happiness of a people, and the good order and preservation
of civil government, essentially depend upon piety, religion, and morality;
and as these cannot be generally diffused through a community but by the
institution of the public worship of GOD and of public instructions in piety,
religion, and morality: Therefore, to promote their happiness, and secure
the good order and preservation of their government, the people of this
commonwealth have a right to invest their legislature with power to authorize and require, and the legislature shall from time to time authorize
and require, the several towns, parishes, precincts, and other bodies politic,
or religious societies, to make suitable provision, at their own expense, for
the institution of the public worship of GOD, and for the support and
maintenance of public Protestant teachers of piety, religion, and morality,
in all cases where such provision shall not be made voluntarily.

And the people of this commonwealth have also a right to, and do,
invest their legislature with authority to enjoin upon all the subjects an
attendance upon the instructions of the public teachers aforesaid. . . .

And every denomination of Christians, demeaning themselves peaceably and as good subjects of the commonwealth, shall be equally under the
protection of the law: and no subordination of any one sect or denomination to another shall ever be established by law.

CONSTITUTION OF NEW HAMPSHIRE, JUNE 2, 1784[16]

Part I. The Bill of Rights

IV. Among the natural rights, some are in their very nature unalienable, because no equivalent can be given or received for them. Of this kind are the RIGHTS OF CONSCIENCE.

V. Every individual has a natural and unalienable right to worship GOD according to the dictates of his own conscience, and reason; and no subject shall be hurt, molested, or restrained in his person, liberty or estate for worshipping GOD, in the manner and season most agreeable to the dictates of his own conscience, or for his religious profession, sentiments or persuasion; provided he doth not disturb the public peace, or disturb others, in their religious worship.

VI. As morality and piety, rightly grounded on evangelical principles, will give the best and greatest security to government, and will lay in the hearts of men the strongest obligations to due subjection; and as the knowledge of these, is most likely to be propagated through a society by the institution of the public worship of the DEITY, and of public instruction in morality and religion; therefore, to promote those important purposes, the people of this state have a right to impower, and do hereby fully impower the legislature to authorize from time to time, the several towns, parishes, bodies-corporate, or religious societies within this state, to make adequate provision at their own expence, for the support and maintenance of public protestant teachers of piety, religion and morality. . . .

And every denomination of christians demeaning themselves quietly, and as good subjects of the state, shall be equally under the protection of the law: and no subordination of any one sect or denomination to another, shall ever be established by law.

The Constitution of the United States of America, 1787

WE THE PEOPLE of the United States, in Order to form a more perfect Union, establish Justice, insure domestic Tranquility, provide for the common defence, promote the general Welfare, and secure the Blessings of Liberty to ourselves and our Posterity, do ordain and establish this CONSTITUTION for the United States of America.

ARTICLE VI

. . . .

The Senators and Representatives before mentioned, and the Members of the several State Legislatures, and all executive and judicial Officers, both of the United States and of the several States, shall be bound by Oath or Affirmation, to support this Constitution; but no religious Test shall ever be required as a Qualification to any Office or public Trust under the United States.

AMENDMENT I [1791]

Congress shall make no law respecting an establishment of religion, or prohibiting the free exercise thereof; or abridging the freedom of speech, or of the press; or the right of the people peaceably to assemble, and to petition the Government for a redress of grievances.

AMENDMENT XIV [1868]

SECTION 1. All persons born or naturalized in the United States, and subject to the jurisdiction thereof, are citizens of the United States and of the State wherein they reside. No State shall make or enforce any law which shall abridge the privileges or immunities of citizens of the United States; nor shall any State deprive any person of life, liberty, or property, without due process of law; nor deny to any person within its jurisdiction the equal protection of the laws.

Appendix Three
Leading Supreme Court Decisions on Religious Liberty

Reynolds v. United States, 98 U.S. 145 (1879) (emphasizing the distinction between religious belief and action in rejecting a Mormon's claim that his criminal conviction for religiously motivated polygamy violated the free exercise clause).

Cantwell v. Connecticut, 310 U.S. 296 (1940) (holding that the Fourteenth Amendment due process clause incorporates the free exercise clause and affording broad protection to proselytizing Jehovah's Witnesses from state regulation).

Murdock v. Pennsylvania, 319 U.S. 105 (1943) (licence tax imposed on religious solicitation violates the free exercise, press, and speech clauses).

West Virginia State Board of Education v. Barnette, 319 U.S. 624 (1943) (sustaining religiously based claim of Jehovah's Witnesses that compulsory flag salute and pledge of allegiance in public schools violates the First Amendment).

Prince v. Massachusetts, 321 U.S. 158 (1944) (government interest in protecting children under child labor laws overrides guardian's free exercise rights).

United States v. Ballard, 322 U.S. 78 (1944) (religious fraud decision concluding that free exercise clause prohibits governmental inquiry into the truth or falsity of religious beliefs, but does not foreclose a determination as to whether the beliefs are sincerely held).

Everson v. Board of Education, 330 U.S. 1 (1947) (incorporating the establishment clause; broadly construing the clause, but over vigorous dissents sustaining state reimbursement for the bus fares of parochial school children).

McCollum v. Board of Education, 333 U.S. 203 (1948) (released time religious education program, held inside public school buildings, breaches the wall of separation erected by the establishment clause).

Zorach v. Clauson, 343 U.S. 306 (1952) (dismissed time religious education program, held off public school grounds, is a permissible accommodation of the religious needs of school children and their parents).

McGowan v. Maryland, 366 U.S. 420 (1961), and *Braunfeld v. Brown,* 366 U.S. 599 (1961) (rejecting establishment and free exercise challenges to Sunday closing laws on the ground that such laws now have a valid secular purpose).

Torcaso v. Watkins, 367 U.S. 488 (1961) (Maryland constitutional provision requiring office holders to declare a belief in God contravenes the religious freedom guaranteed by the First Amendment).

Engel v. Vitale, 370 U.S. 421 (1962) (state-sponsored prayer in the public schools violates the establishment clause).

Abington School District v. Schempp, 374 U.S. 203 (1963) (state-sponsored Bible reading in the public schools violates the establishment clause).

Sherbert v. Verner, 374 U.S. 398 (1963) (state's denial of unemployment benefits to Seventh-Day Adventist who refused to work on Saturday, her Sabbath, contravenes free exercise clause).

Board of Education v. Allen, 392 U.S. 236 (1968) (state loan of textbooks to parochial school students benefits the children, not the religious institution, and therefore is not inconsistent with the establishment clause).

Epperson v. Arkansas, 393 U.S. 97 (1968) (statute prohibiting the teaching of evolution and non-Biblical accounts of origins in the public schools violates the establishment clause because it resulted from "fundamentalist sectarian conviction").

Walz v. Tax Commission, 397 U.S. 664 (1970) (relying largely on historical precedent in rejecting the claim that tax exemptions for religious property violate the establishment clause).

Gillette v. United States, 401 U.S. 437 (1971) (conscientious objector statute affording exemption to pacifists, but not to adherents of the just war ethic, does not contravene the religion clauses).

Lemon v. Kurtzman, 403 U.S. 602 (1971) (direct aid to parochial schools for the teaching of state-mandated secular subjects violates establishment clause under three-prong test that aid must have a secular purpose, must have a primary effect that neither advances nor inhibits religion, and must not foster excessive entanglement between church and state).

Tilton v. Richardson, 403 U.S. 672 (1971) (upholding grants to religiously affiliated higher education to construct buildings to be used for secular purposes).

Wisconsin v. Yoder, 406 U.S. 205 (1972) (sustaining religious claim of Amish parents that free exercise clause requires the exemption of their children from compulsory education beyond the eighth grade).

Jones v. Wolf, 443 U.S. 595 (1979) (sustaining Georgia statute resolving church property disputes on the basis of "neutral principles of law," which operated in favor of a local congregational majority in the absence of explicit church procedures dictating otherwise).

Thomas v. Review Board, 450 U.S. 707 (1981) (extending *Sherbert* to require Indiana to afford unemployment benefits to a Jehovah's Witness who refused to work on armaments because of individual religious convictions).

Widmar v. Vincent, 454 U.S. 263 (1981) (state university regulation prohibiting students from using campus facilities for religious purposes violates First Amendment).

Bob Jones University v. United States, 461 U.S. 574 (1983) (sustaining revocation of religious university's tax-exempt status because government's policy in eradicating racial discrimination constitutes a compelling interest that overrides free exercise rights).

Mueller v. Allen, 463 U.S. 388 (1983) (state tax deduction for "tuition, textbooks and transportation" expenses for parents with children in public and private schools upheld under the *Lemon* test).

Marsh v. Chambers, 463 U.S. 783 (1983) (sustaining Nebraska's legislative chaplaincy against establishment clause challenge on the basis of long historical precedent).

Lynch v. Donnelly, 465 U.S. 668 (1984) (inclusion of a nativity scene in a public park as part of a Christmas holiday display does not violate the establishment clause).

Wallace v. Jaffree, 472 U.S. 38 (1985) (Alabama law authorizing a moment of silence for "meditation or voluntary prayer" in public schools endorses religion in violation of establishment clause).

Goldman v. Weinberger, 475 U.S. 503 (1986) (military's need for uniformity, order, and discipline outweighs free exercise claim of a Jewish officer to wear a yarmulke).

Edwards v. Aguillard, 482 U.S. 578 (1987) (Louisiana law requiring "balanced treatment" for the teaching of evolution and creation science in public schools provides financial and symbolic support for fundamentalist Christianity in violation of the establishment clause).

Corporation of Presiding Bishops v. Amos, 483 U.S. 327 (1987) (law exempting secular activities of religious organizations from the prohibition in the Civil Rights Act of 1964 against religious discrimination in employment does not violate the establishment clause).

Bowen v. Kendrick, 108 S.Ct. 2562 (1988) (rejecting establishment challenge against Adolescent Family Life Act, which provides federal funding to secular and religious organizations not advocating abortion to counsel youth on sexual responsibility).

County of Allegheny v. American Civil Liberties Union Greater Pittsburgh Chapter, 109 S.Ct. 3086 (1989) (invalidating a solitary courthouse nativity scene as officially endorsing Christianity, but sustaining a courthouse menorah as part of a broader holiday display).

Notes

Authorities are generally cited in accordance with HARVARD LAW RE-VIEW ASSOC., A UNIFORM SYSTEM OF CITATION (14th ed. 1986). All documents are dated in the text in accordance with modern reckoning. Quotations in the text from documents written before 1750 were changed to conform to modern usage. Those from documents written after 1750 were not changed, except that abbreviated words were spelled out and ampersands were replaced with "and." These rules are also followed for the documents set forth in appendixes 1 and 2.

Introduction

1. Historian Sanford Cobb concluded that America's solution to the "world-old problem of Church and State" was "so unique, so far-reaching, and so markedly diverse from European principles as to constitute the most striking contribution of America to the science of government." S. COBB, THE RISE OF RELIGIOUS LIBERTY IN AMERICA, at vii (1902).
2. U.S. CONST. amend. I.
3. There is a tendency among legal scholars to disparage the use of history in interpreting the religion clauses. A leading constitutional law treatise concludes, for example, that historical study of the clauses cannot "produce clear answers to current issues," and that the "seemingly irresistible impulse to appeal to history when analyzing issues under the religion clauses . . . is unfortunate because there is no clear history as to the meaning of the clauses." J. NOWAK, R. ROTUNDA & J. YOUNG, CONSTITUTIONAL LAW 1029–30 (2d ed. 1983). See also R. MORGAN, THE SUPREME COURT AND RELIGION 186 (1972) (maintaining "that the historical materials themselves will not settle anything"). This outlook may not only discourage continued historical study of the religion clauses but may reinforce the cynical view among lawyers that history can be invoked to prove anything. See Sutherland, *Historians, Lawyers, and "Establishment of Religion,"* in 5 RELIGION AND THE PUBLIC ORDER 27, 27 (D. Giannella ed. 1969) (questioning whether lawyers and judges can use historical materials objectively).

Chapter One. The Historical Roots of American Religious Liberty

1. Luther articulated his position in M. LUTHER, TEMPORAL AUTHORITY: TO WHAT EXTENT IT SHOULD BE OBEYED (Wittenberg 1523), in 45 LUTHER'S WORKS: THE CHRISTIAN IN SOCIETY II, at 81–129 (W. Brandt ed. 1962). A good biog-

raphy is R. Bainton, Here I Stand: A Life of Martin Luther (1950). Calvin set forth his position in 2 J. Calvin, Institutes of the Christian Religion bk. IV, ch. XX (Geneva 1559 ed.) (J. McNeill ed. 1960). For a recent biography, see W. Bouwsma, John Calvin: A Sixteenth-Century Portrait (1988). For the Reformers' views on religious liberty, see R. Bainton, The Reformation of the Sixteenth Century 211–27 (1952).

2. 1 J. Lecler, Toleration and the Reformation 141 (1960). See T. More, Utopia (Louvain 1518 ed.), in 4 The Complete Works of St. Thomas More 217–47 (E. Surtz & J. Hexter eds. 1965) (discussing religious freedom). A balanced biography is E. Reynolds, The Field is Won: The Life and Death of Saint Thomas More (1968).

3. J. Milton, A Treatise of Civil Power in Ecclesiastical Causes (London 1659), in 7 Complete Prose Works of John Milton 238, 242 (R. Ayers rev. ed. 1980). See D. Bush, John Milton (1964).

4. See J. Locke, A Letter on Toleration (Gouda 1689) (J. Gough ed. & trans. 1968). The Founders looked to J. Locke, Two Treatises of Government (London 1690) more than any other work in justifying the American Revolution. The work rejected the absolutist theory of government and its corollary, the divine right of kings, and espoused a theory premised on the "social compact." See R. Woolhouse, Locke (1983).

5. Accounts focusing on the role of religion in early Virginia include S. Ahlstrom, A Religious History of the American People 184–93 (1972) and S. Cobb, supra Introduction note 1, at 74–115.

6. The legal code is summarized in S. Cobb, supra Introduction note 1, at 77–79.

7. Puritanism embraced Continental Reformed theology and sought to purify the church by inculcating Calvinistic doctrine, reinstating apostolic worship, and reviving piety and discipline. It consisted of several groups and covered a broad spectrum in terms of church polity. Congregational Puritans, in contrast to Presbyterians and Anglicans, believed that Christians who had covenanted with God and with one another constituted a church body capable of ordaining a minister, determining membership, administering the sacraments, and carrying out discipline and excommunication. The Congregationalists, the critical group from the standpoint of colonization, consisted of nonseparatist and separatist factions. Nonseparatists remained in the Church of England in the hope of reforming it; separatists such as the Pilgrims completely renounced ties to the established church. See S. Ahlstrom, supra note 5, at 125, 132–34.

8. See Sources of Our Liberties 55–59 (R. Perry & J. Cooper eds. rev. ed. 1978) [hereinafter Sources]. On the Pilgrims, see the classic account by Plymouth Bay's first governor, W. Bradford, Of Plymouth Plantation: 1620–1647 (Boston 1856) (S. Morison ed. 4th printing 1966).

9. The last half century has witnessed a renaissance in Puritan studies, inaugurated in 1933 by Perry Miller. See P. Miller, Orthodoxy in Massachusetts: 1630–1650 (1933). Other important works include P. Miller, Errand into the

WILDERNESS (1956); P. MILLER, THE NEW ENGLAND MIND (1939 & 1953) (two vols.); E. MORGAN, THE PURITAN DILEMMA: THE STORY OF JOHN WINTHROP (1958); and E. MORGAN, VISIBLE SAINTS: THE HISTORY OF A PURITAN IDEA (1963).

10. S. AHLSTROM, *supra* note 5, at 124 (footnote omitted).

11. *See* T. HANLEY, THEIR RIGHTS AND LIBERTIES: THE BEGINNINGS OF RELIGIOUS AND POLITICAL FREEDOM IN MARYLAND (1959) and T. CURRY, THE FIRST FREEDOMS: CHURCH AND STATE IN AMERICA TO THE PASSAGE OF THE FIRST AMENDMENT 29–53 (1986).

12. Act Concerning Religion (1649), in 1 ARCHIVES OF MARYLAND 244, 246 (W. Browne ed. 1883) [hereinafter MARYLAND ARCHIVES].

13. *See* O. WINSLOW, MASTER ROGER WILLIAMS (1957). Scholars disagree over the extent to which Williams influenced the American tradition. Early biographers glorified his political contributions and overlooked the deeply theological nature of his works. *See, e.g.,* S. BROKUNIER, THE IRREPRESSIBLE DEMOCRAT: ROGER WILLIAMS (1940); V. PARRINGTON, MAIN CURRENTS IN AMERICAN THOUGHT 62–75 (1927). Perry Miller broke ground by asserting that Williams was a radical Christian thinker who had little enduring impact on American religious freedom. *See* P. MILLER, ROGER WILLIAMS: HIS CONTRIBUTION TO THE AMERICAN TRADITION (1953); *cf.* 3 W.K. JORDAN, THE DEVELOPMENT OF RELIGIOUS TOLERATION IN ENGLAND 472–506 (1938) (Williams influenced England more than America in this area). For more sympathetic assessments, see E. MORGAN, ROGER WILLIAMS: THE CHURCH AND THE STATE (1967) and M. HOWE, THE GARDEN AND THE WILDERNESS: RELIGION AND GOVERNMENT IN AMERICAN CONSTITUTIONAL HISTORY 1–18 (1965); *see also* W. MILLER, THE FIRST LIBERTY: RELIGION AND THE AMERICAN REPUBLIC 153–224 (1986).

14. *See* R. WILLIAMS, THE BLOUDY TENENT, OF PERSECUTION, FOR CAUSE OF CONSCIENCE (London 1644), in 3 THE COMPLETE WRITINGS OF ROGER WILLIAMS 1 (Russell & Russell, Inc. 1963) (seven vols.) [hereinafter WRITINGS OF WILLIAMS].

15. *Id.* at 4.

16. R. WILLIAMS, MR. COTTONS LETTER LATELY PRINTED, EXAMINED AND ANSWERED (London 1644), in 1 WRITINGS OF WILLIAMS, *supra* note 14, at 392.

17. *See* J. CLARKE, ILL NEWES FROM NEW-ENGLAND: OR A NARATIVE OF NEW-ENGLANDS PERSECUTION 68 (London 1652). The definitive work on the Baptists in New England is W. McLOUGHLIN, NEW ENGLAND DISSENT 1630–1833: THE BAPTISTS AND THE SEPARATION OF CHURCH AND STATE (1971) (two vols.) [hereinafter W. McLOUGHLIN, NEW ENGLAND DISSENT].

18. *See* CHARTER OF RHODE ISLAND AND PROVIDENCE PLANTATIONS (1663), in 6 THE FEDERAL AND STATE CONSTITUTIONS, COLONIAL CHARTERS, AND OTHER ORGANIC LAWS 3211 (F. Thorpe ed. 1909) [hereinafter THORPE].

19. *Id.* at 3212.

20. Scholarly biographies include E. BRONNER, WILLIAM PENN'S HOLY EXPERIMENT: THE FOUNDING OF PENNSYLVANIA 1681–1701 (1962) and C. PEARE, WILLIAM PENN: A BIOGRAPHY (1956). *See also* M. DUNN, WILLIAM PENN: POLITICS AND CONSCIENCE (1967) (stressing the central role of liberty of conscience in Penn's political thought); M. ENDY, WILLIAM PENN AND EARLY QUAKERISM (1973)

(examining the way Penn's theological views shaped his political theory). For his works, see THE PAPERS OF WILLIAM PENN (R. Dunn & M. Dunn eds. 1981) (five vols.) [hereinafter PAPERS OF PENN].

21. W. PENN, THE GREAT CASE OF LIBERTY OF CONSCIENCE (London 1670), in 1 A COLLECTION OF THE WORKS OF WILLIAM PENN 443, 447 (J. Besse ed. 1726 & photo. reprint 1974) [hereinafter WORKS OF PENN].

22. CONCESSIONS AND AGREEMENTS OF WEST NEW JERSEY of 1677, The Charter or Fundamental Laws, of West New Jersey, Agreed Upon, *reprinted in* SOURCES, *supra* note 8, at 184–88.

23. *Id.* ch. XVI (Liberty of conscience), at 185.

24. PA. FRAME OF GOVERNMENT of 1682, Laws Agreed Upon in England, art. XXXV (1682), in 5 THORPE, *supra* note 18, at 3063; *see also* 2 PAPERS OF PENN, *supra* note 20, at 135–238 (examining Penn's drafting of the document).

25. *See* PA. FRAME OF GOVERNMENT, *supra* note 24, arts. XXXIV, XXXVI & XXXVII, in 5 THORPE, *supra* note 18, at 3062–63.

26. *See* PA. CHARTER OF PRIVILEGES of 1701, art. I (granting religious freedom to theists and limiting public office to Christians) & art. VIII (liberty of conscience shall remain "inviolably for ever"), in 5 THORPE, *supra* note 18, at 3077–78, 3079–80.

27. *See* T. CURRY, *supra* note 11, at 78–104 (discussing church and state in the colonies in the early eighteenth century).

28. J. OTIS, THE RIGHTS OF THE BRITISH COLONIES ASSERTED AND PROVED (Boston 1764), in 1 PAMPHLETS OF THE AMERICAN REVOLUTION: 1750–1776, at 408 (B. Bailyn ed. 1965).

29. *Id.* at 425 n.4.

30. *See* S. ADAMS, A STATE OF THE RIGHTS OF THE COLONISTS (Boston 1772), in TRACTS OF THE AMERICAN REVOLUTION: 1763–1776, at 238 (M. Jensen ed. 1967).

31. *Id.* at 250.

32. A classic exposition is E. CORWIN, THE "HIGHER LAW" BACKGROUND OF AMERICAN CONSTITUTIONAL LAW (1955), which focuses on the centrality of natural law. For an illuminating discussion of colonial political thought, see A. KELLY & W. HARBISON, THE AMERICAN CONSTITUTION: ITS ORIGINS AND DEVELOPMENT 36–46 (5th ed. 1976). P. FURNEAUX, J. PRIESTLEY & W. BLACKSTONE, THE PALLADIUM OF CONSCIENCE (Philadelphia 1773) (L. Levy ed. 1974), contains a debate showing English attitudes concerning religious freedom before the Revolution. *See also* Lutz, *The Origins of American Constitutionalism: The Colonial Heritage*, 2 JURIS 1 (1987) (tracing the influence of colonial church covenants, law codes, and charters on the American constitutional tradition).

33. *See* The Declaration of Independence (U.S. 1776). *See generally* C. BECKER, THE DECLARATION OF INDEPENDENCE (1942) (examining the political and philosophical roots of the document); 1 A. STOKES, CHURCH AND STATE IN THE UNITED STATES 461–66 (1950) (discussing the religious references in the Declaration of Independence); Van Patten, *In the End Is the Beginning: An Inquiry into the Meaning of the Religion Clauses*, 27 ST. LOUIS U.L.J. 1, 36–43 (1983) (the Declaration is "vital" to understanding the American tradition of religious liberty).

34. By 1776, the issue was not a principal source of friction between the colonies and the Crown. The colonists had successfully resisted the establishment of an Anglican episcopate and had exercised significant control over their own religious affairs. *See* 1 A. STOKES, *supra* note 33, at 463.

35. The Declaration of Independence, paras. 1, 2, 31 (U.S. 1776).

36. *Id.* para. 2.

37. *See* 1 A. STOKES, *supra* note 33, at 464.

38. Resolution of the Board of Visitors of the University of Virginia (Mar. 4, 1825), in THE COMPLETE JEFFERSON 1112 (S. Padover ed. 1943). Madison concurred with this assessment, also adding Washington's Inaugural Address. *See* Letter from James Madison to Thomas Jefferson (Feb. 8, 1825), in 9 THE WRITINGS OF JAMES MADISON 218, 221 (G. Hunt ed. 1910) [hereinafter WRITINGS OF MADISON].

39. Connecticut and Rhode Island continued under their liberal colonial charters.

40. *See* JAMES MADISON ON RELIGIOUS LIBERTY 51–52 (R. Alley ed. 1985).

41. VA. DECLARATION OF RIGHTS of 1776, art. 16, in 7 THORPE, *supra* note 18, at 3814.

42. PA. CONST. of 1776, Declaration of Rights, art. II, in 5 THORPE, *supra* note 18, at 3082.

43. N.J. CONST. of 1776, art. XVIII, in 5 THORPE, *supra* note 18, at 2597.

44. *See* DEL. DECLARATION OF RIGHTS of 1776, § 2, *reprinted in* SOURCES, *supra* note 8, at 338; DEL. CONST. of 1776, art. 29, in 1 THORPE, *supra* note 18, at 567; DEL. CONST. of 1792, art. I, § 1, in 1 THORPE, *supra* note 18, at 568.

45. N.Y. CONST. of 1777, art. XXXVIII, in 5 THORPE, *supra* note 18, at 2637.

46. *See* N.C. CONST. of 1776, Declaration of Rights, art. XIX, in 5 THORPE, *supra* note 18, at 2788 ("all men have a natural and unalienable right to worship Almighty God according to the dictates of their own consciences"); GA. CONST. of 1777, art. LVI, in 2 THORPE, *supra* note 18, at 784 (guaranteeing the "free exercise" of religion, and prohibiting compulsory support of ministers); *see also* GA. CONST. of 1789, art. IV, § 5, in 2 THORPE, *supra* note 18, at 789 (similar guarantees).

47. MD. CONST. of 1776, Declaration of Rights, art. XXXIII, in 3 THORPE, *supra* note 18, at 1689.

48. *See* S.C. CONST. of 1778, art. XXXVIII, in 6 THORPE, *supra* note 18, at 3255–57; S.C. CONST. of 1790, art. VIII, § 1, in 6 THORPE, *supra* note 18, at 3264 (worded almost identically to the 1777 New York provision, *see supra* note 45 and accompanying text).

49. MASS. CONST. of 1780, pt. I (Declaration of Rights), arts. II & III, in 3 THORPE, *supra* note 18, at 1889–90.

50. *See* N.H. CONST. of 1776, in 4 THORPE, *supra* note 18, at 2451; N.H. CONST. of 1784, pt. I (Bill of Rights), arts. V & VI, in 4 THORPE, *supra* note 18, at 2454.

51. *See* VT. CONST. of 1777, ch. I (Declaration of Rights), art. III, in 6 THORPE, *supra* note 18, at 3740. This provision was included, with minor variations, in the Vermont constitutions of 1786 and 1793.

52. *See generally* 1 A. STOKES, *supra* note 33, at 447–48 (noting these and other actions that revealed the Founders' belief in the importance of religion to the republic).

53. *See* ARTICLES OF CONFEDERATION of 1781, art. XIII, in 1 THORPE, *supra* note 18, at 15.

54. *See id.* arts. II & III, in 1 THORPE, *supra* note 18, at 10.

55. *See* Northwest Ordinance (1787), *reprinted in* SOURCES, *supra* note 8, at 392.

56. *Id.* § 13 (preamble), arts. I & III, at 395–96.

57. For discussions of the movement towards disestablishment in the various states, see T. CURRY, *supra* note 11, at 134–92; 1 A. STOKES, *supra* note 33, at 358–446.

58. Despite their age, two older works remain authoritative. *See* H. ECKENRODE, SEPARATION OF CHURCH AND STATE IN VIRGINIA (1910) and C. JAMES, DOCU- MENTARY HISTORY OF THE STRUGGLE FOR RELIGIOUS LIBERTY IN VIRGINIA (1900). For recent discussions, see R. ISAAC, THE TRANSFORMATION OF VIRGINIA: 1740–1790, at 273–95 (1982) and 1 A. STOKES, *supra* note 33, at 366–97.

59. References to the Virginia struggle abound in the Justices' opinions. *See* Everson v. Board of Educ., 330 U.S. 1, 33–34 (1947) (Rutledge, J., dissenting) (the religion clauses were the "direct culmination" of the "long and intensive struggle for religious freedom" in Virginia); McGowan v. Maryland, 366 U.S. 420, 437 (1961) (the campaign to enact Jefferson's bill is "particularly relevant in the search for the First Amendment's meaning"); *McGowan*, 366 U.S. at 494 (Frankfurter, J., separate opinion) (the Virginia struggle is "a gloss on the signification of the [First] Amendment"); Reynolds v. United States, 98 U.S. 145, 163 (1879) ("the controversy [over public taxation for religion] was animated in many of the States, but seemed at last to culminate in Virginia"). The Court's heavy reliance on the Virginia struggle has prompted sharp criticisms from legal commentators.

60. *See* G. PILCHER, SAMUEL DAVIES: APOSTLE OF DISSENT IN COLONIAL VIRGINIA 94 (1971).

61. A Memorial of the Presbytery of Hanover (Oct. 24, 1776), *reprinted in part in* C. JAMES, *supra* note 58, at 73.

62. For the text of the Assessment Bill, see *Everson*, 330 U.S. app. at 72–74 (Rutledge, J., dissenting).

63. Assessment Bill, *id.* app. at 74 (Rutledge, J., dissenting). While the measure aided only Christian teachers, this limitation would have made little differ- ence, for in 1784 "there were no non-Christian teachers of religion" in Vir- ginia. L. PFEFFER, CHURCH, STATE, AND FREEDOM 110 (rev. ed. 1967).

64. Madison, *Memorial and Remonstrance Against Religious Assessments* (circa June 20, 1785) [hereinafter *Memorial and Remonstrance*], in 8 THE PAPERS OF JAMES MADISON 295 (W. Hutchison & W. Rachal eds. 1973) [hereinafter PAPERS OF MADISON].

65. *Id.* preamble, paras. 1 & 3, at 299–300.

66. *See* Jefferson, A Bill for Establishing Religious Freedom (1785), in 2 THE PAPERS OF THOMAS JEFFERSON 545–47 (J. Boyd ed. 1950) [hereinafter PAPERS OF JEFFERSON]. The bill, first published in 1779, was introduced several times in the Virginia legislature before its enactment in 1786. When the legislature

enacted the 1785 bill, it deleted some of Jefferson's language. *See* An Act for Establishing Religious Freedom, ch. XXXIV (1786), in 12 Hening's Statutes at Large of Virginia 84 (1823).

67. An Act for Establishing Religious Freedom, art. I, *supra* note 66, at 84.

68. *Id.* art. II, at 86.

69. J. Leland, The Rights of Conscience Inalienable 7 (New London 1791).

70. *Id.* at 10–11.

71. *See* T. Curry, *supra* note 11, at 134–58.

72. S.C. Const. of 1790, art. VIII, § 1, in 6 Thorpe, *supra* note 18, at 3264.

73. U.S. Const. art. VI, cl. 3.

74. *See* N.J. Const. of 1776, art. XIX, in 5 Thorpe, *supra* note 18, at 2597–98; Ga. Const. of 1777, art. VI, in 2 Thorpe, *supra* note 18, at 779; S.C. Const. of 1778, arts. XII & XIII, in 6 Thorpe, *supra* note 18, at 3250–52; *see also id.* art. III, in 6 Thorpe, *supra* note 18, at 3249 (requiring the governor, lieutenant-governor, and members of the privy council to be Protestants); N.H. Const. of 1784, pt. II (Form of Government), in 4 Thorpe, *supra* note 18, at 2460–65; Md. Const. of 1776, Declaration of Rights, art. XXXV, in 3 Thorpe, *supra* note 18, at 1690; Mass. Const. of 1780, pt. 2 (Frame of Government), ch. VI, art. I, in 3 Thorpe, *supra* note 18, at 1908 (requiring "[a]ny person chosen governor, lieutenant-governor, councillor, senator, or representative" to profess "the Christian religion").

75. N.C. Const. of 1776, Form of Government, art. XXXII, in 5 Thorpe, *supra* note 18, at 2793.

76. Pa. Const. of 1776, Frame of Government, § 10, in 5 Thorpe, *supra* note 18, at 3085 (emphasis deleted). Vermont legislators had to make a similar declaration, except that "and own and profess the protestant religion" was added at the end. Vt. Const. of 1777, ch. II (Frame of Government), § IX, in 6 Thorpe, *supra* note 18, at 3743.

77. Del. Const. of 1776, art. 22, in 1 Thorpe, *supra* note 18, at 566.

78. 5 The Debates in the Several State Conventions on the Adoption of the Federal Constitution 131 (J. Elliot 2d ed. 1836) [hereinafter Elliot's Debates] (May 29, 1787).

79. Martin, *The Genuine Information delivered to the Maryland Legislature in 1787*, in Secret Proceedings and Debates of the Convention 3, 89–90 (Louisville 1845).

80. Ellsworth, *Landholder, No. 7* (Dec. 17, 1787), *reprinted in* 4 The Founders' Constitution 639, 639–40 (P. Kurland & R. Lerner eds. 1987) [hereinafter Founders' Constitution].

81. 2 Elliot's Debates, *supra* note 78, at 148–49 (Feb. 4, 1788).

82. 3 *Id.* at 330 (June 12, 1788) (remarks of Madison); *id.* at 204 (June 10, 1788) (remarks of Randolph).

83. 4 *Id.* at 193 (July 30, 1788).

84. On the Jews in early America, see Jews and the Founding of the Republic (J. Sarna, B. Kraut & S. Joseph eds. 1985); L. Schwartz, Jews and the American Revolution: Haym Solomon and Others (1987). *See* Petition to the Council of Censors of Pennsylvania (Dec. 23, 1783), *reprinted in* 1 A. Stokes, *supra* note

33, at 287–89; Petition of Jonas Phillips to the President and Members of the Constitutional Convention (Sept. 7, 1787), *reprinted in* 4 FOUNDERS' CONSTITUTION, *supra* note 80, at 638–39.

85. PA. CONST. of 1790, art. IX, § 4, in 5 THORPE, *supra* note 18, at 3100.

86. Torcaso v. Watkins, 367 U.S. 488, 496 (1961).

87. The responses of the ratifying conventions concerning the absence of a religious liberty guarantee are discussed in C. ANTIEAU, A. DOWNEY & E. ROBERTS, FREEDOM FROM FEDERAL ESTABLISHMENT: FORMATION AND EARLY HISTORY OF THE FIRST AMENDMENT RELIGION CLAUSES 111–42 (1964).

88. *See id.* at 114–22.

89. 1 ELLIOT'S DEBATES, *supra* note 78, at 326.

90. For a discussion of Livermore's contribution to religious freedom, see 1 A. STOKES, *supra* note 33, at 314–18.

91. 1 ANNALS OF THE CONGRESS OF THE UNITED STATES 434 (J. Gales ed. 1834) [hereinafter ANNALS] (June 8, 1789).

92. *Id.* at 434, 435 (June 8, 1789).

93. For the House debates on August 15, see *id.* at 729–31.

94. *See id.* at 749–51, 755 (Aug. 17, 1789).

95. *Id.* at 766–67 (Aug. 20, 1789).

96. *See id.* at 779 (Aug. 24, 1789).

97. 1 DOCUMENTARY HISTORY OF THE FIRST FEDERAL CONGRESS OF THE UNITED STATES OF AMERICA 151 (L. De Pauw ed. 1972) [hereinafter DE PAUW'S FIRST CONGRESS] (Senate Journal, Sept. 3, 1789).

98. *Id.* at 166 (Senate Journal, Sept. 9, 1789).

99. 1 ANNALS, *supra* note 91, at 914 (Sept. 25, 1789).

100. The debates are recounted in C. ANTIEAU, A. DOWNEY & E. ROBERTS, *supra* note 87, at 143–58.

101. JOURNAL OF THE SENATE OF VIRGINIA FOR 1789, *quoted in* C. ANTIEAU, A. DOWNEY & E. ROBERTS, *supra* note 87, at 145.

102. A helpful historical overview can be found in Kurland, *The Origins of the Religion Clauses of the Constitution*, 27 WM. & MARY L. REV. 839 (1986).

103. For authorities supporting the nonpreferentialist position, see Wallace v. Jaffree, 472 U.S. 38, 91–114 (1985) (Rehnquist, J., dissenting); R. CORD, SEPARATION OF CHURCH AND STATE: HISTORICAL FACT AND CURRENT FICTION, at ii, 5–15 (1982); M. MALBIN, RELIGION AND POLITICS: THE INTENTIONS OF THE AUTHORS OF THE FIRST AMENDMENT 9 (1978); R. SMITH, PUBLIC PRAYER AND THE CONSTITUTION 73–105 (1987). For criticisms of this position, see L. LEVY, THE ESTABLISHMENT CLAUSE: RELIGION AND THE FIRST AMENDMENT 91–119 (1986) and Laycock, *"Nonpreferential" Aid to Religion: A False Claim About Original Intent*, 27 WM. & MARY L. REV. 875 (1986).

104. For an insightful argument that the Founders did not think of establishment in terms of the nonpreferential framework, see T. CURRY, *supra* note 11, at 207–10.

105. 44 U.S. (3 How.) 589 (1845).

106. *Id.* at 609.

107. For a definitive examination of the disestablishment struggle, see W. McLoughlin, New England Dissent, *supra* note 17.
108. 1 The Autobiography of Lyman Beecher 252–53 (B. Cross ed. 1961) (emphasis deleted).

Chapter Two. The Founders on Religious Liberty

1. *See, e.g.*, Marsh v. Chambers, 463 U.S. 783, 794–95 (1983) (according the Founders' appointment of legislative chaplains great weight in upholding Nebraska's legislative chaplaincy); Walz v. Tax Comm'n, 397 U.S. 664, 677–80 (1970) (sustaining church tax exemption, in part because of historical examples dating to the Founders); Everson v. Board of Educ., 330 U.S. 1, 8–15 (1947) (interpreting the establishment clause by looking to its historical context). On the religious views of the Founders, see C. Antieau, A. Downey & E. Roberts, *supra* ch. 1 note 87, at 123–42, 189–203; N. Cousins, "In God We Trust": The Religious Beliefs and Ideas of the American Founding Fathers (1958).
2. *See* C. Antieau, A. Downey & E. Roberts, *supra* ch. 1 note 87, at vii & n.*. We often refer to the Founding Fathers as the "Founders."
3. For an excellent synopsis of the current schools of thought on church and state, see Esbeck, *Five Views of Church-State Relations in Contemporary American Thought*, 1986 B.Y.U. L. Rev. 371.
4. Certain parallels can be drawn between these historical classifications and the five schools of thought identified by Carl Esbeck. *See id.* Enlightenment separationists would generally correspond to Esbeck's strict separationist position, although Madison probably falls within the pluralistic separationist camp. While some political centrists could be classified as institutional separationists, most would fall within the nonpreferentialist position. There is a close correlation between the pietistic tradition and Esbeck's institutional separationists.
5. *See* H. Commager, Jefferson, Nationalism, and the Enlightenment 64 (1975) (noting that to Jefferson "church authority and religious superstition" posed a serious threat to freedom of the mind); *see also* H. May, The Enlightenment in America, at xiv–xvi (1976).
6. *See* D. Hawke, Paine (1974). For Paine's works, see The Complete Writings of Thomas Paine (P. Foner ed. 1945) (two vols.) [hereinafter Writings of Paine]. The quoted language is from T. Paine, The Age of Reason (Paris 1794), in 1 *id.* at 464, 596.
7. T. Paine, The Rights of Man (pts. 1 & 2) (London 1791, 1792), in 1 Writings of Paine, *supra* note 6, at 292.
8. The definitive biography is the six-volume, multi-titled work, D. Malone, Jefferson and His Time (1948–81). For a good one-volume account, see M. Peterson, Thomas Jefferson and the New Nation (1970). Jefferson's writings are collected in Papers of Jefferson, *supra* ch. 1 note 66, a compilation presently under way which is complete through the early 1790s. References to

later works are to THE WRITINGS OF THOMAS JEFFERSON (H. Washington ed. 1853) [hereinafter WRITINGS OF JEFFERSON].

9. Letter from Thomas Jefferson to Dr. Benjamin Rush (Apr. 21, 1803), in 4 WRITINGS OF JEFFERSON, *supra* note 8, at 482.

10. A brief discussion appears in 6 D. MALONE, THE SAGE OF MONTICELLO, *supra* note 8, at 499 (1981).

11. Jefferson, Reply to the Danbury Baptist Association (Jan. 1, 1802), in 8 WRITINGS OF JEFFERSON, *supra* note 8, at 113.

12. 98 U.S. 145, 164 (1879).

13. 330 U.S. 1 (1947).

14. *Id.* at 18. The Court reaffirmed this view in McCollum v. Board of Educ., 333 U.S. 203, 212 (1948).

15. In Zorach v. Clauson, 343 U.S. 306 (1952), the Court suggested that the "common sense of the matter" was that the wall did not effect separation "in every and all respects." *Id.* at 312. By 1971, when the Court announced the tripartite establishment clause test in Lemon v. Kurtzman, 403 U.S. 602 (1971), "the line of separation, far from being a 'wall,'" had become "a blurred, indistinct, and variable barrier depending on all the circumstances of a particular relationship." *Id.* at 614. More recently, Justice Rehnquist asserted that the wall metaphor is "based on bad history," and "has proved useless as a guide to judging." Wallace v. Jaffree, 472 U.S. 38, 107 (1985) (Rehnquist, J., dissenting).

16. *See* Konvitz, *Separation of Church and State: The First Freedom*, 14 LAW & CONTEMP. PROBS. 44, 46, 57 (1949); *see also* L. PFEFFER, *supra* ch. 1 note 63, at 131–35 (arguing that the *Everson* Court's adoption of the wall metaphor accords with history and sound constitutional doctrine).

17. For criticisms of the wall metaphor, see R. MICHAELSEN, PIETY IN THE PUBLIC SCHOOL 216 (1970) (to the layman the phrase presents an "unfortunate, albeit dramatically effective, metaphor"); Hutchins, *The Future of the Wall*, in THE WALL BETWEEN CHURCH AND STATE 17, 18 (D. Oaks ed. 1963) (words in "a routine acknowledgement of a complimentary address" should not be accorded such weight); Kauper, *Church, State, and Freedom: A Review*, 52 MICH. L. REV. 829, 845 (1954) (the "metaphor is hardly apt as a description" of church-state relations).

18. Letter from Thomas Jefferson to the Rev. Millar (Jan. 23, 1808), in 5 WRITINGS OF JEFFERSON, *supra* note 8, at 236–37.

19. These bills are reprinted in 2 PAPERS OF JEFFERSON, *supra* ch. 1 note 66, at 555–58.

20. *See infra* ch. 4 notes 15–18 and accompanying text. For an analysis of Jefferson's political philosophy and the issue of federalism, see Comment, *Jefferson and the Church-State Wall: A Historical Examination of the Man and the Metaphor*, 1978 B.Y.U. L. REV. 645, 673–74 (regarding the states as free to determine church-state relations, Jefferson developed a standard of "impartial accommodation" in Virginia).

21. For an exhaustive biography, see the six-volume work, I. BRANT, JAMES MADISON (1941–61). A good one-volume biography is R. RUTLAND, JAMES MADISON: THE FOUNDING FATHER (1987). Madison's papers were first collected in

WRITINGS OF MADISON, *supra* ch. 1 note 38. This will be superseded by PAPERS OF MADISON, *supra* ch. 1 note 64, a compilation now complete through the early 1790s.

22. *See* Berman, *Religion and Law: The First Amendment in Historical Perspective*, 35 EMORY L.J. 777, 786 (1986).

23. For works expressing doubt that Madison authored the First Amendment, see C. ANTIEAU, A. DOWNEY & E. ROBERTS, *supra* ch. 1 note 87, at 131; Corwin, *The Supreme Court as National School Board*, 14 LAW & CONTEMP. PROBS. 3, 11–13 (1949); Drakeman, *Religion and the Republic: James Madison and the First Amendment*, in JAMES MADISON ON RELIGIOUS LIBERTY 231, 234 (R. Alley ed. 1985).

24. These veto messages to the House, dated February 21, 1811, and February 28, 1811, respectively, are reprinted in 1 J. RICHARDSON, A COMPILATION OF THE MESSAGES AND PAPERS OF THE PRESIDENTS 1789–1908, at 489–90 (1908).

25. For these proclamations, see 1 J. RICHARDSON, *supra* note 24, at 513 (July 9, 1812); *id.* at 532–33 (July 23, 1813); *id.* at 558 (Nov. 16, 1814); *id.* at 560–61 (Mar. 4, 1815).

26. Letter from James Madison to Edward Livingston (July 10, 1822), in 9 WRITINGS OF MADISON, *supra* ch. 1 note 38, at 103.

27. *See* Fleet, *Madison's "Detatched Memoranda,"* 3 WM. & MARY Q. 534, 558–62 (3d ser. 1946).

28. Letter from James Madison to Frederick Beasley (Nov. 20, 1825), in 9 WRITINGS OF MADISON, *supra* ch. 1 note 38, at 230.

29. Letter from James Madison to Edward Livingston (July 10, 1822), in 9 WRITINGS OF MADISON, *supra* ch. 1 note 38, at 102.

30. Biographies include J. FLEXNER, GEORGE WASHINGTON (1965–72) (four vols.) and J. ALDEN, GEORGE WASHINGTON: A BIOGRAPHY (1984); *see also* P. BOLLER, GEORGE WASHINGTON AND RELIGION (1963). For his papers, see THE WRITINGS OF GEORGE WASHINGTON (J. Fitzpatrick ed. 1931–44) [hereinafter WRITINGS OF WASHINGTON].

31. The first quotation is found in Letter from George Washington to the clergy of Philadelphia (Mar. 3, 1797), in 35 WRITINGS OF WASHINGTON, *supra* note 30, at 416; the second in Letter from George Washington to the General Assembly of Presbyterian Churches (n.d.), in 30 WRITINGS OF WASHINGTON, *supra* note 30, at 336 n.12.

32. *See* N. COUSINS, *supra* note 1, at 50–52 (reprinting orders).

33. Washington, Proclamation: A National Thanksgiving (Oct. 3, 1789), in 1 J. RICHARDSON, *supra* note 24, at 64. Washington issued a second thanksgiving proclamation on January 1, 1795, which is reprinted in *id.* at 179–80.

34. First Inaugural Address by George Washington (Apr. 30, 1789), in 1 J. RICHARDSON, *supra* note 24, at 52.

35. Letter from George Washington to the Hebrew Congregation of Newport (Aug. 17, 1792), in 31 WRITINGS OF WASHINGTON, *supra* note 30, at 93 n.65.

36. Farewell Address by George Washington (Sept. 17, 1796), in 1 J. RICHARDSON, *supra* note 24, at 220.

37. Recent biographies of Adams include R. Brown, The Presidency of John Adams (1975) and P. Smith, John Adams (1962) (two vols.). For his writings, see The Works of John Adams (C. Adams ed. 1850–56 & reprint 1971) [hereinafter Works of J. Adams].

38. Letter from John Adams to a unit of the Massachusetts militia (Oct. 11, 1798), in 9 Works of J. Adams, *supra* note 37, at 229.

39. The first proclamation, quoted in the text, was issued on March 23, 1798. It is reprinted in 1 J. Richardson, *supra* note 24, at 268–70. The second proclamation, issued on March 6, 1799, is reprinted in *id.* at 284–86.

40. For biographies of the Carroll family, see M. Geiger, Daniel Carroll: A Framer of the Constitution (1943); T. Hanley, Charles Carroll of Carrollton: The Making of a Revolutionary Gentleman (1970). On the contributions of Roman Catholicism to America, see J. Ellis, Catholics in Colonial America (1965); J. Hennesey, American Catholics: A History of the Roman Catholic Community in the United States (1981). Important documents are reprinted in Documents of American Catholic History (J. Ellis 4th ed. 1987).

41. A biography, which contains little on Marshall's religious views, is A. Beveridge, The Life of John Marshall (1916–19) (four vols.); *see also* L. Baker, John Marshall: A Life in Law (1974). On Story's views, see J. McClellan, Joseph Story and the American Constitution 21 (1971) (Story believed "Christianity necessary to the support of civil society"); R. Newmyer, Supreme Court Justice Joseph Story: Statesman of the Old Republic 183 (1985) ("the state should promote the religious beliefs of individuals, for, no less than property rights, they were the foundation of republican social order").

42. Letter from John Marshall to Jasper Adams (May 9, 1833) (available in University of Michigan Library). Marshall was responding to a sermon by the Rev. Jasper Adams, who argued that the American people "have retained the Christian religion as the foundation of their civil, legal and political institutions; while they have refused to continue a legal preferenc[e] to any one of its forms over any other." *See* J. Adams, The Relation of Christianity to Civil Government in the United States 12–13 (Charleston 1833) (emphasis deleted).

43. 3 J. Story, Commentaries on the Constitution § 1867, at 724 (Boston 1833).

44. *Id.* § 1871, at 728.

45. *See* W. Brown, The Life of Oliver Ellsworth (1905).

46. Ellsworth, *Landholder, No. 7* (Dec. 17, 1787), *reprinted in* Founders' Constitution, *supra* ch. 1 note 80, at 640.

47. On the importance of the pietistic tradition of separation, see M. Howe, supra ch. 1 note 13, W. McLoughlin, New England Dissent, *supra* ch. 1 note 17, and W. McLoughlin, Isaac Backus and the American Pietistic Tradition (1967) [hereinafter W. McLoughlin, Isaac Backus]. In referring to this tradition, we have adopted the term "pietistic" rather than "evangelical" to avoid confusion with contemporary Protestant Evangelicalism.

48. I. Backus, An Appeal to the Public for Religious Liberty (Boston 1773), in Isaac Backus on Church, State, and Calvinism: Pamphlets, 1754–1789, at 308, 312 (W. McLoughlin ed. 1968) [hereinafter W. McLoughlin, Pamphlets].

49. For biographical information, see W. McLoughlin, Isaac Backus, *supra* note 47; W. McLoughlin, Pamphlets, *supra* note 48.

50. I. Backus, A Fish Caught in His Own Net (Boston 1768), in W. McLoughlin, Pamphlets, *supra* note 48, at 190–91.

51. Backus, A Declaration of the Rights, of the Inhabitants of the State of Massachusetts-Bay, in New-England (1779), in W. McLoughlin, Pamphlets, *supra* note 48, app. 3, at 487.

52. McLoughlin, *Introduction* to W. McLoughlin, Pamphlets, *supra* note 48, at 49–52.

53. His life is recounted in V. Collins, President Witherspoon (1925 & reprint 1969) (two vols.) and M. Stohlman, John Witherspoon: Parson, Politician, Patriot (1976). For his writings, see The Works of the Rev. John Witherspoon (2d ed. Philadelphia 1802) (four vols.) [hereinafter Works of Witherspoon].

54. J. Witherspoon, The Dominion of Providence over the Passions of Men (Philadelphia 1776), in 3 Works of Witherspoon, *supra* note 53, at 37.

55. J. Witherspoon, Lectures on Moral Philosophy 159–61 (J. Scott ann. ed. 1982).

56. Sherman's private papers have been lost, but his support for thanksgiving proclamations and adherence to evangelical religion suggest his affinities to pietistic separation. *See* R. Boardman, Roger Sherman: Signer and States-man 319 (1938) (Sherman's "faith in the new republic was largely because he felt it was founded on Christianity as he understood it"); C. Collier, Roger Sherman's Connecticut: Yankee Politics and the American Revolution 323–29 (1971) (Sherman staunchly supported "New Light" revivalism).

57. 1 A. Stokes, *supra* ch. 1 note 33, at 460–61 (quoting the committee of the Continental Congress consisting of Sherman, John Adams, and George Wythe).

58. 1 The Records of the Federal Convention of 1787, at 452 (M. Farrand rev. ed. 1937) [hereinafter Farrand's Records] (Madison, June 28, 1787).

59. *See* 1 Annals, *supra* ch. 1 note 91, at 707–08 (Aug. 13, 1789).

Chapter Three. The Supreme Court and Religious Liberty

1. U.S. Const. art. III, § 2, cl. 1.
2. U.S. Const. amend XIV, § 1.
3. 302 U.S. 319 (1937).
4. *Id.* at 325.
5. 310 U.S. 296, 303 (1940).
6. 330 U.S. 1 (1947).
7. *Id.* at 8.

8. *See, e.g.*, Snee, *Religious Disestablishment and the Fourteenth Amendment*, 1954 WASH. U.L.Q. 371, 389, 397–407.

9. E. CORWIN, A CONSTITUTION OF POWERS IN A SECULAR STATE 114 (1951) (emphasis deleted).

10. P. FREUND, THE SUPREME COURT OF THE UNITED STATES 58–59 (1961).

11. *Everson*, 330 U.S. at 15–16, 18.

12. *Id.* at 41 (Rutledge, J., dissenting).

13. For an excellent analysis of *Everson*, see Kauper, Everson v. Board of Education: *A Product of the Judicial Will*, 15 ARIZ. L. REV. 307 (1973).

14. *See* Paulsen, *Religion, Equality, and the Constitution: An Equal Protection Approach to Establishment Clause Adjudication*, 61 NOTRE DAME L. REV. 311, 318–22 (1986); *see also* J. O'NEILL, RELIGION AND EDUCATION UNDER THE CONSTITUTION 194–95 (1949) (the importance attached by Justices Black and Rutledge to the Virginia struggle is "invalid"); Kauper, *supra* note 13, at 318–19 ("It would be a mistake . . . to interpret the establishment clause wholly in terms of what Madison and Jefferson thought."); Murray, *Law or Prepossessions?*, 14 LAW & CONTEMP. PROBS. 23, 27 (1949) (history contradicts the view that the religion clauses incorporated the "total personal ideology of James Madison").

15. *See, e.g.*, R. CORD, *supra* ch. 1 note 103, at 121–22 (criticizing the *Everson* Court's use of Madison and Jefferson and its failure to explore the legislative history of the establishment clause). Not until 1985 did a Justice examine the legislative history in any detail. *See* Wallace v. Jaffree, 472 U.S. 38, 94–114 (1985) (Rehnquist, J., dissenting).

16. M. HOWE, *supra* ch. 1 note 13, at 6.

17. *See, e.g.*, Meiklejohn, *Educational Cooperation Between Church and State*, 14 LAW & CONTEMP. PROBS. 61, 70–71 (1949).

18. *See, e.g.*, R. CORD, *supra* ch. 1 note 103, at 15.

19. *See supra* ch. 1 note 103 & ch. 2 note 16.

20. *See* Meese, *Toward a Jurisprudence of Original Intention*, 2 BENCHMARK 1, 5 (1986) and W. Brennan, The Constitution of the United States: Contemporary Ratification, Speech delivered at Georgetown University (Oct. 12, 1985), *reprinted in* A. MASON & D. STEPHENSON, AMERICAN CONSTITUTIONAL LAW 607, 609 (8th ed. 1987). *See also* Rehnquist, *The Notion of a Living Constitution*, 54 TEX. L. REV. 693 (1976) (rejecting the view of a living constitution which accords judges a role in solving society's problems independent of popular will).

21. Marsh v. Chambers, 463 U.S. 783, 816 (1983) (Brennan, J., dissenting).

22. *Id.* at 816 (Brennan, J., dissenting) (quoting Abington School Dist. v. Schempp, 374 U.S. 203, 241 (1963) (Brennan, J., concurring)).

23. Works emphasizing the importance of history in interpreting the religion clauses, include J. MURRAY, WE HOLD THESE TRUTHS: CATHOLIC REFLECTIONS ON THE AMERICAN PROPOSITION (1960); A. REICHLEY, RELIGION IN AMERICAN PUBLIC LIFE (1985); R. SMITH, *supra* ch. 1 note 103, at 1–13; McConnell, *Accommodation of Religion*, 1985 SUP. CT. REV. 1; Van Patten, *supra* ch. 1 note 33.

For works discussing the use of history in law, see B. CARDOZO, THE NATURE OF THE JUDICIAL PROCESS 51-58 (1921); C. MILLER, THE SUPREME COURT AND THE USES OF HISTORY (1969).

24. 374 U.S. 203, 305 (Goldberg, J., concurring). There appears to be a growing consensus among scholars that the core value of the religion clauses is religious liberty. *See, e.g.*, Choper, *The Religion Clauses of the First Amendment: Reconciling the Conflict*, 41 U. PITT. L. REV. 673, 678 (1980) (the "central aim of the Religion Clauses [is] protection of religious liberty"); Katz, *Radiations From Church Tax Exemption*, 1970 SUP. CT. REV. 93, 101 (the establishment clause requires only separation of church and state "compatible with full religious freedom"); McConnell, *supra* note 23, at 1 ("religious liberty is the central value and animating purpose of the Religion Clauses").

25. *See, e.g.*, Pfeffer, *Freedom and/or Separation: The Constitutional Dilemma of the First Amendment*, 64 MINN. L. REV. 561 (1980) (footnote omitted).

26. *Id.* at 564.

27. "Liberty of conscience" and "religious liberty" are used interchangeably in this book. An examination of the historical record from seventeenth-century England, when numerous pamphleteers campaigned for civil and religious freedom, to the early national period in America yields the conclusion that liberty of conscience was commonly, if not exclusively, understood in religious terms. *See generally* 3 W.K. JORDAN, *supra* ch. 1 note 13; TRACTS ON LIBERTY OF CONSCIENCE AND PERSECUTION: 1614–1661 (E. Underhill ed. 1846 & reprint 1966).

28. *See* 1 ANNALS, *supra* ch. 1 note 91, at 434 (June 8, 1789).

29. *Id.* at 730 (August 15, 1789).

30. *Id.* at 730–31.

31. *See id.* at 731 (the House passed Rep. Livermore's proposal prohibiting Congress from "infringing the rights of conscience"); *id.* at 755 (Aug. 17, 1789) (the House adopted Madison's proposal prohibiting the states from infringing "the equal rights of conscience"); *id.* at 766 (Aug. 20, 1789) (the House passed a proposal protecting "rights of conscience," which included establishment and free exercise clauses); *see also* 1 DE PAUW'S FIRST CONGRESS, *supra* ch. 1 note 97, at 151 (Senate Journal, Sept. 3, 1789) (in debating several proposals prohibiting infringement of "the rights of conscience," the Senate struck the conscience clause, probably because it was redundant in view of explicit nonestablishment and free exercise guarantees).

32. JOURNAL OF THE SENATE OF VIRGINIA FOR 1789, *quoted in* C. ANTIEAU, A. DOWNEY & E. ROBERTS, *supra* ch. 1 note 87, at 145.

33. *See supra* ch. 1 notes 39–51 and accompanying text.

34. Northwest Ordinance § 13 (1787), *reprinted in* SOURCES, *supra* ch. 1 note 8, at 395.

35. *See* Declaration of the Causes and Necessity of Taking Up Arms (1775), *reprinted in* SOURCES, *supra* ch. 1 note 8, at 295–96, 300.

36. Essay in the National Gazette (Mar. 27, 1792), in 14 PAPERS OF MADISON, *supra* ch. 1 note 64, at 267.

37. Fleet, *supra* ch. 2 note 27, at 555 (quoting Madison's "Detatched Memoranda," n.d.).

38. Jefferson, A Bill for Establishing Religious Freedom (1785), in 2 PAPERS OF JEFFERSON, *supra* ch. 1 note 66, at 545–46.

39. Jefferson, Reply to the Danbury Baptist Association (Jan. 1, 1802), in 8 WRITINGS OF JEFFERSON, *supra* ch. 2 note 8, at 113.

40. *See* J. COTTON, THE BLOUDY TENENT, WASHED, AND MADE WHITE IN THE BLOUD OF THE LAMBE (London 1647).

41. R. WILLIAMS, THE BLOUDY TENENT, OF PERSECUTION, FOR CAUSE OF CONSCIENCE, *supra* ch. 1 note 14, at 3.

42. R. WILLIAMS, THE BLOODY TENENT YET MORE BLOODY (London 1652), in 4 WRITINGS OF WILLIAMS, *supra* ch. 1 note 14, at 481–82.

43. Plantation Agreement at Providence (1640), in 6 THORPE, *supra* ch. 1 note 18, at 3206.

44. W. PENN, THE GREAT CASE OF LIBERTY OF CONSCIENCE, *supra* ch. 1 note 21, at 447.

45. In Wallace v. Jaffree, 472 U.S. 38 (1985), the Court referred to a First Amendment "concept of individual freedom of mind" or "freedom of conscience" when it invalidated an Alabama moment of silence statute under the establishment clause. *Id.* at 52–53. However, the *Wallace* Court did not clearly delineate the contours of this concept. *See also* Wooley v. Maynard, 430 U.S. 705, 714 (1977) (invoking a First Amendment "right of freedom of thought" in holding that New Hampshire could not require display, over religious objections, of the state motto on license plates); West Va. Bd. of Educ. v. Barnette, 319 U.S. 624, 642 (1943) (invalidating a compulsory flag salute and pledge of allegiance ceremony in public schools because it invaded "the sphere of intellect and spirit" protected by the First Amendment).

46. The Court's failure to articulate principles reconciling the clauses is most evident in cases involving aid to religious schools. Wolman v. Walter, 433 U.S. 229 (1977), which considered an Ohio statute providing such aid, illustrates the Court's inability to reach a consensus. Eight opinions were filed, as the Justices voted over six forms of aid. The Court's inconsistent school-aid precedent has evoked harsh criticisms. *See, e.g.*, Howard, *Up Against the Wall: The Uneasy Separation of Church and State*, in CHURCH, STATE, AND POLITICS 5, 21 (J. Hensel ed. 1981) (reading these decisions is like "stumbl[ing] into the forest of Hansel and Gretel, the birds having eaten all the crumbs that mark the way out"); Kurland, *The Irrelevance of the Constitution: The Religion Clauses of the First Amendment and the Supreme Court*, 24 VILL. L. REV. 3, 18 (1978) (these decisions reveal that even "within this narrow but important area there is again no sign of consistency"); Marty, *Of Darters and Schools and Clergymen: The Religion Clauses Worse Confounded*, 1978 SUP. CT. REV. 171, 190 (the decisions fail to disclose "any [consistent] principle except fear of entanglement—which is not a principle at all"). For an admirable attempt to reconcile the Court's establishment clause precedent on the basis of symbolic endorsement, see Marshall, *"We Know It When We See It": The Supreme Court and Establishment*, 59 S. CAL. L. REV. 495 (1986).

47. 397 U.S. 664, 668–69 (1970).
48. 374 U.S. 398 (1963).
49. *See id.* at 409.
50. *See* Hobbie v. Unemployment Appeals Comm'n, 480 U.S. 136, 144–45 (1987) (dismissing an establishment clause argument on the basis of *Sherbert*); Thomas v. Review Bd., 450 U.S. 707, 719–20 (1981) (payment of benefits to Jehovah's Witnesses does not violate the establishment clause but merely reflects "the tension between the two Religious Clauses which the Court resolved in *Sherbert*").
51. Choper, *The Free Exercise Clause: A Structural Overview and an Appraisal of Recent Developments*, 27 WM. & MARY L. REV. 943, 949–50 (1986).
52. *See* Moore, *The Supreme Court and the Relationship Between the "Establishment" and "Free Exercise" Clauses*, 42 TEX. L. REV. 142, 194–97 (1963); *see also* Choper, *supra* note 24, at 686 (the view that free exercise is dominant fulfills "the historic and contemporary aims of both clauses to further religious liberty"); Giannella, *Religious Liberty, Nonestablishment, and Doctrinal Development: The Religious Liberty Guarantee* (pt. 1), 80 HARV. L. REV. 1381, 1389 (1967) (the free exercise clause should predominate because it is "premised on a vital civil right," rather than on "outmoded eighteenth century political theory").
53. *See* W. MARNELL, THE FIRST AMENDMENT 225–29 (1964).
54. *See, e.g.,* Pfeffer, *The Case for Separation*, in RELIGION IN AMERICA: ORIGINAL ESSAYS ON RELIGION IN A FREE SOCIETY 52, 60 (J. Cogley ed. 1958) (the two clauses are of equal dignity and were intended to promote the "unitary freedom-separation principle").
55. 454 U.S. 263, 269 (1981).
56. *See* Johnson, *Concepts and Compromise in First Amendment Religious Doctrine*, 72 CALIF. L. REV. 817, 820–25 (1984).

Chapter Four. The Animating Principles of the Religion Clauses

1. This discussion of animating principles is not intended to be exhaustive; history may well yield other principles.
2. THE BOOK OF THE GENERAL LAWES AND LIBERTYES CONCERNING THE INHABITANTS OF THE MASSACHUSETS, at A2 (Cambridge, Mass. 1648).
3. J. COTTON, *supra* ch. 3 note 40, at 12.
4. Farewell Address by George Washington (Sept. 17, 1796), in 1 J. RICHARDSON, *supra* ch. 2 note 24, at 220; *see also* A. REICHLEY, *supra* ch. 3 note 23, at 340 ("Almost all of the principal founders of the United States, including Thomas Jefferson, were convinced that the health of republican government depends on moral values derived from religion.").
5. THE FEDERALIST NO. 47, at 336 (J. Madison) (B. Wright ed. 1961).
6. U.S. CONST. amend. X. As Professor Tribe states, the Constitution called for the division of governmental authority along two lines: "vertically (along the axis of federal, state and local authority) and horizontally (along the axis of

legislative, executive, and judicial authority)." L. TRIBE, AMERICAN CONSTITU-
TIONAL LAW § 1–2, at 2 (1978).

7. Daniel Carroll supported a religious freedom amendment on this ground in
   the House debates held on August 15, 1789. *See supra* ch. 1 note 93 and
   accompanying text.

8. In the House debates over Madison's proposed amendment prohibiting the
   states from infringing the "equal rights of conscience," Rep. Thomas Tucker
   of South Carolina opposed the measure because he thought it best "to leave
   the State Governments to themselves, and not to interfere with them more
   than we already do." 1 ANNALS, *supra* ch. 1 note 91, at 755 (Aug. 17, 1789).

9. This may explain Madison's proposed amendment that "[n]o State shall
   violate the equal rights of conscience, or the freedom of the press, or the trial
   by jury in criminal cases." 1 ANNALS, *supra* ch. 1 note 91, at 435 (June 8, 1789).
   He later described this as "the most valuable" of the amendments. *Id.* at 755
   (Aug. 17, 1789).

10. 1 ANNALS, *supra* ch. 1 note 91, at 434–35 (June 8, 1789).

11. DE PAUW'S FIRST CONGRESS, *supra* ch. 1 note 97, at 166 (Sept. 9, 1789).

12. Gaustad, *A Disestablished Society: Origins of the First Amendment*, 11 J. CHURCH
    & ST. 409, 414 (1969). This helpful article advances four sources that con-
    tributed to the movement for disestablishment in the late colonial and early
    republican periods: "the principles of radical religion; the pragmatism of
    conservative religion; the position of natural religion; and the indifference to
    and hostility toward religion." *Id.* at 409.

13. *See* Hamilton, *Remarks on the "Quebec Bill"* (1775), *reprinted in part in* 1 A.
    STOKES, *supra* ch. 1 note 33, at 510–11. Hamilton noted that with an established
    religion "[c]ertain precise dues, (tithes &c.,) are legally annexed to the clerical
    office, independent of the liberal contributions of the people." *Id.* at 510.

14. Declaration and Resolves of the First Continental Congress (Oct. 14, 1774),
    reprinted in SOURCES, *supra* ch. 1 note 8, at 289.

15. Letter from Thomas Jefferson to the Rev. Millar (Jan. 23, 1808), in 5 WRITINGS
    OF JEFFERSON, *supra* ch. 2 note 8, at 237.

16. THE FEDERALIST NO. 28, at 225 (A. Hamilton) (B. Wright ed. 1961).

17. When Madison introduced his series of proposed amendments on June 8,
    1789, he conceded that this was "one of the most plausible arguments" against
    a federal bill of rights. 1 ANNALS, *supra* ch. 1 note 91, at 439 (June 8, 1789). *See
    also id.* at 442 (remarks of Rep. Jackson); *id.* at 730 (Aug. 15, 1789) (Rep.
    Sherman asserted that a religious freedom guarantee was "altogether unnec-
    essary, inasmuch as Congress had no authority whatever delegated to them by
    the Constitution to make religious establishments").

18. This outlook is illustrated by the Constitutional Convention's handling of
    Jonas Phillips's petition objecting to Pennsylvania's 1776 test oath for legis-
    lators. The petition received committee reference, but ultimately the issue was
    resolved at the state level. *See supra* ch. 1 notes 84–85 and accompanying text.

19. In his analysis of the House debates held on August 15, 1789, Thomas Curry
    argues that Benjamin Huntington's remarks reveal a fear that "the [proposed
    religious freedom] amendment might give Congress power to interfere with

existing arrangements in the individual states." T. CURRY, *supra* ch. 1 note 11, at 203.

20. U.S. CONST. art. I, § 8, cl. 18; *see also* 1 ANNALS, *supra* ch. 1 note 91, at 438 (June 8, 1789) (reporting Madison's concern over the broad scope of the general government's discretionary powers).

21. This was the wording proposed by Madison. *See* 1 ANNALS, *supra* ch. 1 note 91, at 434 (June 8, 1789).

22. Madison noted that there were "two methods of removing the causes of faction: the one, by destroying the liberty which is essential to its existence; the other, by giving to every citizen the same opinions, the same passions, and the same interests." THE FEDERALIST No. 10, at 130 (J. Madison) (B. Wright ed. 1961). He rejected the first as "worse than the disease" and the second as "impracticable." *Id.*

23. *Id.* at 136.

24. THE FEDERALIST No. 51, at 358 (J. Madison) (B. Wright ed. 1961).

25. 374 U.S. 203, 310 (1963) (Stewart, J., dissenting).

26. For discussions of the incorporation debate, see R. CORD, *supra* ch. 1 note 103, at 84–101; L. LEVY, *supra* ch. 1 note 103, at 165–85; R. SMITH, *supra* ch. 1 note 103, at 133–70.

27. In Jaffree v. Board of School Comm'rs, 554 F. Supp. 1104, 1124 (S.D. Ala. 1983), Chief Judge Hand refused to enjoin teacher-initiated prayer activity in Alabama's public schools because he concluded that the historical record showed that the Fourteenth Amendment did not incorporate the establishment clause. He was promptly reversed in Jaffree v. Wallace, 705 F.2d 1526, 1532 (11th Cir. 1984), *aff'd*, 472 U.S. 38 (1985).

28. Kauper, *supra* ch. 3 note 13, at 316. Professor Kauper asks what fundamental liberty interest is embodied in the establishment clause: "Is it simply a right to be free from establishment, or is it a right not to be deprived of life, liberty or property by a law respecting establishment of religion?" *Id.*

29. *Schempp*, 374 U.S. at 256 (Brennan, J., concurring). This concurring opinion contains the most extensive defense by a Justice of the incorporation of the establishment clause.

30. For a discussion of the threat to religious liberty posed by church labor relations, see Laycock, *Towards a General Theory of the Religion Clauses: The Case of Church Labor Relations and the Right to Church Autonomy*, 81 COLUM. L. REV. 1373, 1382–84 (1981); *cf.* Adams & Hanlon, Jones v. Wolf: *Church Autonomy and the Religion Clauses of the First Amendment*, 128 U. PA. L. REV. 1291 (1980).

31. Excellent overviews of the federal tax provisions affecting religious organizations are contained in Schwarz, *Limiting Religious Tax Exemptions: When Should the Church Render Unto Caesar?*, 29 U. FLA. L. REV. 50 (1976) and Slye, *Rendering Unto Caesar: Defining "Religion" for Purposes of Administering Religion-Based Tax Exemptions*, 6 HARV. J.L. & PUB. POL'Y 219 (1983).

32. *See* Slye, *supra* note 31, at 242–78 (discussing the federal tax exemption for religious organizations and the substantive tests used by the Internal Revenue Service to determine eligibility).

33. J.S. MILL, ON LIBERTY 98 (London 1859) (D. Spitz ed. 1975).
34. *See* Schauer, *May Officials Think Religiously?*, 27 WM. & MARY L. REV. 1075, 1076 (1986).
35. L. HAND, THE BILL OF RIGHTS 73 (1958).
36. 473 U.S. 402, 404–06 & n.1, 409, 414 (1985). Leading scholars have denounced the excessive entanglement test as a vague tool designed to justify subjective decision making, as an unwelcome return to the rigidity of strict separation, as the death knell for using neutral principles to interpret the establishment clause, and as a potential threat to historic free exercise values. *See* Kauper, *Public Aid for Parochial Schools and Church Colleges: The Lemon, DiCenso and Tilton Cases*, 13 ARIZ. L. REV. 567, 584–87 (1971) and Ripple, *The Entanglement Test of the Religion Clauses—A Ten Year Assessment*, 27 UCLA L. REV. 1195, 1201, 1217, 1230 (1980).
37. P. BERGER & R. NEUHAUS, TO EMPOWER PEOPLE: THE ROLE OF MEDIATING STRUCTURES IN PUBLIC POLICY 2 (1977) (emphasis deleted). The authors stress that "[mediating] institutions have a private face, giving private life a measure of stability, and they have a public face, transferring meaning and value to the megastructures." *Id.* at 3. *See also* CHURCH, STATE, AND PUBLIC POLICY: THE NEW SHAPE OF THE CHURCH-STATE DEBATE (J. Mechling ed. 1978).
38. R. FROST, *Mending Wall* (1914), in THE POETRY OF ROBERT FROST 33, 34 (E. Lathem ed. 1969).
39. *See* 1 ANNALS, *supra* ch. 1 note 91, at 914 (Sept. 25, 1789); R. CORD, *supra* ch. 1 note 103, at 53–55.
40. *See* R. CORD, *supra* ch. 1 note 103, at 57–61.
41. As Professor Berman states, the Framers "almost certainly would have agreed . . . that law, the Constitution itself, could not survive the disappearance of religious faith in this country." H. BERMAN, THE INTERACTION OF LAW AND RELIGION 140 (1974). *See also* C. ANTIEAU, A. DOWNEY & E. ROBERTS, *supra* ch. 1 note 87, at 159–88 (discussing practices in the late eighteenth century, including grants of public land and funds to religious institutions, tax exemptions for churches and religious schools, legal incorporation of churches, legislative and military chaplains, days of thanksgiving, and blasphemy and Sunday closing laws).
42. 343 U.S. 306, 313 (1952). The Supreme Court has repeatedly quoted this statement and lower courts have often employed it in addressing religious liberty issues. Indeed, the maxim has acquired a prominence overshadowed only by the wall of separation metaphor. The Court's continued use of both the maxim and the wall metaphor compounds the tension in its religion decisions. The statement probably embodies the notions that religion, particularly the Judeo-Christian tradition, has played an important role in shaping American institutions and that these institutions depend for vitality on belief in a Supreme Being. *See* C. RICE, THE SUPREME COURT AND PUBLIC PRAYER: THE NEED FOR RESTRAINT 53–68 (1964) (the practices of American institutions and government indicate that "the existence and supremacy of God have been repeatedly recognized"); *see also* Engel v. Vitale, 370 U.S. 421, 446 (1962) (Stewart, J., dissenting) (discussing "the history of the religious

traditions of our people, reflected in countless practices of the institutions and officials of our government").

43. Freund, *Public Aid to Parochial Schools*, 82 HARV. L. REV. 1680, 1686 (1969). The Court cited this article in Lemon v. Kurtzman, 403 U.S. 602 (1971), when it announced, without citing any historical evidence, that "political division along religious lines was one of the principal evils against which the First Amendment was intended to protect." *Id.* at 622. This political divisiveness concept, a corollary of the excessive entanglement test, has been criticized on constitutional and historical grounds. *See, e.g.*, Gaffney, *Political Divisiveness Along Religious Lines: The Entanglement of the Court in Sloppy History and Bad Public Policy*, 24 ST. LOUIS U.L.J. 205, 236 (1980); Choper, *supra* ch. 3 note 24, at 683–84. In 1983, the Court largely interred the concept by restricting its use to cases involving direct financial aid to parochial schools. Mueller v. Allen, 463 U.S. 388, 403–04 & n.11 (1983).

44. *See* Bernardin, Marty & Adams, *The Role of the Religious Leader in the Development of Public Policy*, 34 DE PAUL L. REV. 1 (1984). Even Jefferson eventually agreed with Madison that the establishment clause did not foreclose ministers from becoming legislators. For a discussion of their views and early state constitutional provisions prohibiting clergy from holding public office, see McDaniel v. Paty, 435 U.S. 618, 622–25 (1978), which invalidated a Tennessee law implementing a state constitutional provision barring ministers from serving as legislators.

45. 397 U.S. 664, 670 (1970).

46. *See* Derr, *The First Amendment as a Guide to Church-State Relations: Theological Illusions, Cultural Fantasies, and Legal Practicalities*, in CHURCH, STATE, AND POLITICS 75 (J. Hensel ed. 1981).

47. E. BETHGE, COSTLY GRACE 185 (1979) (quoting a testimonial given by Reinhold Niebuhr in June 1945).

48. *See* A. REICHLEY, *supra* ch. 3 note 23, at 350–59 (while churches should speak to the moral issues of the day, they must be careful not to become merely political); *Findings and Recommendations*, in CHURCH, STATE, AND POLITICS, *supra* note 46, at 131–32 (setting forth propositions on "Church in Politics" considered by the conferees of the 1981 Chief Justice Earl Warren Conference).

49. An Act to restore to the Crown the ancient Jurisdiction over the Estate Ecclesiastical and Spiritual, and abolishing all foreign Powers repugnant to the same, 1 Eliz., ch. 1, §§ 1, 18 (1558).

50. *See id.* § 19; An Act for the Uniformity of Common Prayer and Service in the Church, and Administration of the Sacraments, 1 Eliz., ch. 2 (1558). Perhaps the Senate had the English establishment in mind when it adopted a proposal on September 9, 1789, prohibiting Congress from making any "law establishing articles of faith or a mode of worship." *See* 1 DE PAUW'S FIRST CONGRESS, *supra* ch. 1 note 97, at 166 (Senate Journal, Sept. 9, 1789).

51. THE CAMBRIDGE PLATFORM (Cambridge, Mass. 1648), in W. WALKER, THE CREEDS AND PLATFORMS OF CONGREGATIONALISM 194, 235 (1960).

52. *Id.* at 237.

53. R. WILLIAMS, THE BLOODY TENENT YET MORE BLOODY (London 1652), in 4 WRITINGS OF WILLIAMS, *supra* ch. 1 note 14, at 389.

54. *Id.* at 390–91. This passage appears to be the clearest definition of establishment in Williams's writings.

55. Act Concerning Religion (1649), in 1 MARYLAND ARCHIVES, *supra* ch. 1 note 12, at 246.

56. *See supra* ch. 1 notes 13–26 and accompanying text. Referring to the New England Way in church and state, for example, Clarke declared in 1652: "But this outward forcing of men in matters of conscience towards God to believe as others believe, and to practice and worship as others do, cannot stand with the peace, liberty, prosperity, and safety of a place, commonwealth, or nation." J. CLARKE, *supra* ch. 1 note 17, at 72.

57. *See supra* ch. 1 notes 24–26 and accompanying text.

58. *See supra* ch. 1 notes 39–51 and accompanying text.

59. *See, e.g.,* A Memorial of the Presbytery of Hanover (Oct. 24, 1776), *reprinted in part in* C. JAMES, *supra* ch. 1 note 58, at 73 (petitioning the Virginia legislature to exempt members of religious sects "from all taxes for the support of any church whatever, farther than what may be agreeable to their own private choice, or voluntary obligation"); Memorial from the Warren Baptist Association to the Massachusetts Assembly (Sept. 1775), *quoted in* 2 I. BACKUS, A HISTORY OF NEW ENGLAND WITH PARTICULAR REFERENCE TO THE BAPTISTS 203–04 (2d ed. 1871 & reprint 1969) (asserting that "an entire freedom from being taxed by civil rulers to religious worship, is not a mere favor, from any man or men in the world, but a right and property granted us by God").

60. *See supra* ch. 1 notes 64–68 and accompanying text; *see also* McConnell, *Coercion: The Lost Element of Establishment*, 27 WM. & MARY L. REV. 933, 938 (1986) (using the *Memorial and Remonstrance* to support the proposition that "legal compulsion to support or participate in religious activities would seem to be the essence of an establishment").

61. *See* 1 ANNALS, *supra* ch. 1 note 91, at 730–31 (Aug. 15, 1789).

62. Choper, *supra* ch. 3 note 51, at 948. For an article exploring the use of a similar test in public education, see Choper, *Religion in the Public Schools: A Proposed Constitutional Standard*, 47 MINN. L. REV. 329 (1963). *See also* McConnell, *supra* note 60, at 940 (a test based on coercion "would lead to a proscription of all government action that has the purpose and effect of coercing or altering religious belief or action"); Paulsen, *supra* ch. 3 note 14, at 336 (proposing an analysis that would ask "whether government policy has coercive or discriminatory effects on an individual's religious exercise"); Schwarz, *No Imposition of Religion: The Establishment Clause Value*, 77 YALE L.J. 692, 693 (1968) (the clause "should be read to prohibit only aid which has as its motive or substantial effect the imposition of religious belief or practice").

63. *See* Engel v. Vitale, 370 U.S. 421, 430 (1962) ("[t]he Establishment Clause, unlike the Free Exercise Clause, does not depend upon any showing of direct governmental compulsion"); Lemon v. Kurtzman, 403 U.S. 602, 612–13 (1971).

64. Miller, *Roger Williams: An Essay in Interpretation*, in 7 WRITINGS OF WILLIAMS, *supra* ch. 1 note 14, at 6.

65. I. BACKUS, AN APPEAL TO THE PUBLIC FOR RELIGIOUS LIBERTY, *supra* ch. 2 note 48, at 334.

66. As Backus stated: "We view it to be our incumbent duty to render unto Caesar the things that are his but also that it is of as much importance not to render unto him anything that belongs only to God, who is to be obeyed rather than any man." *Id.* at 317.

67. *Romans* 13:1 (King James).

68. PA. FRAME OF GOVERNMENT of 1682, preface, in 5 THORPE, *supra* ch. 1 note 18, at 3053.

69. *See* Letter from Roger Williams to the Town of Providence (Jan. 1655), in 6 WRITINGS OF WILLIAMS, *supra* ch. 1 note 14, at 278–79.

70. E. MORGAN, *supra* ch. 1 note 13, at 134.

71. *See Exodus* 20:3–11. For an insightful discussion of Williams's views concerning the role of government, see E. MORGAN, *supra* ch. 1 note 13, at 115–42.

72. R. WILLIAMS, THE HIRELING MINISTRY NONE OF CHRISTS (London 1652), in 7 WRITINGS OF WILLIAMS, *supra* ch. 1 note 14, at 178.

73. The concept is discussed in Adams & Gordon, *The Doctrine of Accommodation in the Jurisprudence of the Religion Clauses*, 37 DE PAUL L. REV. 317 (1988) and McConnell, *supra* ch. 3 note 23.

74. For sources collecting and discussing cases in both categories, see A. JOHNSON & F. YOST, SEPARATION OF CHURCH AND STATE IN THE UNITED STATES (1948); D. MANWARING, RENDER UNTO CAESAR: THE FLAG-SALUTE CONTROVERSY 38–52 (1962); W. TORPEY, JUDICIAL DOCTRINES OF RELIGIOUS RIGHTS IN AMERICA (1948); Giannella, *supra* ch. 3 note 52; Pfeffer, *The Supremacy of Free Exercise*, 61 GEO. L.J. 1115 (1973).

75. For cases involving religious exemptions from laws prohibiting conduct, see Cantwell v. Connecticut, 310 U.S. 296, 307–11 (1940) (reversing breach of peace conviction of a Jehovah's Witness on free exercise and free speech grounds); Braunfeld v. Brown, 366 U.S. 599 (1961) (sustaining application of Sunday closing laws to Orthodox Jewish merchants); City of St. Louis v. Hellscher, 295 Mo. 293, 242 S.W. 652 (1922) (upholding a law against commercial fortune telling despite claim that it constituted a religious ritual); State *ex rel.* Swann v. Pack, 527 S.W.2d 99 (Tenn. 1975) (enjoining members of the Holiness Church from handling poisonous snakes), *cert. denied*, 424 U.S. 954 (1976); United States v. Ballard, 322 U.S. 78 (1944) (reversing convictions of "I Am" adherents for mail fraud); State v. Verbon, 167 Wash. 140, 8 P.2d 1083 (1932) (sustaining application of medical standards and licensing to faith healers); People v. Woody, 61 Cal. 2d 716, 394 P.2d 813, 40 Cal. Rptr. 69 (1964) (reversing drug convictions of American Indians for using peyote in a religious ceremony).

76. For cases involving religious exemptions from civic duties, see *In re* Jenison, 276 Minn. 136, 125 N.W.2d 588 (1963) (*per curiam*) (reversing contempt conviction of a person refusing on religious grounds to serve as a juror); United States v. Seeger, 380 U.S. 163 (1965) (person opposed to war because of

religiously based moral principles entitled to conscientious objector status);
Kolbeck v. Kramer, 46 N.J. 46, 214 A.2d 408 (1965) (*per curiam*) (indicating
legality of requiring vaccinations for college students without granting any
religious exemptions); Hamilton v. Regents of University of California, 293
U.S. 245 (1934) (Fourteenth Amendment does not require exemption of
religious pacifists from a college course in military science); West Va. Bd. of
Educ. v. Barnette, 319 U.S. 624 (1943) (compulsory flag salute and pledge of
allegiance in public schools violates First Amendment); Girouard v. United
States, 328 U.S. 61 (1946) (Seventh-Day Adventist opposed to bearing arms
entitled to citizenship); United States v. Lee, 455 U.S. 252 (1982) (requiring
Amish farmer who employs workers to pay social security taxes does not
violate the free exercise clause); Jehovah's Witnesses in Wash. v. King County
Hosp., 278 F. Supp. 488 (W.D. Wash. 1967) (three-judge court) (sustaining
a law authorizing children of Jehovah's Witnesses to be made wards of the
state to receive medical care), *aff'd*, 390 U.S. 598, *reh'g denied*, 391 U.S. 961
(1968).

77. D. MANWARING, *supra* note 74, at 51 (emphasis deleted).

78. 98 U.S. 145, 166 (1879).

79. 406 U.S. 205 (1972); *see also* Sherbert v. Verner, 374 U.S. 398 (1963) (the free
exercise clause compelled South Carolina to grant unemployment benefits to
a Seventh-Day Adventist who could not find employment because she refused
to work on her Sabbath).

80. 343 U.S. 306 (1952).

81. *See* Walz v. Tax Comm'n, 397 U.S. 664 (1970). One school of thought argues
that the free exercise clause compels tax exemption for religious property, but
the Court refused to adopt this rationale in *Walz*. For a defense of the
religious tax exemption on social policy grounds, see D. KELLEY, WHY
CHURCHES SHOULD NOT PAY TAXES (1977).

82. In the Selective Draft Law Cases, 245 U.S. 366 (1918), the Court dismissed the
contention that the religious exemptions of the 1917 draft law violated the
religion clauses. *Id.* at 389–90. In Gillette v. United States, 401 U.S. 437 (1971),
the Court sustained the Military Selective Service Act of 1967 against the claim
that the act's failure to exempt those objecting to particular wars, along with
objectors to all war, violated the religion clauses. *Id.* at 448–60. The Court's
decisions construing the exemption also strongly suggest its constitutionality.
See United States v. Seeger, 380 U.S. 163, 165–66 (1965) (avoiding the constitutional issue by broadly interpreting the exemption's requirement of a belief
in a Supreme Being); *see also* Welsh v. United States, 398 U.S. 333, 335 (1970)
(avoiding the constitutional issue on the basis of *Seeger*).

83. 472 U.S. 703, 710–11 (1985). In a concurring opinion joined by Justice Marshall, Justice O'Connor distinguished the Connecticut statute from provisions in Title VII of the Civil Rights Act of 1964 which require private
employers reasonably to accommodate the religious practices of employees.
She reasoned that the Title VII provisions were neither compelled by the free
exercise clause nor forbidden by the establishment clause. *Thornton*, 472 U.S.
at 712 (O'Connor, J., concurring).

In Corporation of Presiding Bishop v. Amos, 483 U.S. 327 (1987), the Court held that exempting the secular activities of religious organizations from Title VII's prohibition against religious discrimination in employment did not violate the establishment clause. *Amos* suggests that the Court is attempting to reconcile the tension between its establishment clause jurisprudence and the accommodation principle by broadening the "permissible zone" between the clauses.

84. Act Concerning Religion (1649), in 1 MARYLAND ARCHIVES, *supra* ch. 1 note 12, at 245.

85. *See* Stansbury v. Marks, 2 U.S. (2 Dall.) 213 (1793). This presumably was the same citizen who petitioned Congress about the religious test oath in the Pennsylvania Constitution of 1776. *See supra* ch. 1 note 84 and accompanying text.

86. U.S. CONST. art. VI, cl. 3 (emphasis added). Before assuming office the President-elect must take an "Oath or Affirmation" requiring him or her to "solemnly swear (or affirm)" to faithfully execute the office and to defend the Constitution. U.S. CONST. art. II, § 1, cl. 8. The wording of the presidential oath undoubtedly derived from the same religious considerations that motivated the wording of article VI.

87. *See* 4 FARRAND'S RECORDS, *supra* ch. 2 note 58, at 123 (listing references in legislative history to art. VI, cl. 3).

88. 2 FARRAND'S RECORDS, *supra* ch. 2 note 58, at 461 (Journal, Aug. 30); *id.* at 468 (Madison, Aug. 30).

89. 3 J. STORY, *supra* ch. 2 note 43, § 1838, at 703.

90. MD. CONST. of 1776, Declaration of Rights, art. XXXVI, in 3 THORPE, *supra* ch. 1 note 18, at 1690.

91. DEL. CONST. of 1776, art. 22, in 1 THORPE, *supra* ch. 1 note 18, at 566.

92. *See* PA. CONST. of 1776, Frame of Government, §§ 10 & 40, in 5 THORPE, *supra* ch. 1 note 18, at 3085, 3090 (requiring legislators and public officials to take an oath or affirmation of office); N.H. CONST. of 1784, Form of Government, "Oaths and Subscriptions," in 4 THORPE, *supra* ch. 1 note 18, at 2468 (loyalty oath for civil officers permitted Quakers and others "scrupulous of swearing," merely to make an affirmation). Vermont did not become a state until 1791, but it enacted a constitution in 1777 which contained loyalty provisions almost identical to those of Pennsylvania. *See* VT. CONST. of 1777, ch. II, §§ IX, XXXVI, in 6 THORPE, *supra* ch. 1 note 18, at 3743, 3747.

93. N.J. CONST. of 1776, art. XXIII, in 5 THORPE, *supra* ch. 1 note 18, at 2598.

94. N.Y. CONST. of 1777, art. VIII, in 5 THORPE, *supra* ch. 1 note 18, at 2631.

95. GA. CONST. of 1777, art. XIV, in 2 THORPE, *supra* ch. 1 note 18, at 780; S.C. CONST. of 1778, art. XIII, in 6 THORPE, *supra* ch. 1 note 18, at 3252.

96. S.C. CONST. of 1778, art. XXXVIII, in 6 THORPE, *supra* ch. 1 note 18, at 3256.

97. 2 JOURNALS OF THE CONTINENTAL CONGRESS 189 (W. Ford ed. 1905).

98. 1 ANNALS, *supra* ch. 1 note 91, at 434 (June 8, 1789).

99. PA. CONST. of 1776, Declaration of Rights, art. VIII, in 5 THORPE, *supra* ch. 1 note 18, at 3083. For the Delaware, New Hampshire, and Vermont provisions, see DEL. DECLARATION OF RIGHTS of 1776, § 10, *reprinted in* SOURCES, *supra* ch.

1 note 8, at 339; N.H. CONST. of 1784, pt. I (Bill of Rights), art. XIII, in 4 THORPE, *supra* ch. 1 note 18, at 2455; VT. CONST. of 1777, ch. I (Declaration of Rights), art. IX, in 6 THORPE, *supra* ch. 1 note 18, at 3741.

100. N.Y. CONST. of 1777, art. XL, in 5 THORPE, *supra* ch. 1 note 18, at 2637.

101. For this interchange on the conscientious objector provision, see 1 ANNALS, *supra* ch. 1 note 91, at 749–51 (Aug. 17, 1789).

102. *Id.* at 766–67 (Aug. 20, 1789).

103. *Id.* at 751.

104. For an article exploring the Court's reasons for affording religion a unique status, see Smith, *The Special Place of Religion in the Constitution*, 1983 SUP. CT. REV. 83.

105. This discussion shows that the principle of accommodation receives substantial support from history. For articles exploring the principle at length, see Adams & Gordon, *supra* note 73, and McConnell, *supra* ch. 3 note 23.

106. Board of Educ. v. Allen, 392 U.S. 236, 249 (1968) (Harlan, J., concurring).

107. *See supra* ch. 1 notes 33–36 and accompanying text. Although minorities, immigrants, women, and other segments of our society have struggled to attain equal treatment, their success in appealing to and achieving equality derives, in the first instance, from the nation's normative commitment to the ideal of equality.

108. For extended discussions of the ideal of equality as a value animating the religion clauses, see Garvey, *Freedom and Equality in the Religion Clauses*, 1981 SUP. CT. REV. 193; Paulsen, *supra* ch. 3 note 14, at 326–71; *see also* Karst, *Equality as a Central Principle in the First Amendment*, 43 U. CHI. L. REV. 20 (1975) (arguing that equal liberty of expression is the basic principle underlying the First Amendment).

109. Giannella, *Religious Liberty, Nonestablishment, and Doctrinal Development: The Nonestablishment Principle* (pt. 2), 81 HARV. L. REV. 513, 517 (1968) (footnote omitted).

110. Abington School Dist. v. Schempp, 374 U.S. 203, 222 (1963). The Court's tripartite establishment clause test, often referred to as the *Lemon* test, is discussed briefly in *supra* text accompanying note 63.

111. *Schempp*, 374 U.S. at 225. According to Justice Goldberg, neutrality requires that "government neither engage in nor compel religious practices, that it effect no favoritism among sects or between religion and nonreligion, and that it work deterrence of no religious belief." *Id.* at 305 (Goldberg, J., concurring).

112. Epperson v. Arkansas, 393 U.S. 97, 103–04 (1968) (footnote omitted).

113. 397 U.S. 664, 669 (1970).

114. The thesis that the founding generation understood nonestablishment primarily, if not exclusively, as a prohibition against the granting of a preference to any one religious denomination is advanced in C. ANTIEAU, A. DOWNEY & E. ROBERTS, *supra* ch. 1 note 87, at 204–09.

115. 1 ANNALS, *supra* ch. 1 note 91, at 731 (Aug. 15, 1789).

116. 1 ELLIOT'S DEBATES, *supra* ch. 1 note 78, at 328 (July 26, 1788).

117. *See id.* at 334 (May 29, 1790).

118. Del. Const. of 1776, art. 29, in 1 Thorpe, *supra* ch. 1 note 18, at 567.

119. *See* Ga. Const. of 1798, art. IV, § 10, in 2 Thorpe, *supra* ch. 1 note 18, at 801; N.J. Const. of 1776, art. XIX, in 5 Thorpe, *supra* ch. 1 note 18, at 2597; N.C. Const. of 1776, Form of Government, art. XXXIV, in 5 Thorpe, *supra* ch. 1 note 18, at 2793; Pa. Const. of 1790, art. IX, § 3, in 5 Thorpe, *supra* ch. 1 note 18, at 3100. *See also* Ky. Const. of 1792, art. XII, § 3, in 3 Thorpe, *supra* ch. 1 note 18, at 1274 (including a bill of rights drafted by Jefferson containing a no-preference provision virtually identical to that in the Pennsylvania Constitution of 1790).

120. N.Y. Const. of 1777, art. XXXVIII, in 5 Thorpe, *supra* ch. 1 note 18, at 2637; S.C. Const. of 1790, art. VIII, § 1, in 6 Thorpe, *supra* ch. 1 note 18, at 3264.

121. Mass. Const. of 1780, pt. I (Declaration of Rights), art. III, in 3 Thorpe, *supra* ch. 1 note 18, at 1890; N.H. Const. of 1784, pt. I (Bill of Rights), art. VI, in 4 Thorpe, *supra* ch. 1 note 18, at 2454 (adding a comma after the word "another").

122. Conn. Const. of 1818, art. 1 (Declaration of Rights), § 4, in 1 Thorpe, *supra* ch. 1 note 18, at 537.

123. Madison, *Memorial and Remonstrance, supra* ch. 1 note 64, paras. 4 & 8, at 300, 302.

124. I. Backus, An Appeal to the Public for Religious Liberty, *supra* ch. 2 note 48, at 333, 335.

125. Larson v. Valente, 456 U.S. 228, 244 (1982); *see also* Gillette v. United States, 401 U.S. 437, 449 (1971) ("An attack founded on disparate treatment of 'religious' claims invokes what is perhaps the central purpose of the Establishment Clause—the purpose of ensuring governmental neutrality in matters of religion.").

126. *See, e.g., Gillette*, 401 U.S. at 450 ("the Establishment Clause prohibits government from abandoning secular purposes in order to put an imprimatur on one religion, or on religion as such, or to favor the adherents of any sect or religious organization"); *see also* Abington School Dist. v. Schempp, 374 U.S. 203, 216 (1963) (confirming view advanced in *Everson* that government may not aid religion in general).

127. *See supra* ch. 1 notes 102–04 and accompanying text.

128. Sherbert v. Verner, 374 U.S. 398 (1963), and its progeny held that under the free exercise clause, South Carolina and other states had to give public funds to Mrs. Sherbert and those similarly situated precisely because of their religious convictions. *See supra* ch. 3 notes 48–50.

129. The focus on "no-aid" perhaps resulted because of fears in the 1940s that the legislatures would support Catholic schools. Many Protestants and secularists expressed this fear, often in intemperate language. *See, e.g.,* P. Blanshard, American Freedom and Catholic Power 54–78 (1949) (interpreting strict separation primarily in terms of prohibiting state aid to Catholic education); J. Dawson, Separate Church and State Now 52–53 (1948) (expressing the view that *Everson* was wrongly decided and that the Catholic Church poses the most serious threat to separation); C. Moehlman, The Wall of Separation Between Church and State, at xiii (1951) (defending strict separation

and asserting that Catholic views are "antithetical" to the American tradition of church and state); V. THAYER, RELIGION IN PUBLIC EDUCATION (1947) (glorifying the secular school and opposing inclusion of religion in public education). Justice Rutledge's dissent in *Everson*, written during this era, reflects the misplaced emphasis on "no-aid." *See* Everson v. Board of Educ., 330 U.S. 1, 31–32 (1947) (Rutledge, J., dissenting).

130. *See supra* notes 55–63 and accompanying text.

131. Madison, *Memorial and Remonstrance, supra* ch. 1 note 64, para. 3, at 300 (emphasis added).

132. *See id.* paras. 1, 4, 7, 9, 11, 13, 14, at 299–303.

133. Madison's views on church and state as a younger statesman and Framer of the religion clauses are best understood in light of federalism, the centrality of coercion, and a recognition that in many respects he stood between the Enlightenment and pietistic separationists. In his retirement, Madison rejected some of his earlier views and extended others. *See supra* ch. 2 notes 21–29 and accompanying text.

134. *See supra* notes 39–42 and accompanying text. It is not suggested that all of these practices would pass constitutional muster either in the founding generation or today, but merely that, taken as a whole, they demonstrate that the Founders had a far more intrusive view of establishment than do modern separationists.

135. Justice Brennan offered a variation of this thesis in Marsh v. Chambers, 463 U.S. 783 (1983). In rejecting the Court's reliance on history in sustaining legislative chaplains, he labeled as "questionable" the majority's assumption "that the Framers of the Establishment Clause would not have themselves authorized a practice that they thought violated the guarantees contained in the Clause." *Id.* at 814 (Brennan, J., dissenting). This argument might have more credence if Congress had appointed chaplains years after ratification of the First Amendment, but it lacks force since the First Congress appointed paid chaplains just days before arriving at the final wording of the Bill of Rights.

136. *See* McConnell, *supra* ch. 3 note 23, at 8–13 (discussing the various meanings of strict neutrality between religion and nonreligion); Paulsen, *supra* ch. 3 note 14, at 332–34 (criticizing the Court's use of the term "nonreligion").

137. R. WILLIAMS, THE BLOODY TENENT YET MORE BLOODY (London 1652), in 4 WRITINGS OF WILLIAMS, *supra* ch. 1 note 14, at 209.

138. M. ENDY, *supra* ch. 1 note 20, at 323.

139. *See* McConnell, *supra* ch. 3 note 23, at 11 (under the religion clauses, "[t]he protection of religious opinion will equally benefit religion and unbelief; the protection of religious action will primarily benefit religion") Nonreligious conduct, however, may well find protection under the free speech clause or under the First Amendment's "penumbral" right of freedom of thought.

140. P. KURLAND, RELIGION AND THE LAW 18 (1962). The similarity between Kurland's approach and the secular regulation rule is evident from his assessment of *Reynolds*, which he regards as essentially sound because it followed a religion-blind approach. *See id.* at 22.

141. Katz, *supra* ch. 3 note 24, at 102. The view is developed at length in W. KATZ, RELIGION AND AMERICAN CONSTITUTIONS (1964).
142. 1 A. DE TOCQUEVILLE, DEMOCRACY IN AMERICA 295 (1835) (J. Mayer ed. & G. Lawrence trans. 1969) (two vols. in one).

Chapter Five. Religious Liberty in Contemporary America

1. *See* United States v. Dubré, 820 F.2d 886, 889 (7th Cir. 1987) (congregant's discussions with his pastor concerning income tax problems were not covered by the clergy-penitent privilege, at least when the discussions were unrelated to spiritual matters).
2. *See* Paul v. Watchtower Bible and Tract Soc'y of New York, Inc., 819 F.2d 875, 876–77 (9th Cir.) (the free exercise clause bars an action alleging defamation, invasion of privacy, fraud, and outrageous conduct against the Jehovah's Witness Church, which had "shunned" plaintiff), *cert. denied*, 108 S. Ct. 289 (1987); Nally v. Grace Community Church of the Valley, 240 Cal. Rptr. 215, 219 (Ct. App. 1987) (the First Amendment does not shield church-related counselors from parents' tort action alleging "negligent failure to prevent [their son's] suicide"), *rev'd on other grounds*, 47 Cal. 3d 278, 297–98, 763 P.2d 948, 954–55, 253 Cal. Rptr. 97, 108–09 (1988).
3. *See* Smith v. Board of School Comm'rs, 827 F.2d 684, 693–95 (11th Cir. 1987) (reversing a decision that numerous public school textbooks violated the establishment clause by advancing the religion of secular humanism; finding it unnecessary to determine whether secular humanism was a religion because the books did not advance or inhibit any religion); Mozert v. Hawkins County Bd. of Educ., 827 F.2d 1058, 1070 (6th Cir. 1987) (free exercise rights of fundamentalist Christian parents were not violated by a public school's failure to accommodate their religious objections to offensive reading materials), *cert. denied*, 108 S. Ct. 1029 (1988).
4. *See* United States v. Merkt, 794 F.2d 950, 954–57 (5th Cir. 1986) (conviction of church sanctuary workers for violating immigration laws did not violate free exercise clause because the governmental interest in enforcing such laws was compelling), *cert. denied*, 480 U.S. 946 (1987).
5. *See* International Ass'n of Machinists, Lodge 751 v. Boeing Co., 833 F.2d 165, 168–69 (9th Cir. 1987) (employee opposed to union membership on religious grounds entitled under Title VII of the Civil Rights Act to make a charitable contribution in lieu of union dues).
6. A common view in the new nation, for example, was that the concept of institutional separation required the exclusion of ministers from sitting in the state legislatures or from holding any political office. *See supra* ch. 4 note 44 and accompanying text. Jefferson initially embraced this view because he regarded ministers a threat to America's political experiment: "The clergy, by getting themselves established by law, and ingrafted into the machine of government, have been a very formidable engine against the civil and religious rights of man." Letter from Thomas Jefferson to Jeremiah Moor (Aug.

14, 1800), in 7 THE WRITINGS OF JEFFERSON 455 (P. Ford ed. 1904). Witherspoon, Madison, and others strongly opposed clergy exclusion provisions
and, years later, Jefferson adopted the same view on the ground that the
clergy no longer posed a political threat to the republic. *See id.* Whatever its
justifications to the founding generation, scholars agree that institutional
separation neither requires nor counsels clergy exclusion in today's society.

7. For a thoughtful defense of the equal-access rights of student religious groups,
see Laycock, *Equal Access and Moments of Silence: The Equal Status of Religious
Speech by Private Speakers*, 81 Nw. U.L. REV. 1, 9–57 (1986). Applying a strict
neutrality standard, Laycock concludes that the free speech and free exercise
clauses require a right of equal access for religious speech. Because we believe
the Constitution compels "benevolent" rather than "strict" neutrality, we
arrive at the same conclusion, but on somewhat different premises.

8. Dewey, *Religion and Our Schools*, 6 HIBBERT J. 796, 807 (1908).

9. For articles asserting that the government is impermissibly advancing the
"religion" of secular humanism, see Bird, *Freedom from Establishment and
Unneutrality in Public School Instruction and Religious School Regulation*, 2
HARV. J.L. & PUB. POL'Y 125, 177–80, 182–83 (1979); Whitehead & Conlan, *The
Establishment of the Religion of Secular Humanism and Its First Amendment
Implications*, 10 TEX. TECH. L. REV. 1, 15–24 (1978).

10. *See* PANEL ON RELIGION IN THE CURRICULUM, ASSOCIATION FOR SUPERVISION AND
CURRICULUM DEVELOPMENT, RELIGION IN THE CURRICULUM 7–8 (1987) ("references to religion have been all but excised from the public school curriculum,"
largely because of educators' concern over breaching Jefferson's wall); P.
VITZ, CENSORSHIP: EVIDENCE OF BIAS IN OUR CHILDREN'S TEXTBOOKS 56 (1986)
(investigation of eight major American history textbooks used in the eleventh
and twelfth grades disclosed that not one "acknowledges, much less emphasizes, the great religious energy and creativity of the United States").

11. Abington School Dist. v. Schempp, 374 U.S. 203, 306 (1963) (Goldberg, J.,
concurring).

12. C. MALIK, THE TWO TASKS 27 (1980).

13. J.S. MILL, *supra* ch. 4 note 33, at 98.

14. *Id.* at 99.

15. McCollum v. Board of Educ., 333 U.S. 203, 236 (1948) (Jackson, J., concurring). *See generally* C. COX, THE FOURTH R: WHAT CAN BE TAUGHT ABOUT
RELIGION IN THE PUBLIC SCHOOLS 125–26, 165–69 (1969) (there is a need for
educationally sound materials about religion, as well as for better training and
supervision of teachers to ensure objectivity).

16. *See* Brandon v. Board of Educ., 635 F.2d 971, 977–79 (2d Cir. 1980) (rejecting
students' free exercise claim that the school board must allow them to meet
before classes and finding in the alternative that the establishment clause
would compel exclusion of religious groups from the school), *cert. denied*, 454
U.S. 1123 (1981); *infra* notes 20–26 and accompanying text (discussing *Bender*);
see also Lubbock Civil Liberties Union v. Lubbock Indep. School Dist., 669
F.2d 1038, 1044–46 (5th Cir. 1982) (school board policy permitting students
to meet voluntarily at school before or after regular hours for any "educa-

tional, moral, religious or ethical purposes" violates the establishment clause), *cert. denied*, 459 U.S. 1155 (1983).

17. Some commentators assert on the basis of Widmar v. Vincent, 454 U.S. 263 (1981), that equal access for student religious groups in public high schools is required by the free speech clause. *See, e.g.*, Laycock, *supra* note 7. While we share this view, analysis of the equal-access issue under the free speech clause is beyond the scope of this book. For a brief discussion of *Widmar*, see *supra* text accompanying ch. 3 note 55.

18. The Equal Access Act, Pub. L. No. 98-377, 98 Stat. 1302 (codified at 20 U.S.C. §§ 4071–74 (Supp. IV 1986)). The Act is considered in Laycock, *supra* note 7, at 4–5, 35–45.

19. The Equal Access Act § 4071(a).

20. 741 F.2d 538 (3d Cir. 1984), *vacated on other grounds*, 475 U.S. 534 (1986).

21. *See id.* at 543 n.8; *id.* at 565 n.5 (Adams, J., dissenting).

22. *Id.* at 555.

23. *Id.* at 561.

24. *Id.* at 565 (Adams, J., dissenting).

25. 454 U.S. 263 (1981).

26. Bender v. Williamsport Area School Dist., 475 U.S. 534, 554–55 (1986) (Burger, C.J., dissenting); *see id.* at 556 (Powell, J., dissenting) ("I do not believe— particularly in this age of massive media information—that the few years difference in age between high school and college students justifies departing from *Widmar*.").

27. Mergens v. Board of Educ. of the Westside Community Schools, 867 F.2d 1076 (8th Cir. 1989), *cert. granted*, 109 S.Ct. 3240 (1989).

28. *See, e.g.*, O'Hair v. Andrus, 613 F.2d 931, 934–35 (D.C. Cir. 1979) (rejecting an establishment clause challenge to the Pope's use of the National Mall because any "meaningful perception" of endorsing religion was eliminated by the availability of the mall to all speakers and groups).

29. For a discussion of Kurland's religion-blind approach, see *supra* ch. 4 note 140 and accompanying text. Laycock sets forth his position in Laycock, *supra* note 7.

30. *Bender*, 741 F.2d at 570 (Adams, J., dissenting).

31. S. Hook, Religion in a Free Society 87 (1967). In Hall v. Bradshaw, 630 F.2d 1018 (4th Cir. 1980), the court reasoned that historical references to the Deity in public life should be treated as "grandfathered" exceptions to establishment clause doctrine because they have little "entangling theological significance" and can "safely occupy their own small, unexpandable niche." *Id.* at 1023 n.2. This approach fails to recognize religion's dynamic character, relegating it instead to a stagnant historical role.

32. 1 A. De Tocqueville, *supra* ch. 4 note 142, at 293.

33. C. Geertz, *Ethos, World View, and the Analysis of Sacred Symbols*, in The Interpretation of Cultures 126, 127 (1973).

34. P. Tillich, Theology of Culture 42 (1959). The Supreme Court used Tillich's definition of religion as "ultimate concern" in United States v. Seeger, 380 U.S. 163, 187 (1965).

35. 463 U.S. 783 (1983).

36. Justice Stevens asserted that "the designation of a member of one religious faith to serve as the sole official chaplain of a state legislature for a period of 16 years constitutes the preference of one faith over another in violation of the Establishment Clause." *Id.* at 823 (Stevens, J., dissenting).

37. 822 F.2d 1406 (6th Cir. 1987).

38. *Id.* at 1407.

39. *Id.* at 1408.

40. *Id.*

41. *Id.* at 1409 (footnote omitted).

42. In a concurring opinion, Judge Milburn stressed that in order to pass constitutional muster, ceremonial prayers must be "nonsectarian and nondenominational" and as "secular" as those approved in *Marsh. Id.* at 1410 (Milburn, J., concurring).

43. *Stein*, 822 F.2d at 1411 (Wellford, J., dissenting).

44. *Id.* at 1412 (Wellford, J., dissenting) (quoting *Marsh*, 463 U.S. at 794–95).

45. *Id.* at 1415 (Wellford, J., dissenting).

46. In holding that a state could not censor a controversial motion picture as "sacrilegious," the Supreme Court stated: "[I]t is enough to point out that the state has no legitimate interest in protecting any or all religions from views distasteful to them which is sufficient to justify prior restraints upon the expression of those views." Joseph Burstyn, Inc. v. Wilson, 343 U.S. 495, 505 (1952).

47. B. CARDOZO, *supra* ch. 3 note 23, at 141 (footnote omitted).

48. Such a review invokes images of Queen Elizabeth's Act of Uniformity, which granted Parliament the right to dictate the content of the prayer book used by the Church of England. *See supra* ch. 4 note 50 and accompanying text. For the pietistic separationists, opposition to this and similar acts stood at the core of the struggle for religious freedom. *See also* Engel v. Vitale, 370 U.S. 421, 425 (1962) (invalidating state-sponsored school prayer largely because the establishment clause precludes government officials from composing official prayers).

49. R. BELLAH, THE BROKEN COVENANT: AMERICAN CIVIL RELIGION IN TIME OF TRIAL 139 (1975); *see also* Little, *American Civil Religion and the Rise of Pluralism*, 38 UNION SEMINARY Q. REV. 401, 410–11 (1984) (questioning the notion of civil religion as a unifying force in any sense other than agreement on legal process). The *Stein* court relied on Mirsky, *Civil Religion and the Establishment Clause*, 95 YALE L.J. 1237 (1986), rather than on the works of the scholars who initially formulated the concept of civil religion. *See Stein*, 822 F.2d at 1409 n.5.

50. *See, e.g.*, Bogen v. Doty, 598 F.2d 1110, 1114 (8th Cir. 1979) (sustaining invocations at county board meetings, but warning that constitutional problems would arise if the board limited participation to Christians).

51. For the view that the ideology of secularism—the exclusion of "religion and religiously grounded values from the conduct of public business"—poses a dangerous threat to democracy, see R. NEUHAUS, THE NAKED PUBLIC SQUARE: RELIGION AND DEMOCRACY IN AMERICA, at ix (2d ed. 1986).

52. Among the numerous articles on this issue, see in particular Choper, *Defining "Religion" in the First Amendment*, 1982 U. ILL. L. REV. 579; Greenawalt, *Religion as a Concept in Constitutional Law*, 72 CALIF. L. REV. 753 (1984); *see also* Freeman, *The Misguided Search for the Constitutional Definition of "Religion,"* 71 GEO. L.J. 1519, 1519 n.3 (1983) (listing other authorities).

53. 662 F.2d 1025 (3d Cir. 1981), *cert. denied*, 456 U.S. 908 (1982). Judge Adams wrote the opinion of the court.

54. *Id.* at 1032 (citing Malnak v. Yogi, 592 F.2d 197, 207–10 (3d Cir. 1979) (Adams, J., concurring in result)).

55. *Id.* at 1028 (quoting Frank Africa, Brief to Define the Importance of MOVE's Religious Diet).

56. *Id.* at 1033.

57. *Id.* at 1034 (relying on Wisconsin v. Yoder, 406 U.S. 205, 215–16 (1972)).

58. Torcaso v. Watkins, 367 U.S. 488, 495 n. 11 (1961). For older cases espousing a theistic definition, see Davis v. Beason, 133 U.S. 333, 342 (1890) (defining religion in the context of an antipolygamy case as belief in a Supreme Being); *see also* United States v. Macintosh, 283 U.S. 605, 633–34 (1931) (Hughes, C.J., dissenting) ("[t]he essence of religion is belief in a relation to God involving duties superior to those arising from any human relation").

59. 380 U.S. 163, 166 (1965); *see also* Welsh v. United States, 398 U.S. 333, 343–44 (1970) (conscientious objector decision expanding the *Seeger* test's definition of "religious").

60. 406 U.S. 205, 216 (1972).

61. Thomas v. Review Board, 450 U.S. 707, 715 (1981).

62. VA. DECLARATION OF RIGHTS of 1776, art. 16, in 7 THORPE, *supra* ch. 1 note 18, at 3814.

63. T. JEFFERSON, AUTOBIOGRAPHY, in 1 THE WRITINGS OF JEFFERSON 71 (P. Ford ed. 1904).

64. *See* R. WILLIAMS, THE BLOUDY TENENT, OF PERSECUTION, FOR CAUSE OF CONSCIENCE, *supra* ch. 1 note 14, at 3.

65. As Justice White indicated, "It cannot be ignored that the First Amendment itself contains a religious classification." Welsh v. United States, 398 U.S. 333, 372 (1970) (White, J., dissenting).

66. A more extended defense of the unitary definition of religion is contained in Malnak v. Yogi, 592 F.2d 197, 210–13 (3d Cir. 1979) (Adams, J., concurring in result).

67. *See, e.g.*, Slye, *supra* ch. 4 note 31, at 240 & n.121 (because the *Africa* test requires analogization to orthodox beliefs, it may result in judges ruling in favor of traditional religions, but against "less well-established religious groups").

Conclusion

1. *See* epigraph, F. MAITLAND, *England Before the Conquest*, in DOMESDAY BOOK AND BEYOND 356 (1897).

2. Pepper, *Reynolds, Yoder, and Beyond: Alternatives for the Free Exercise Clause*, 1981 UTAH L. REV. 309, 377–78.
3. Mansfield, *The Religion Clauses of the First Amendment and the Philosophy of the Constitution*, 72 CALIF. L. REV. 847, 904 (1984).
4. Letter from John Adams to a unit of the Massachusetts militia (Oct. 11, 1798), in 9 WORKS OF J. ADAMS, *supra* ch. 2 note 37, at 229.

Appendixes

1. R. WILLIAMS, MR. COTTONS LETTER LATELY PRINTED, EXAMINED AND ANSWERED (London 1644), in 1 THE COMPLETE WRITINGS OF ROGER WILLIAMS 392 (Russell & Russell, Inc. 1963) [hereinafter WRITINGS OF WILLIAMS].
2. R. WILLIAMS, THE BLOUDY TENENT, OF PERSECUTION, FOR CAUSE OF CONSCIENCE (London 1644), in 3 WRITINGS OF WILLIAMS, *supra* note 1, at 3–4.
3. Letter from Roger Williams to the Town of Providence (Jan. 1655), in 6 WRITINGS OF WILLIAMS, *supra* note 1, at 278–79.
4. W. PENN, THE GREAT CASE OF LIBERTY OF CONSCIENCE (London 1670), in 1 A COLLECTION OF THE WORKS OF WILLIAM PENN 444, 446–48 (J. Besse ed. 1726 & photo. reprint 1974).
5. I. BACKUS, AN APPEAL TO THE PUBLIC FOR RELIGIOUS LIBERTY (Boston 1773), in ISAAC BACKUS ON CHURCH, STATE, AND CALVINISM: PAMPHLETS, 1754–1789, at 309, 315, 317, 321, 332–35 (W. McLoughlin ed. 1968).
6. Madison, *Memorial and Remonstrance Against Religious Assessments* (circa June 20, 1785), in 8 THE PAPERS OF JAMES MADISON 298–304 (W. Hutchison & W. Rachal eds. 1973).
7. Jefferson, A Bill for Establishing Religious Freedom (1785), in 2 THE PAPERS OF THOMAS JEFFERSON 545–47 (J. Boyd ed. 1950); An Act for Establishing Religious Freedom, ch. XXXIV (1786), in 12 HENING'S STATUTES AT LARGE OF VIRGINIA 84–86 (1823). When the Virginia legislature enacted the bill in 1786, it deleted the italicized words in brackets and added the numerals, the "WHEREAS" after numeral I, and the introductory clause after numeral II. The italicized language in brackets is taken from Jefferson's bill, while the remaining language is from the bill as enacted.
8. Jefferson, Reply to the Danbury Baptist Association (Jan. 1, 1802), in 8 THE WRITINGS OF THOMAS JEFFERSON 113–14 (H. Washington ed. 1853).
9. Washington, Proclamation: A National Thanksgiving (Oct. 3, 1789), in 1 J. RICHARDSON, A COMPILATION OF THE MESSAGES AND PAPERS OF THE PRESIDENTS 1789–1908, at 64 (1908).
10. Farewell Address by George Washington (Sept. 17, 1796), in 1 J. RICHARDSON, *supra* note 9, at 220.
11. The Declaration of Independence paras. 1, 2, 31 (U.S. 1776).
12. All state constitutional provisions, except as otherwise noted, are taken from THE FEDERAL AND STATE CONSTITUTIONS, COLONIAL CHARTERS, AND OTHER ORGANIC LAWS (F. Thorpe ed. 1909) (seven vols.). Rhode Island and Connecticut continued under their colonial charters. Although Vermont adopted

two constitutions prior to the adoption of the Federal Constitution, it was not admitted as a state until 1791.

13. Technically, this provision is section 16 of the Virginia Bill of Rights of 1776. The provision, however, is now almost uniformly referred to as article 16 of the Virginia Declaration of Rights.

14. DEL. DECLARATION OF RIGHTS of 1776, § 2, *reprinted in* SOURCES OF OUR LIBERTIES 338 (R. Perry & J. Cooper eds. rev. ed. 1978).

15. South Carolina's first constitution, adopted in 1776, did not contain a religious freedom provision.

16. New Hampshire's first constitution, adopted in 1776, did not contain a religious freedom provision.

Bibliography

I. PRIMARY SOURCES

ANNALS OF THE CONGRESS OF THE UNITED STATES (J. Gales ed. 1834).

THE DEBATES IN THE SEVERAL STATE CONVENTIONS ON THE ADOPTION OF THE FEDERAL CONSTITUTION (J. Elliot 2d ed. 1836) (five vols.).

DOCUMENTARY HISTORY OF THE FIRST FEDERAL CONGRESS OF THE UNITED STATES OF AMERICA (L. De Pauw ed. 1972–).

THE FEDERAL AND STATE CONSTITUTIONS, COLONIAL CHARTERS, AND OTHER ORGANIC LAWS (F. Thorpe ed. 1909) (seven vols.).

THE FOUNDERS' CONSTITUTION (P. Kurland & R. Lerner eds. 1987) (five vols.).

C. JAMES, DOCUMENTARY HISTORY OF THE STRUGGLE FOR RELIGIOUS LIBERTY IN VIRGINIA (1900).

JOURNALS OF THE CONTINENTAL CONGRESS (W. Ford ed. 1905).

PAMPHLETS OF THE AMERICAN REVOLUTION: 1750–1776 (B. Bailyn ed. 1965).

THE RECORDS OF THE FEDERAL CONVENTION OF 1787 (M. Farrand rev. ed. 1937) (four vols.).

J. RICHARDSON, A COMPILATION OF THE MESSAGES AND PAPERS OF THE PRESIDENTS 1789–1908 (1908).

SOURCES OF OUR LIBERTIES (R. Perry & J. Cooper eds. rev. ed. 1978).

II. MAJOR SECONDARY SOURCES

S. AHLSTROM, A RELIGIOUS HISTORY OF THE AMERICAN PEOPLE (1972).

AMERICAN CIVIL RELIGION (R. Richey & D. Jones eds. 1974).

C. ANTIEAU, A. DOWNEY & E. ROBERTS, FREEDOM FROM FEDERAL ESTABLISHMENT: FORMATION AND EARLY HISTORY OF THE FIRST AMENDMENT RELIGION CLAUSES (1964).

H. BERMAN, THE INTERACTION OF LAW AND RELIGION (1974).

P. BONOMI, UNDER THE COPE OF HEAVEN: RELIGION, SOCIETY AND POLITICS IN COLONIAL AMERICA (1986).

CHURCH AND STATE IN AMERICA: A BIBLIOGRAPHIC GUIDE (J. Wilson ed. 1986–87) (two vols.).

CHURCH AND STATE IN AMERICAN HISTORY (J. Wilson & D. Drakeman eds. 2d rev. ed. 1987).

CHURCH AND STATE: THE SUPREME COURT AND THE FIRST AMENDMENT (P. Kurland ed. 1975).

CHURCH, STATE, AND POLITICS (J. Hensel ed. 1981).

CHURCH, STATE, AND PUBLIC POLICY: THE NEW SHAPE OF THE CHURCH-STATE DEBATE (J. Mechling ed. 1978).

S. COBB, THE RISE OF RELIGIOUS LIBERTY IN AMERICA (1902).

R. CORD, SEPARATION OF CHURCH AND STATE: HISTORICAL FACT AND CURRENT FICTION (1982).

E. CORWIN, THE "HIGHER LAW" BACKGROUND OF AMERICAN CONSTITUTIONAL LAW (1955).

N. COUSINS, "IN GOD WE TRUST": THE RELIGIOUS BELIEFS AND IDEAS OF THE AMERICAN FOUNDING FATHERS (1958).

T. CURRY, THE FIRST FREEDOMS: CHURCH AND STATE IN AMERICA TO THE PASSAGE OF THE FIRST AMENDMENT (1986).

A DOCUMENTARY HISTORY OF RELIGION IN AMERICA (E. Gaustad ed. 1982–83) (two vols.).

R. DRINAN, RELIGION, THE COURTS, AND PUBLIC POLICY (1963).

H. ECKENRODE, SEPARATION OF CHURCH AND STATE IN VIRGINIA (1910).

D. FELLMAN, RELIGION IN AMERICAN PUBLIC LAW (1965).

E. GAUSTAD, THE FAITH OF OUR FATHERS: RELIGION AND THE NEW NATION (1987).

K. GREENAWALT, RELIGIOUS CONVICTIONS AND POLITICAL CHOICE (1988).

S. HOOK, RELIGION IN A FREE SOCIETY (1967).

M. HOWE, THE GARDEN AND THE WILDERNESS: RELIGION AND GOVERNMENT IN AMERICAN CONSTITUTIONAL HISTORY (1965).

JAMES MADISON ON RELIGIOUS LIBERTY (R. Alley ed. 1985).

A. JOHNSON & F. YOST, SEPARATION OF CHURCH AND STATE IN THE UNITED STATES (1948).

W.K. JORDAN, THE DEVELOPMENT OF RELIGIOUS TOLERATION IN ENGLAND (1932–40) (four vols.).

W. KATZ, RELIGION AND AMERICAN CONSTITUTIONS (1964).

P. KAUPER, RELIGION AND THE CONSTITUTION (1964).

A. KELLY & W. HARBISON, THE AMERICAN CONSTITUTION: ITS ORIGINS AND DEVELOPMENT (5th ed. 1976).

M. KONVITZ, RELIGIOUS LIBERTY AND CONSCIENCE: A CONSTITUTIONAL INQUIRY (1968).

P. KURLAND, RELIGION AND THE LAW: OF CHURCH AND STATE AND THE SUPREME COURT (1962).

L. LEVY, THE ESTABLISHMENT CLAUSE: RELIGION AND THE FIRST AMENDMENT (1986).

W. McLOUGHLIN, NEW ENGLAND DISSENT 1630–1833: THE BAPTISTS AND THE SEPARATION OF CHURCH AND STATE (1971) (two vols.).

M. MALBIN, RELIGION AND POLITICS: THE INTENTIONS OF THE AUTHORS OF THE FIRST AMENDMENT (1978).

D. MANWARING, RENDER UNTO CAESAR: THE FLAG-SALUTE CONTROVERSY (1962).

M. MARTY, RELIGION AND REPUBLIC: THE AMERICAN CIRCUMSTANCE (1987).

S. MEAD, THE LIVELY EXPERIMENT: THE SHAPING OF CHRISTIANITY IN AMERICA (1963).

————, THE NATION WITH THE SOUL OF A CHURCH (1975).

R. MICHAELSEN, PIETY IN THE PUBLIC SCHOOL (1970).

R. MILLER & R. FLOWERS, TOWARD BENEVOLENT NEUTRALITY: CHURCH, STATE, AND THE SUPREME COURT (3d ed. 1987).

W. MILLER, THE FIRST LIBERTY: RELIGION AND THE AMERICAN REPUBLIC (1986).

E. Morgan, Roger Williams: The Church and the State (1967).

R. Morgan, The Supreme Court and Religion (1972).

J. Murray, We Hold These Truths: Catholic Reflections on the American Proposition (1960).

R. Neuhaus, The Naked Public Square: Religion and Democracy in America (2d ed. 1986).

M. Noll, One Nation Under God? Christian Faith and Political Action in America (1988).

J. Noonan, The Believers and the Powers That Are: Cases, History, and Other Data Bearing on the Relation of Religion and Government (1987).

L. Pfeffer, Church, State, and Freedom (rev. ed. 1967).

L. Pfeffer, Religion, State, and the Burger Court (1985).

A. Reichley, Religion in American Public Life (1985).

Religion and American Politics: From the Colonial Period to the 1980's (M. Noll ed. 1990).

Religion and the Public Order (D. Giannella ed. 1964–69) (five vols.).

Religion in America: Original Essays on Religion in a Free Society (J. Cogley ed. 1958).

R. Smith, Public Prayer and the Constitution (1987).

F. Sorauf, The Wall of Separation: The Constitutional Politics of Church and State (1976).

A. Stokes, Church and State in the United States (1950) (three vols.).

A. Stokes & L. Pfeffer, Church and State in the United States (rev. ed. 1964) (one vol.).

W. Sweet, Religion in Colonial America (1942).

W. Torpey, Judicial Doctrines of Religious Rights in America (1948).

The Virginia Statute for Religious Freedom: Its Evolution and Consequences for American History (M. Peterson & R. Vaughan eds. 1988).

The Wall Between Church and State (D. Oaks ed. 1963).

G. Wood, The Creation of the American Republic, 1776–1787 (1969).

C. Zollman, American Church Law (1933).

Index